Praise for *The Character Edge*

"*The Character Edge* artfully combines scholarly research and practical experience in an interesting, persuasive way. I think character matters more today than at any time in my memory. Bob Caslen and Michael Matthews get it right."

—General Martin E. Dempsey, US Army (Retired), 18th Chairman of the Joint Chiefs of Staff, author of *Radical Inclusion: What the Post-9/11 World Should Have Taught Us About Leadership*

"The world needs leaders with strong character more than ever, and *The Character Edge* will show you how that is done in two institutions that carry the trust and respect of all Americans: the United States Military Academy at West Point, and the United States Army. This book is a must-read for anyone who aspires to live a life of character."

—General (Retired) Raymond T. Odierno, 38th Chief of Staff of the United States Army

"As school administrators, be it at the state, local, and campus levels, we have much in common with the sacred responsibility of military leaders, especially in light of what LTG (Ret.) Caslen terms the 'Bank of Public Trust.' Caslen and Matthews give compelling illustrations of how trust accounts must be cherished and nurtured over time and modeled consistently with 'deposits of competence, character, and caring.' As educators and public servants, there is much we can draw from the stories, the exquisite scholarship, and the 'right way' lessons found throughout *The Character Edge*."

—Mary M. Keller, Ed.D., former President & CEO of the Military Child Education Coalition

"In *The Character Edge*, Caslen and Matthews offer the definitive guide to how individuals and organizations may build and utilize positive character to flourish and win. Corporations who 'get' this message excel; those who do not will fail in the long run."

—Indra Nooyi, former Chairman & CEO of PepsiCo

"Blending behavioral science with lessons learned in the crucible of military service, Bob Caslen and Mike Matthews have written a leadership book that is both timely and timeless. They examine the complex nature of character in both individuals and organizations with vivid examples from the military, sports, education, and business. In a time of polarization and incivility, the authors have created a how-to manual for counteracting these destructive forces in ourselves and our institutions."

—Stefanie Sanford, Chief of Global Policy & External Relations of the College Board

"We believe it is the quality and character of the leader that determines the results. In *The Character Edge* we discover a blueprint for instilling values-based leadership to achieve significance and success."

—Frances Hesselbein, Chairman of the Frances Hesselbein Leadership Forum, former CEO of Girl Scouts of the USA, and Presidential Medal of Freedom recipient

THE CHARACTER EDGE

ROBERT L. CASLEN, JR.
AND
DR. MICHAEL D. MATTHEWS

— THE —

CHARACTER
EDGE

LEADING AND WINNING
WITH INTEGRITY

ST. MARTIN'S PRESS ≋ NEW YORK

First published in the United States by St. Martin's Press, an imprint of St. Martin's Publishing Group

THE CHARACTER EDGE. Copyright © 2020 by Robert L. Caslen, Jr. and Dr. Michael D. Matthews. Foreword copyright © 2020 by Martin E. P. Seligman. All rights reserved. Printed in the United States of America. For information, address St. Martin's Press, 120 Broadway, New York, NY 10271.

www.stmartins.com

The Library of Congress Cataloging-in-Publication Data is available upon request.

ISBN 978-1-250-25908-0 (hardcover)
ISBN 978-1-250-25907-3 (ebook)

Our books may be purchased in bulk for promotional, educational, or business use. Please contact your local bookseller or the Macmillan Corporate and Premium Sales Department at 1-800-221-7945, extension 5442, or by email at MacmillanSpecialMarkets@macmillan.com.

First Edition: 2020

10 9 8 7 6 5 4 3 2 1

We are deeply grateful for the numerous men and women who live lives of character and who allowed us to tell their story. May their character be a shining light that will help guide our readers through their own challenges and triumphs.

CONTENTS

CONTENTS

ACKNOWLEDGMENTS

Our ideas for this book evolved from many decades of experience and study of character and leadership. Many of the leaders and scientists discussed in *The Character Edge* shaped our view that positive character is a fundamental requirement for individuals, leaders, and organizations to flourish and prosper, to wit, to win in the right way. Moreover, we enjoyed the benefit of working for values-based, high-performing organizations. We learned important lessons from our own leaders who were competent, of high character, and caring. Owing to our combined eighty-plus years of experience, we cannot begin to recognize each individual who contributed to our views. But for all who influenced us, you will see your mark in the pages of this book.

We thank our agent, Gillian MacKenzie, and her team for believing in us and helping us develop the proposal that grew into *The Character Edge*. Gillian helped transform our raw ideas into a coherent plan. We appreciate how she shares our vision of the importance of character to individuals and organizations, and her enthusiasm in turning an idea into a viable proposal, and a proposal into a book. She was with us at every stage of the project, from inception to completion. Gillian's mentoring made this book better in all respects, and for that we are grateful. Thank you as well to Larry James, for introducing us to Gillian.

Our publisher, St. Martin's Press, was terrific. Marc Resnick and Hannah O'Grady understood our vision for the book and empowered us to tell our story in our own way. Their feedback on drafts of the book was timely and immensely helpful. Because of their competence, character, and caring, we trusted them implicitly to transform our proposal into a finished product. Everyone we worked with at St. Martin's Press, from copy editors to the marketing team, were true professionals. It takes a village to raise a child, and it takes a top-drawer publishing house to raise a book. We cannot thank Marc, Hannah, and their team enough for their support and guidance.

We thank Martin Seligman for his support and for providing the foreword for *The Character Edge*. Also, we are indebted to the many people who reviewed the book and provided blurbs. Among these, we single out Angela Duckworth because of her fifteen-year collaborative relationship with West Point. Angela conducted one of her first studies on grit at West Point in 2004 and has since then spoken to thousands of cadets and faculty about grit and other character strengths linked to leadership.

Tufts University professor Richard Lerner has helped us to better understand character development within an institution. The principal investigator of a five-year longitudinal study of character development at West Point, Project Arete, Rich has researched positive youth development for thirty years, and his work has guided our efforts to better understand character and how to develop it among cadets. We are grateful for Rich's un-wavering support of West Point's efforts to fully integrate char-acter into its officer-development model.

This brings us to our project manager, Gretchen Bain Mat-thews. First a bit about Gretchen's background. The careful reader will see she shares her last name with one of the authors. This is not a coincidence; she is the second author's spouse. Gretchen is an experienced and talented writer and editor, who assists scientists in preparing top-quality manuscripts ranging from dissertations to top-tier-journal submissions. Gretchen has worked in technical writing and editing since graduating with a bachelor's degree in English from Pomona College. As well honed as her writing and editing skills are, her organizational skills are what set her apart. The reader only sees the tip of the iceberg—the book—but below the surface lurks the real work that goes into publishing a book. Keeping track of drafts, edit-ing for style and content, corresponding with stakeholders, and making sure everything is completed on time are just as import-ant as the writing. Without Gretchen's amazing organizational acumen, this book would never have been completed.

—ROBERT L. CASLEN, JR., *and* DR. MICHAEL D. MATTHEWS

I also thank my wife, Shelly, and my sons Robert III, Nicholas, and Jeffrey, and their families, who have put up with a husband and father struggling to balance his life while trying to achieve excellence in husband-hood and fatherhood, and within his chosen profession as well. God has blessed us with family, health, unconditional love, and challenges to our character every day. I am so fortunate to have a wife and children who love me unconditionally and who lift me up every day.

—ROBERT L. CASLEN, JR.

FOREWORD

This book catapults General Robert Caslen and Professor Michael Matthews into the front rank of the legion of people now working on good character across the world.

Part of the reason for the success of this book is the character and hugely different experiences of the two people who wrote this gem. I want tell you about each of them.

I first met General Caslen when he was the brigadier general who had just taken his new assignment as commandant of West Point. I was a visitor lecturing to the cadets about resilience and post-traumatic growth. We met to discuss the future of his counseling service. General Caslen was concerned that the counseling service was exclusively occupied with bad stuff: drug abuse, low-level criminality, and sexual harassment.

"Couldn't counseling do better than just this, by giving advice and measuring the good stuff as well," he asked, "like how to become an exemplary soldier or how to make academic choices based on one's strengths, not just how to be less bad?" I could see that we were on the same wavelength. His interest was military excellence and academic excellence and so was mine. My specific interest there was in transforming counseling services in psychology generally into being about what makes life worth living as opposed to just about how to deal with the negative stuff and with the bad apples. So he and I talked about the possibility that the counseling center could be a place where cadets find out about the best things about themselves. I left the meeting thinking, "This guy is a visionary."

Fast-forward a few years later: General Caslen has now become the superintendent of West Point, the officer in charge of the whole shebang. As you will read, the theme of his tenure was the building of character. His many years of experience in the field at every level of command had taught him that building character is the cornerstone of military leadership. And this is what he brings to this book: thousands of hours of actual leadership ranging from in extremis on the battlefield to the more pastoral setting of West Point.

His partner in this book is Professor Michael Matthews, a scholar, researcher, and teacher of long experience. I first met Mike more than fifteen years ago when I was organizing the future of positive psychology. We invited Mike to become a senior fellow for several months at the University of Pennsylvania under a grant from the John Templeton Foundation and Atlantic Philanthropies. Angela Duckworth and I had just begun to work on grit, and Mike and Angela began a collaboration with West Point to study who quits the academy after Beast Barracks, the grueling summer program that new cadets face as their first introduction to the Army. Grit proved to be a significant predictor of not quitting, and this expanded into Mike's work on character as a predictor of military success and also launched Angela's remarkable career. So what Mike brings to this book are serious behavioral science, rigor, and many years of experience teaching and measuring the minds and behavior of cadets.

As you will see, this results in a unique, unprecedented collaboration between a member of the highest ranks of military leadership with a lifetime of extensive experience in instilling character in soldiers in the field with a senior behavioral scientist, experienced in measurement and experimental design. So, you have in front of you the first book on character resulting from a partnership between long experience with the reality of the battlefield combined with long experience in behavioral science.

Joining two good heads together is only a potential, but the actuality is a book on character that they and the entire field can be proud of.

I am going to avoid spoilers in this foreword, but I want to tell you what I liked the most:

Duty, Honor, Country is the traditional motto of West Point. But merely mouthing that motto over and over does not translate it into the actions of its graduates. It is Caslen and Matthews's insight that the molding of character during a cadet's four years at West Point transforms the words of the motto into a lifetime of noble deeds. How this is achieved, how this is measured, and how it applies to the world beyond the Army is the treat that awaits you now.

—MARTIN E. P. SELIGMAN
PROFESSOR OF PSYCHOLOGY
DIRECTOR, POSITIVE PSYCHOLOGY CENTER
UNIVERSITY OF PENNSYLVANIA

PREFACE

The Character Edge springs from more than eighty years of collective experience by the authors. General Caslen served in the Army for forty-three years following his commissioning as a second lieutenant from West Point in 1975. From second lieutenant to lieutenant general, he commanded at every level from platoon to division, in peace and in war. As a second lieutenant Caslen was part of an Army recovering from the Vietnam War, an Army plagued with racial unrest, drug use, and a lack of purpose and direction. Caslen, with the help of his generation of Army officers, helped repair the fractures plaguing the Army and helped prepare it for the first Gulf War and for the wars in Afghanistan and Iraq that followed the events of September 11, 2001. Caslen capped his distinguished Army career by serving as West Point's fifty-ninth superintendent from 2013 to 2018.

Throughout his years in the Army, Caslen observed leaders and soldiers in the most challenging situations. It became clear to him that character and leadership were inextricably linked. From his perspective as the leader of a platoon of thirty soldiers

to a division of more than twenty-three thousand soldiers, it
became evident that character was essential to winning. As his
views on the essential role of character in leadership developed,
he came to prioritize character development—both his own
and that of his soldiers—as a core component of his leadership
philosophy. This culminated during his tenure as West Point's
superintendent, when he formalized character development as
a primary institutional goal along with cadet academic, physical,
and military development.

Dr. Matthews, born the same year as Caslen, brings a different perspective to *The Character Edge*. A military psychologist
for forty years, Matthews employs scientific methods to study
character and its influence on individual performance and leadership. Both a former law enforcement officer and Air Force
officer, he is keenly interested in the ways that character may
be measured and how it interacts with other factors, such as
intelligence, in influencing how we adapt individually and lead
others in challenging, sometimes dangerous, situations. He
is interested in the theory of character and its relationship to
other important psychological and social attributes, but he is
also interested in how character plays out in the types of real-
world situations that Caslen has experienced throughout his
long and distinguished Army career. Like Caslen, Matthews
believes that character forms the basis of leadership, as well as
being of fundamental importance in personal adjustment and
social relationships.

Retired generals have written many books on these topics,
just as psychologists have written many books on leadership and
character. Those books in the first category are based on the

unique experiences of the leader and lack a foundation in behavioral sciences. While often insightful, such books are easily criticized as presenting simply opinions. Leadership and character books written by psychologists, on the other hand, are well grounded in the behavioral and social sciences. Scientifically sound, they may lack relevance. Things that work well in the laboratory often fail to play out in the real world.

The purpose of *The Character Edge* is to blend together these two complementary perspectives on character and leadership. No other book on character and leadership is based on the combined experiences and perspectives of both a strategic leader *and* a scientist. We weave together the science and practice of character and character-based leadership into a narrative that both educates and inspires readers.

We frame this preface with two stories, one written by General Caslen and one by Dr. Matthews, that illustrate our passionate interest in character and leadership.

IRAQ, 2009—LIEUTENANT GENERAL (RETIRED) ROBERT L. CASLEN, JR.

On February 9, 2009, during Operation Iraqi Freedom, the Third Battalion of the Eighth Cavalry Regiment was securing the western part of Mosul, Iraq, as part of the famous "surge." Coalition casualties and enemy contact had dropped significantly throughout most of Iraq. But northern Iraq, specifically Nineveh province with its capital city of Mosul, was still seeing frequent combat. Lieutenant Colonel Gary Derby—a tough, no-nonsense, scrappy officer both loved and admired by his soldiers—had been in command of the battalion for a couple months, and already significant progress was being made under his leadership. A soldier's soldier, Derby led from the front, and through his constant presence and authority, he continually brought his troops confidence, hope, and optimism, regardless of whatever challenging circumstances they were facing.

At about one o'clock in the afternoon of February 9, I received the call that no commander ever wants to receive. En route to a combat outpost in western Mosul, Derby's vehicle was hit by a suicide-vehicle-borne improvised explosive device. Derby, three other soldiers, and one interpreter in his vehicle were instantly killed. With a heavy heart, I immediately got into a helicopter and flew to battalion headquarters to meet with its surviving leaders, to console and put my arm around them, and to assure them that our division and the rest of the theater leadership would do whatever we could to assist them through their loss. I promised to get another commander for the battalion as quickly as possible.

Lieutenant Colonel Derby's impact on the culture and values and effectiveness of his unit was obvious not only by the gains he had made in the field but also by the shock his loss had on his soldiers. A leader's influence is significant, and I learned through my career that in settings of crisis and stress, this impact is exponentially higher. In dangerous conditions, people are drawn closer as they sense their vulnerability. They are more attuned to the actions of their leaders because they must depend so heavily on them for guidance through the perilous circumstances. The glue that holds these people together is their trust in their leader. Trust—perhaps the most important ingredient in effective leadership—is arguably the most important quality fostered in troops by their leaders. The love and respect the troops had for

Gary Derby was in great part because he delivered for them again and again. Their trust was about as high as one can imagine; they would follow him anywhere because they trusted he would lead them there safely and competently.

Where was that trust engendered? In part, it came out of the competence that Gary Derby demonstrated every day as a battalion commander in combat. But trust is also built on something that is as important as competence, and that is character. Quite simply, you can be the most effective and competent battalion commander in my division in combat, but if you fail in character you fail in leadership. Lieutenant Colonel Derby showed the highest qualities of character—he was honest, he was selfless, he was full of grit and determination, and he was compassionate. His character came through in subtle ways and in less subtle ways, but it was obvious. He listened to his troops' concerns, demonstrated care for each and every one of them, and put his life on the line for them. It was the basis of his troopers' trust in him.

When Lieutenant Colonel Derby was killed, the soldiers in his unit were not only grieving over the loss of a friend and comrade; they were mourning the loss of someone they trusted with their lives. They felt rudderless without him. I knew they needed a good new leader, and fast. Western Mosul was a critical location in the fight against radical Sunni Islam, and we needed to get this battalion emotionally sound and back into the fight as quickly as possible.

Working with the commander from the First Cavalry Division, we had to find a capable officer who we could quickly place in charge to lead Derby's battalion. Fortunately, a good candidate—an officer who was already selected for battalion command, although scheduled for a year later—was already in theater. He was tough, personable, and accepted by the battalion's leadership. He quickly proved, through his competence, that he would be an effective leader in this critical location in western Mosul.

The new battalion commander had been in place for only a couple months when I received a call from his superior—the brigade commander—about an issue that needed to be resolved. As I listened to the brigade commander's report, all I could do was shake my head.

Gary Derby created a culture of honor and integrity, so that when leaders in his unit saw something out of standard, they chose to confront and report it. This was the case when these leaders saw something going on with their new commander that they recognized as being outside the values and character of their unit. The new commander had developed an inappropriate online relationship with the spouse of a staff officer. Some of the senior leaders had observed the online dialog and they immediately knew it was wrong. One of the hardest things a subordinate can do is to report a leader's alleged misconduct, but that is what these leaders had to do.

When the brigade commander reported the allegations to me, I initiated an investigation. While the investigation was going on, we temporarily suspended the new commander and sent him home. Sure enough, the investigation substantiated the allegations, and this new commander was relieved of command. That this commander was a highly competent leader did not make him effective in practice. Time and again, I'd seen that no matter how competent you are in the skill sets demanded of your high position, if you fail in character, you fail in leadership.

Shortly after the new commander was sent packing, I went on patrol with the battalion for a day. The soldiers were out of uniform, the noncommissioned officers were not making corrections, and disrespectful comments were made over the radio that we all were able to hear. It was concerning. The Third Battalion, Eighth Cavalry Regiment had suffered the loss of its trusted and competent leader, Gary Derby, and then the loss of its moral compass with the character defects of Derby's replacement. The battalion would continue to work hard at its mission, but it was never the same.

Quite simply, the failure of character in leadership not only has an impact on the individual, but also a significant impact on the climate of the organization, and its ability to accomplish its assigned task. In combat, a unit with a defective organizational climate because of character failure in leadership has impacts not only on mission accomplishment but also the lives of each and every subordinate.

This battalion commander character issue was unfortunately not the only ethical issue of senior leaders I had to deal with during my twelve months as a division commander in Iraq. While in command, I assumed responsibility for the adjudication of any senior-leader misconduct within my division. Most issues of misconduct were not violations of the law of land warfare, but simple character issues linked to living in close quarters while on our forward operating bases. Treating subordinates improperly, hostile command climates, inappropriate relationships, sexual harassment, and sexual assault were alarmingly common themes. Failure to report for duty or violations of General Order Number 1 were also common offenses.[1] They were mostly moral issues of inappropriate behavior, all of which illustrated a breakdown of character.

For each of these cases, not only did these incidents have a severe consequence and in most cases a termination of a career for the accused leader, but they also negatively impacted the health, welfare, morale, and discipline of their units—critical to a unit's success while in combat. I was stunned by the dangerous level of misconduct that I had to contend with and the negative impact that these compromised leaders had on the combat effectiveness of their units. I committed myself to restoring character to its place of critical importance in leadership. I vowed that when I returned to the States, I would seek to make character building and nurturing a focus of my ongoing military career.

After my return from Iraq, the Army assigned me to a position from which I was able to do something about this character crisis I'd witnessed in Iraq—superintendent of the United States Military Academy at West Point. The mission of West Point is to educate, train, and inspire the Corps of Cadets so that each graduate is a commissioned leader of character committed to the values of duty, honor, and country and is prepared for a career of professional excellence and service to the nation as an officer in the US Army. Through one of the best academic and training programs in the country, cadets at West Point are developed intellectually, physically, and militarily. But you notice that the mission statement does not say "educate, train, and inspire leaders who are intellectually or physically competent." It is implied cadets will be intellectually, militarily, and physically competent. Instead, the mission statement says "educate, train, and inspire leaders of character."

"Leaders of character." You can be number one in your class intellectually, but if you fail in character you fail in leadership. Understanding, codifying, and building character was my focus and top priority for the five years I was the superintendent. West Point graduates will not only prosecute war in the crucible of ground combat under the most challenging conditions, but many will also find themselves later in careers as senior officers of great influence in the military, senior leaders in government, and top managers and CEOs in business. As I started to witness the growing character crisis here at home across all disciplines, my mission expanded: if we can instill a set of values to live honorably in each of our graduates, we can change the moral compass of military units, corporate businesses and nonprofits, sports organizations, and many other institutions throughout the country and around the globe. Building leaders of character became my passion for my years as West Point's superintendent. There I met Dr. Mike Matthews, a celebrated West Point professor of psychology noted for his work in helping the Army formulate its strategy and doctrine to build soldier resilience in a time of protracted war.

I retired from the Army in June of 2018, and my mission now is to bring this message about character-driven leadership and how to deliver it to the public at large. Mike and I knew that the first step was a book that would bring our experiences in the field and in the lab to the world, for readers such as you, to understand how to succeed, and to do so in a way that allows one to go to bed proud and able to sleep soundly at night.

We do not have to look far to find breaches of moral conduct and character everywhere in today's society—in government, the corporate world, universities, or elsewhere. Whether we turn on the news or read any paper or magazine in the country, we will find moral, ethical, and character transgressions. But my time at West Point gave me great confidence in the abilities of the next generation of leaders who are preparing themselves on college and university campuses for service across our nation. If they remain focused on strong character, they have great potential to provide the leadership to unify us and to inspire us to the potential of what the American spirit is capable of. The capacity to be a leader in ways big and small resides in all of us, with the proper attention on character. Dr. Matthews and I intend this book to provide a catalyst for this journey to building and sustaining character in each and every one of you.

UNIVERSITY OF PENNSYLVANIA, SUMMER 2005—
PROFESSOR MICHAEL D. MATTHEWS, WEST POINT

I first learned of Dr. Martin Seligman's psychology research when I was in graduate school in the 1970s. Seligman began his career studying how animals learn to avoid electric shock, and the implications of that learning on how humans deal with adversity. By 1975, his work on learned helplessness had worked its way into the popular culture. Seligman had demonstrated that dogs initially exposed to inescapable shock had difficulty in the future learning to avoid escapable shock. Besides their learning deficit, the dogs appeared sad and listless, as if they had given up on life. Seligman saw in this a model for human depression. People who are faced with unsolvable issues and problems also may give up on life and develop depression.[2]

Flashing forward thirty years, Seligman had moved from studying aversive conditioning in animals to founding a new approach to psychology, one that focuses on how humans excel and flourish, rather than their descent into depression and pathology, called positive psychology. In 2005 the John Templeton Foundation funded a summerlong conference for the world's leading positive psychologists. I had met Seligman two years earlier when he visited West Point's Behavioral Sciences & Leadership Department. We shared a common interest in positive psychology. Like Seligman's, my early psychological research looked at aversive conditioning in animals, and like Seligman's, my interests had shifted to understanding optimal human adjustment. Based on this mutual interest, I applied for and was awarded a John Templeton Foundation fellowship to be part of the gathering of positive psychologists at the University of Pennsylvania in 2005, a meeting that Seligman dubbed the Medici II Conference.

I spent that summer thinking about the role of positive psychology in the military and focused on the role of character in shaping individual-soldier performance and leadership. I was greatly influenced by Dr. Christopher Peterson, a University of Michigan positive psychologist and a core member of the Medici II Conference. Together, Peterson and Seligman had previously crafted an inventory of positive character traits and developed and validated a measure for these character traits.[3] Much of the science in *The Character Edge* is based on these ideas, and on research that was inspired by the Medici II.

Seligman also introduced me to one of his graduate students, Angela Duckworth, who was interested in exploring the role of determination and willpower in human accomplishments. He described her as his best graduate student in decades. Having come up with something she called grit, she was looking at how grit influences achievement. Duckworth defines grit as "the passionate pursuit of long-term goals." When we talked about grit, it became clear to me that grit was essential in understanding soldier performance.

I was so taken with the concept of grit that I helped Duckworth collect grit scores of thousands of West Point cadets. Along with data from other groups she had studied, the West Point data formed part of her dissertation. We found that grit was the only factor that reliably predicted which new cadets would successfully complete West Point's grueling basic training, a regimen that begins with their arrival at West Point each summer around the first of July and concludes with the beginning of academic classes in the fall. Some years and many studies later, Duckworth published her book *Grit: The Power of Passion and Perseverance,* which quickly became a *New York Times* bestseller.[4]

Since 2005 I have continued my character research and have along the way spoken with leaders from the military, industry, education, and sports about character as a multiplier of talent and as a core component of effective leadership. I have yet to encounter a leader who does not get the importance of character. As you will see in the pages that follow, successful individuals and leaders grasp the importance of character and are hungry to learn more about what it is, how to measure it, how it develops, and, most important, how to foster an organizational climate that nurtures good character.

COLUMBIA, SOUTH CAROLINA, AND WEST POINT, NEW YORK, SUMMER 2020—
ROBERT CASLEN AND MICHAEL MATTHEWS

We close with a comment on the book's title, *The Character Edge*. Character and leadership are intertwined. Positive character is essential to personal well-being. Your talent can take you a long way in life, but talent alone is not sufficient to perform at your peak. Talent in the absence of integrity, grit, self-regulation, kindness, and a host of other character strengths is simply not enough to allow you to excel and flourish at the highest levels. Character-based leadership also creates organizational climates that enable sustained success, whether on the battlefield or in the corporate boardroom. Character provides individuals and organizations with an edge. By learning about and adopting the ideas we present, you, too, may give yourself an edge in school, your work, or your personal relationships.

The subtitle, *Leading and Winning with Integrity*, is equally important. Individuals and organizations may cheat and so attain a short-term victory. But these short-term wins are at the expense of long-term success. A theme throughout the book is that character allows individuals and organizations to win consistently. We argue that it is better to take a short-term loss or setback than to win at all costs and, in doing so, compromise one's character or the reputation of the organization. Throughout the book, you will meet individuals and leaders of diverse organizations who reinforce this view. We feel so strongly about this that our final chapter focuses entirely on this essential theme.

We invite you to explore our views on the science and practice of character and character-based leadership. Unlike other books on these topics, our ideas are formulated on the solid foundation of leadership experience *and* scientific study. We firmly believe that what you learn here will give you the edge you need to be successful and to win the right way.

HAVE GOOD CHARACTER, DON'T BE ONE

I am aware that a man of real merit is never seen in so favorable
a light as seen through the medium of adversity. The clouds that
surround him are shades that set off his good qualities.

—ALEXANDER HAMILTON[1]

Most tombstones are engraved with a name and a date of birth
and death, separated by a hyphen. The hyphen is a simple
symbol—a mere dash—but it is emblematic of everything that
person was as a human being. It represents both what we call
one's "résumé virtues," the aggregate of the notable events of a
life, and one's "eulogy virtues," the summation of the manner in
which a life was lived—in other words, one's character. For a little
line, it packs a lot of meaning.

And it makes us think. What do you want to be remembered
for? What will the hyphen represent when your time has come?
How do you want to be remembered—for your résumé virtues, or your eulogy virtues? For what you've accomplished
on paper, or for who you are as a person, your core attributes?

Most of us instinctively want to be remembered for our

qualities of character. They are more about who we are as people, our essences. Our desire to be memorialized for the values we exemplified rather than for our undertakings may well have an evolutionary reason, for these essential values are critical to our ability to succeed. Think of the most successful leaders through history: Aristotle, Joan of Arc, Lincoln, Gandhi, Marie Curie, Martin Luther King, Jr., MacArthur. Some of them were brilliant scientists; others were creative visionaries; still others were masterful at strategic planning. They led huge organizations, built grand businesses, led armies to defeat fascism, or inspired whole movements. Their mastery of their field was important to their success. But it wasn't the secret to their highly effective leadership. Their skills, grit, resiliency, charisma, courage, and credibility all emanated from one thing: their strength of character. Raw competence and talent are not strong enough to stand on their own; all successful leadership relies on the critical foundation of a strong character.

The latest research underscores the connection between character and leadership. Leaders who are competent in their field but who lack critical positive character traits such as integrity and honesty may be successful over the short run, but will ultimately fail. Sports teams led by unscrupulous coaches may succeed for a season or two, but fail over the long run. Companies led by CEOs that foster a culture of deceptive practices might report strong quarterly gains for a handful of years, but will ultimately collapse. Governments run by leaders who bully their way out of international treaties and global norms may gain a short-term political or economic upper hand, but will soon find themselves weaker and less secure in critical ways.

A CHARACTER CRISIS?

Character—the moral values and habits of an individual—is in the spotlight more now than perhaps at any other point in history. People through the ages have looked to public figures and institutions for examples of strong character to follow and emulate, but it is hard not to feel that this core quality is now under siege. We are daily bombarded both in the news and on social media with apparent failures of character. Politicians of all stripes lie so frequently that some news organizations keep a running tally of their lies and half-truths. Long-standing and well-established corporations cheat customers and investors. Previously highly regarded individuals are found to have engaged in illegal or socially harmful behavior, including sexual assault and harassment. Powerful people, more often men, use their prestige and position to sexually assault, exploit, and harass others (think #MeToo). Athletes are caught using illegal supplements to enhance on-field performance. Soldiers are accused of abusing prisoners or harming civilians on the battlefield. Students cheat on exams to improve their chances of gaining admission to the best schools. A win-at-any-cost attitude seems to prevail across all major social institutions.

In addition to harming individuals, this character crisis causes great harm to our culture at large. When major institutions are led by people who do not embrace positive values, confidence in the institutions they represent erodes. How can you trust the well-being of your child to a church whose priests are accused of assaulting their most vulnerable members? Why call the police if you do not trust them to treat you fairly and with dignity? Why do you have to pay taxes if you don't trust politicians to spend your money with principle? What about your financial investments? Reports of greed and abuse of customers by large financial institutions make one want to hide cash in a mattress or bury it in the backyard rather than trust a broker to look out for one's best interests.

Even our schools are not exempt. More and more people homeschool their children in no small part because they fear public schools are failing to instill high character and moral values in their children. In speaking with public school leaders around the globe, positive psychologist Martin Seligman has found keen interest in K–12 institutions in developing explicit, scientifically valid approaches to educate children about character. Dr. Seligman has done just this. In several large-scale studies, he reports that the benefits of character education include a higher sense of well-being and better academic performance. Seligman writes, "From my point of view, improvement in grades is a positive byproduct of positive education. But regardless of its influence on success, more well-being is every young person's birthright and we now know that it can and should be taught."[2]

More evidence comes from Mike Erwin, a former Army officer, who founded a nonprofit organization called The Positivity Project.[3] This project provides evidence-based instruction on character development in schools across the United States. Each week, tailored to their age group, students learn about a different character strength and, through interactive exercises, learn how to express this trait in their dealings with others. The Positivity Project has been a smashing success, with so many schools wanting to adopt the program that Erwin has had to scramble to keep up with demand. This hunger for character education in our schools underscores the perception that more needs to be done to set children on the path toward a value-driven life.

A CAUSE FOR HOPE

In psychology's first century as an independent discipline, the psychology of positive character was largely ignored. Sigmund Freud, a medical doctor, focused on psychological approaches to treating mental disorders. Ivan Pavlov, the Russian physiologist, studied basic principles of learning. B. F. Skinner, the American behaviorist, thought that psychologists should only study overt actions and behaviors of animals and humans. For him, delving into unobservable traits and states was essentially nonscientific. More recently, cognitive psychologists have looked at perception, attention, memory, and decision-making, but haven't factored character into their conceptions of how people interpret the world and solve problems.

But things are changing. Today, at any meeting of psychologists, you will find character to be a major topic of discussion. The psychological science of character is increasingly sophisticated. Dr. Matthews and his psychology colleagues are actively designing new ways of classifying, measuring, and developing character, building their understanding of the role character plays in leadership and trust, and in overcoming adversity. They are establishing empirical links between character and personal and social resilience. Organizations are taking notice of this connection. Now colleges and universities, along with the military and private corporations, are systematically integrating character assessment and development into how they select, educate, train, and develop their students and employees. Sports teams—both amateur and professional—are seeking the advice of psychologists who specialize in the study of character to help them build and sustain highly competitive teams. Fortune 500 companies, nonprofits, and other organizations are calling in experts to help them understand how to instill a culture of character. In short, rapid advances in the psychological science of character promise to help remedy the character crisis that the nation is now experiencing.

We sense the public's hunger for a return to core values and high character. The emerging science of character combined with character-based leadership provide hope for a better tomorrow. As you will see in the chapters ahead, character and leadership are directly correlated. This is not limited to the military and CEOs at Fortune 500 companies. We wrote this book because the advantage of strong character and how to foster it should be available to everyone. Gaining the character edge will help you succeed in all aspects of your life. Your bottom line and your relationships will improve. Most important, the world will be a better place.

You are probably asking, What exactly is character? Why does it matter so much to success? Can mine be changed? How? What can I do to show better character? How can I sustain it? How can I develop it in others? Addressing these questions is our mission in *The Character Edge*. We will teach you about the science of character and also, based on decades of leading others in the most dire of circumstances, the art of nurturing and cultivating character in yourself and others. Character will give you a personal competitive edge, and you may then offer others a model to follow and help everyone thrive.

WHAT IS CHARACTER?

Autumn at West Point is a glorious time. The foliage glows gold and orange against the blue of the Hudson River winding below the hills. The football team is hard at practice getting ready for the next big matchup. Plebes are nervous and full of promise. In West Point's Thayer Hall, juniors (known as cows in West Point's lexicon) sit in a classroom in a course required of all cadets, Military Leadership, ready to learn about the value of character. They read a chapter authored by Dr. Matthews on character, what it is, how to assess it, and what it means in leading soldiers in combat. Cadets readily engage in discussion. They want to know more, and the questions fly. Does West Point help me develop character? How? What can I do to strengthen my character? How can I use this self-knowledge to improve my leadership skills? Will my positive character stand up to the adversity of combat and life? This lesson sets the table for a semester of probing character and leadership.

Cadets are challenged to think of the ways we use the word *character:*

- *Lisa is quite a character!*
- *Wow, that is completely out of character for Jim.*
- *We want to encourage our children to be of good character.*
- *He shoplifted because he is a bad character.*

What they learn is what we set out to do here in *The Character Edge*. To understand the idea of character more precisely, to know how to assess it, to learn how to nurture it in ourselves and others, and to develop the skill of using character to achieve desired goals, a formal definition of character is needed.

We define character as "a person acting on his or her world in ways that benefit it and, in turn, the world thereby providing benefits for the person."[4] This definition has three important parts: (1) character involves actual behavior; (2) this behavior has benefits to the world; and (3) these benefits to the world in turn provide benefits to the person. It is not enough to just think the right way about others and the world (although this is laudable)—thoughts and feelings must translate into actions, and these actions must have a positive impact beyond the individual. One might feel sorry for a panhandler one passes on the street, but that same sense of empathy might compel a person of strong character to organize a charity drive to raise funds for blankets and coats for homeless people. Cadets understand the distinction. Many give up spring break to help people in need around the nation and the world, whether helping the homeless in New York City or with hurricane relief in Puerto Rico.

The third part of this definition is often overlooked, but it is the critical piece to convince people—and you readers—that cultivating and maintaining core character is worth your time. It has empirically been proven that exercising positive character traits to do good for others and make the world a better place improves happiness and individual well-being. Scholars agree that character is an attribute of human nature that involves mutually beneficial exchanges between a person and his or her environment or context. Stanford psychologist Bill Damon has spent his career studying moral virtues. He consistently finds that these virtues are linked to life satisfaction. Damon reports, "People who pursue noble purposes are filled with joy, despite the constant sacrifices they feel called upon to make."[5] It is a case of "you scratch my back, and I will scratch yours." But this "back-scratching" involves genuinely beneficial actions.

Another feature of character is consistency over place and time. At West Point, it is not good enough to be honest in the classroom if you then lie to others about your accomplishments or actions outside the classroom. A cadet can't live honorably at West Point and abandon his or her values after leaving the academy grounds. And, importantly, character plays out over time. As you will discover in the pages ahead, research overwhelmingly shows that character is learned like other behaviors and attributes and, if mindfully attended to, may grow as we mature. We recognize this at West Point, where more discretion is given to plebes (who would be called freshman at other universities) who violate the honor code than is given to firsties (called seniors at other colleges), who have had more time to learn and internalize these values. Living honorably is to have these values become part of our essence, so that if we are faced with a compromising situation, we do not have to think about what is right or wrong—our natural reaction is the manifestation of these internalized principles.

Another way to consider this is to picture yourself holding a cup of coffee filled to the top when someone accidently bumps into your arm. What is in that cup is going to spill out whether you want it to or not. What spills out is the essence of what was inside. Say someone cuts you off while you are driving. Do you swear and blare your horn? Or do you take a deep breath and be grateful that neither of you were harmed? When a colleague gleefully gossips to you about another colleague's home troubles, do you find yourself contributing to the gossip or do you step away, suggesting that the person's home life is likely difficult and definitely none of your business? When you discover a mistake on an invoice and find a client has overpaid your company, do you look the other way and deposit the check, or do you email the client to rectify the problem? In the myriad of unexpected situations confronting us daily, we find ourselves instinctively reacting. Our actions are the true manifestation of the values we have internalized. If we actively and consistently develop our character over time, our actions in all situations will be consistent with the values of our character.

So, in part, strengthening one's character involves doing good things that benefit others, which therefore brings benefits to oneself, and doing it consistently over time and place. This is a necessary condition for the establishment of trust. In our experience, trust is the most important aspect in being an effective leader. We as humans naturally and through socialization have a sense of what good character means. The scientific study of character shows that where you live, your culture, your ethnicity, your nationality, have little bearing on character. People throughout the world share a common view of what constitutes positive character and virtue. Different cultures may emphasize or value certain character attributes more than others, but there is consensus on what right character looks like.

A CLASSIFICATION OF CHARACTER STRENGTHS

We can all think of strengths of character. Who doesn't know the apocryphal story of George Washington and the cherry tree? But what exactly are the traits that count? Are they the same for everyone, or do values depend on the culture in which one is raised? Modern psychology provides us with a more comprehensive way of classifying and understanding the full range of positive character strengths. The broadest and most useful classification of these strengths was first proposed in 2004 by two founders of positive psychology—Dr. Christopher Peterson of the University of Michigan and Dr. Martin Seligman of the University of Pennsylvania.[6] Together, they studied everything that psychologists and other social scientists had learned about character over the past hundred years. They also studied the world's major religions and the writings of philosophers from around the globe, beginning with Aristotle up to contemporary times. Seligman and Peterson identified twenty-four character strengths that are common in the human species. These twenty-four character strengths are universal and not dependent on specific cultures. Honesty, it turns out, is valued by all people in all cultures. Not all individuals are honest (far from it, unfortunately), but across the planet the trait is treasured and considered a hallmark of a virtuous life.

Seligman and Peterson's ideas spawned thousands of studies of character. A study of more than twelve thousand adults in the United States and Germany revealed that the character strengths of love, hope, curiosity, zest, and (particularly) gratitude were linked to high life satisfaction.[7] In parents of children with cancer, the parents who are higher in optimism do a better job of coping with the challenges of dealing with their child's disease than do pessimistic parents.[8] In another study, Dr. Matthews investigated the impact of character among US Army combat commanders. One commander had endured several of his soldiers killed in combat action. Another commander's wife announced to him, halfway through his combat tour, that she was divorcing him. Yet another worked for an unethical commander who allowed graft and corruption in his battalion. Matthews found that, whatever the challenge, certain strengths of character were called upon to deal with the adversities. These officers most frequently turned to five specific strengths described by Peterson and Seligman to cope with such tough situations: teamwork, bravery, capacity to love, persistence, and integrity.[9]

Seligman and Peterson classify these twenty-four character strengths into six overarching categories called moral virtues. These six moral virtues, with their associated character strengths, are:

- *wisdom and knowledge* (creativity, curiosity, open-mindedness, love of learning, perspective)

- *courage* (bravery, persistence, integrity, zest)

- *justice* (teamwork, fairness, leadership)

- *humanity* (capacity to love, kindness, social intelligence)

- *temperance* (forgiveness, humility, prudence, self-regulation)

- *transcendence* (appreciation of beauty, gratitude, hope/optimism, humor, and spirituality)

We each have a unique profile of character strengths. This helps define who we are as individuals. Artists may find that their top character strengths cluster in the moral virtue of transcendence. A soldier may be particularly strong in the moral virtue of courage. Frequently, our highest strengths are scattered across the six moral virtues. A professor needs to embrace and display love of learning and curiosity in her role as a teacher and scholar. But in her role as a family member and parent, strengths of humanity such as capacity to love and kindness are important. A full, well-lived life is enhanced by having strengths from across the moral virtues.

WHAT ARE MY CHARACTER STRENGTHS?

Now it is time to learn about your own character strengths. It turns out we are pretty good at recognizing our strengths of character, especially if given a set of questions to consider. For a quick assessment of your twenty-four character strengths, complete Exercise 1.1.

EXERCISE 1.1. RATE YOUR CHARACTER STRENGTHS.

Use the following 9-point scale to rate yourself on each of the twenty-four character strengths.

For example, if you feel you are quite open-minded, rate yourself 7 or above. If you feel you are rather rigid in your beliefs, rate yourself 3 or below. If you feel you are moderately open-minded, or if it depends on the topic, then a rating of 4, 5, or 6 would be appropriate.

CREATIVITY

1	2	3	4	5	6	7	8	9

CURIOSITY

1	2	3	4	5	6	7	8	9

OPEN-MINDEDNESS

1	2	3	4	5	6	7	8	9

LOVE OF LEARNING

1	2	3	4	5	6	7	8	9

THE CHARACTER EDGE

PERSPECTIVE								
1	2	3	4	5	6	7	8	9

BRAVERY								
1	2	3	4	5	6	7	8	9

PERSISTENCE								
1	2	3	4	5	6	7	8	9

INTEGRITY								
1	2	3	4	5	6	7	8	9

ZEST								
1	2	3	4	5	6	7	8	9

TEAMWORK								
1	2	3	4	5	6	7	8	9

FAIRNESS								
1	2	3	4	5	6	7	8	9

LEADERSHIP								
1	2	3	4	5	6	7	8	9

CAPACITY TO LOVE								
1	2	3	4	5	6	7	8	9

KINDNESS								
1	2	3	4	5	6	7	8	9

SOCIAL INTELLIGENCE								
1	2	3	4	5	6	7	8	9

FORGIVENESS								
1	2	3	4	5	6	7	8	9

HUMILITY								
1	2	3	4	5	6	7	8	9

PRUDENCE								
1	2	3	4	5	6	7	8	9

SELF-REGULATION								
1	2	3	4	5	6	7	8	9

APPRECIATION OF BEAUTY								
1	2	3	4	5	6	7	8	9

GRATITUDE								
1	2	3	4	5	6	7	8	9

HOPE AND OPTIMISM								
1	2	3	4	5	6	7	8	9

SENSE OF HUMOR								
1	2	3	4	5	6	7	8	9

SPIRITUALITY								
1	2	3	4	5	6	7	8	9

To determine your highest character strengths, simply note which of the twenty-four strengths have the highest numbers. Look for your six or seven highest strengths. There may be some ties; that is okay. Then, to see how your strengths are distributed across the six moral virtues, circle your highest character strengths in Table 1.1.

TABLE 1.1 MORAL VIRTUES & CHARACTER STRENGTHS					
WISDOM & KNOWLEDGE	COURAGE	JUSTICE	HUMANITY	TEMPERANCE	TRANSCENDENCE
CREATIVITY	BRAVERY	TEAMWORK	CAPACITY TO LOVE	FORGIVENESS	APPRECIATION OF BEAUTY
CURIOSITY	PERSISTENCE	FAIRNESS	KINDNESS	HUMILITY	GRATITUDE
OPEN-MINDEDNESS	INTEGRITY	LEADERSHIP	SOCIAL INTELLIGENCE	PRUDENCE	HOPE/ OPTIMISM
LOVE OF LEARNING	ZEST			SELF-REGULATION	HUMOR
PERSPECTIVE					SPIRITUALITY

The nice thing about character strengths is that they are all good. Think about how you use your top strengths in the many roles you play in your daily life, both at home, work, or school, and with your family, friends, colleagues, and others.

Peterson and Seligman provide a more systematic way of assessing character strengths—the Values-in-Action Inventory of Strengths (VIA-IS). The VIA-IS consists of multiple questions that tap into each character strength and provide insight into one's personal, unique profile of strengths. The VIA-IS is available online at no charge. Go to www.authentichappiness.org, register, and then look at the menu for the VIA-IS. Complete the test. You can request different types of feedback. We suggest that you ask for a rank ordering, from highest to lowest, of your character strengths.

How did you come out? Again, keep in mind there are no bad character strengths. Peterson and Seligman believe it is particularly instructive to look at your top five or six strengths, which they refer to as *signature strengths*. By this, they mean the character strengths that are not only your highest, but are also the ones that you may find the easiest to use to achieve goals, respond to setbacks, excel at school or work, or enhance personal and social well-being. You may also find it insightful to see if your signature strengths tend to group within one or two of the moral virtues or are scattered across all six.

It may also be instructive to look at your lowest character strengths. Don't be dismayed if a character trait you value falls relatively lower on your hierarchy of strengths. Remember, this is a rank ordering. Even if all of your strengths, compared to those of other people, are relatively high, your rank ordering of strengths will still produce some at the bottom. A strength you value, such as spirituality, could appear low on your hierarchy but still be strong overall when compared to that of other people.

When thinking about your profile of character strengths, also keep in mind that we intuitively turn to specific strengths of character depending on the situation in which we find ourselves. Perhaps spirituality is not one of your signature strengths, but at certain times and in certain situations in your life, spirituality may be of overarching importance. (An axiom of combat: "There are no atheists in foxholes.") Being a successful and well-adjusted person not only requires knowing your character strengths, but also matching them to the different challenges we all face in life's journey. Think of your strengths as being a toolbox. The goal is to learn to match the right strength to the right job.

GROWING CHARACTER

You now have a better idea of your character strengths. What use is this information? A major theme of this book is that character can be nurtured and grown. We are not stuck with whatever character we currently have. We see this at West Point, where the academic, military, and physical-fitness curriculum is explicitly designed to allow cadets to learn about their character, and to hone the attributes of character necessary to lead soldiers in combat. Parents know that they have a huge influence on the character development of their children. Schools from kindergarten through the twelfth grade recognize "citizenship" and character as vital parts of a complete education. Both science and practice agree that the actions of leaders, parents, and teachers are vital in character development. And character does not display itself in a vacuum. The culture of the organization you are in plays a significant role in whether you reliably display positive character. In later chapters we will take a close look at how a variety of organizations including West Point may impact both the development and display of positive character.

CHARACTER, CULTURE, AND LEADERSHIP

You can alter your character. But it is not just something inside you; it is influenced by the culture around you. The culture of a military unit, a school, a workplace, or any other organization is critical to its growth, values, morale, learning, development, and mission success. The person responsible for that culture is the commander, the principal, the CEO, or the leader.

Trusted Army leaders, such as Lieutenant Colonel Derby, described in the preface, are first and foremost competent at their jobs. They know strategy, tactics, and procedures and demonstrate general combat expertise. But that is not enough to lead effectively in combat. Effective leaders are also of high character. They are honest and courageous and of high integrity. But even this is not enough. They have to be perceived as having a true interest in their soldiers' well-being. These leaders put the needs and welfare of their soldiers far above their own needs for personal glory or promotion. And putting soldiers first has to be genuine; if not, it is quickly discovered.

Sadly, some leaders fail in this regard. We learned the story of the battalion commander who, although technically competent, failed in character and therefore failed in trust and leadership. Most soldiers would prefer a leader with average competence who exemplified high character and cared for his or her troops over a highly competent commander who did not possess high character and caring. Character and caring may be less tangible than competence, but they are just as vital to effective trusted leadership.

Think about leaders in your personal experience, including workplace managers, coaches, or teachers. You don't have to be a combat soldier to need a leader who is competent, of high character, and who cares about you. The coach who knows all of the X's and Y's but fails in integrity will fail both as a leader and in leading his or her team to consistent success. The police lieutenant who is competent and of high integrity, but puts his or her career ahead of those he or she leads, will never be fully trusted or respected. The boss who assumes credit for your idea in a meeting with the company head cannot ever hold your trust or respect.

ORGANIZATIONS CAN AND MUST SET THE STANDARD

In his book *Black Hearts,* Jim Frederick describes the actions of First Platoon, Bravo Company, First Battalion, 502nd Infantry Regiment. Deployed to Iraq in late 2005, without enough soldiers and equipment, the regiment was assigned to the so-called Triangle of Death south of Baghdad.[10] Undermanned and stationed in outposts subject to near-daily enemy fire, with heavy casualties, the soldiers were poorly fed, sleep-deprived, and constantly dealing with the death or wounding of their comrades.

These soldiers rarely felt safe and secure from the enemy. Isolated from higher headquarters, First Platoon soon established unique norms and ways of doing things, and these did not reflect the standards of conduct and discipline expected of Army soldiers. On March 12, 2006, four First Platoon soldiers exacted revenge for their hardships on a local Iraqi family. Fueled by anger and frustration, and enabled by a questionable command climate, these soldiers brutally raped a fourteen-year-old girl, before murdering her and setting her body on fire. They also murdered her parents and her sixteen-year-old sister. Ultimately, five soldiers were charged and either found guilty or pleaded guilty to charges stemming from this incident. Charges against a sixth soldier were dropped in exchange for his testimony, and he accepted an administrative discharge from the Army.

The *Black Hearts* story illustrates an extreme example of what can go wrong when leaders fail to adequately monitor, embrace, and reinforce positive values and character among their members. Many other examples come from athletics, education, politics, and the corporate world. Positive character must be a focus for leaders in all organizations. Equally important, the organization itself must have a clear values statement and provide explicit structure and support that promotes and rewards positive character. The Army, for example, formally embraces seven values necessary to fight and win wars. Leaders and soldiers are constantly reminded of these seven values, through formal training and by artifacts such as key chains or posters listing these values. The seven Army values are loyalty, duty, respect, selfless service, honor, integrity, and personal courage. Had these values been emphasized and practiced by those involved in the *Black Hearts* incident, the legacy of First Platoon may have been far different.

High-character organizations inculcate their values into the fabric of their culture. This does not happen by chance. Leaders at every level must internalize and live these values and, in doing so, set an example for others within the organization—whether it's the Army, the local Parent Teacher Association, the Transit Authority, an investment firm, or other institution. This topic is so important that we devote an entire chapter to it later in this book and explore and describe specific examples from a variety of organizations of how to achieve a consistent positive occupational climate and culture. Positive character comes not just from within individuals, but from outside by living and working in settings where positive character is modeled and valued. Learning to form a positive culture in an organization is the most important thing that a leader may do to promote individual positive character among its employees, students, or members.

WHAT YOU DO AND WHO YOU ARE OUTSIDE THE LINES MATTERS

Following each Major League Baseball season, a single player from the hundreds of players among the thirty teams is selected for a great honor, the Roberto Clemente Award. This award is not given to the player who hits the most home runs or the pitcher who leads the league in strikeouts. Rather, it is given to the one player who "best represents the game of Baseball through extraordinary character, community involvement, philanthropy and positive contributions, both on and off the field."[11]

Baseball fans will know that this award is given in Roberto Clemente's honor not just because he was a Hall of Fame player, but because he placed the good of his community above his own safety and personal needs. Roberto Clemente was killed in an air crash just weeks after the 1972 baseball season while delivering supplies and aid to victims of an earthquake in Nicaragua.

In 2018, the Roberto Clemente Award was given to St. Louis Cardinals catcher Yadier Molina. A great player indeed, Molina may perhaps find himself in baseball's Hall of Fame in Cooperstown following his playing days, but he is much more than just an amazingly talented catcher. Growing up in Puerto Rico in a baseball-obsessed family, young Molina heard his father tell stories about the great Roberto Clemente, and a picture of Clemente was proudly displayed in the family home.[12] Molina's father told tales of how great a player Clemente was, but praised him for being "even better outside the lines." Yadier Molina must have taken his father's words to heart. His good deeds and actions outside the lines consistently demonstrate character strengths from the moral virtue of humanity. Several years ago, Molina established a charitable organization, called Foundation 4, to assist youths impacted by adversity, including poverty, abuse, and cancer. Foundation 4 has built a safe house for children and purchases state-of-the-art equipment to help hospitals in Puerto Rico treat children with cancer and other severe ailments. Molina led efforts to provide aid to Puerto Rico as it recovered from Hurricane Maria. He raised more than $800,000 to support relief efforts and personally labored from dawn to dusk in Puerto Rico for fourteen consecutive days immediately after the storm, offering aid and comfort to victims.

To be a leader, whether of a baseball team, a military unit, or other organization, it is not enough to just do your job. Molina's actions are those of a trusted leader. He is competent between the lines and outside the lines, and he applies the character strengths of kindness and capacity to love to every aspect of his life. In sports, as in other walks of life, we depend on our teammates to support and nurture us, and to help us fulfill our potential. Molina is this kind of person—through his own positive character, he raises up his teammates. Fans of all teams know well the deep impact that both good and bad role models have on team morale and performance.

THE CHARACTER EDGE AHEAD

In the chapters that follow, we dig deep into what aspects of character are most important in leadership. We explore individual and organizational attributes that are vital to effective leadership. We break these down into character strengths of the head, heart, and gut—that is to say, character strengths pertaining to good thinking, compassion for others, and courage. These are followed by a chapter focusing entirely on trust, expanding the ideas presented here, and a chapter devoted to the role of the organization in promoting, influencing, and sustaining positive character.

After expanding on the character attributes that make you a better leader, *The Character Edge* then examines how to select people for your organization that are not just competent, but also of high character. We then focus on how to cultivate individual positive character, looking at state-of-the-art approaches to this goal, including West Point's Leader Development System. Instrumental to character development is learning from adversity and challenge, and we look at how this is accomplished, examine why people fail to display positive character, and discuss ways to mitigate against such failures. Even the best people sometimes fall short of their goal of honorable living, and we identify tactics that each of us may employ to guard against these failures.

We conclude with a chapter called "Winning the Right Way." Here, we articulate the critical importance of character in all aspects of our lives and provide an integrated approach to achieving this goal. Throughout *The Character Edge,* we emphasize and illustrate the relationship between character and leadership. We look forward to leading you through this exploration. Character is significant to your well-being and to those whom you lead, follow, or teach. By learning to build and sustain character, you will be gaining the edge to success in life.

STRENGTHS OF THE GUT

I learned that courage was not the absence of fear, but the triumph over it. The brave man is not he who does not feel afraid, but he who conquers that fear.

—NELSON MANDELA[1]

Patriotism runs high in Bladenboro, North Carolina. This was especially so in the years following World War II. Barry Bridger was adopted in 1945 by H. C. Bridger, Jr., the son of the founder of Bladenboro. Barry had faint recollections of the war, but as he grew up, he knew he wanted to serve his country, just like the adults he loved had done around the globe during the war. His stepbrother, McCrea Bridger, flew in the Ferry Command in World War II and served as an early inspiration for Barry to some-day join the military. Barry went to high school at the Sewanee Military Academy in Sewanee, Tennessee. There, his interest in military service was further strengthened, and he matriculated at the University of North Carolina in 1958. With the advent of the jet age and early space exploration, Barry eagerly joined the Air Force Reserve Officer Training Corps (ROTC) at the univer-sity and, upon graduation in 1962, received his commission as a second lieutenant in the US Air Force. Flight school and assignments to operational Air Force fighter squadrons soon followed. The US involvement in the Vietnam War was rapidly escalating, and Bridger, now a captain, was soon flying combat missions over both South and North Vietnam.

January 23, 1967, is a day that Captain Bridger will never forget. Flying with the 497th Tactical Fighter Squadron based at Ubon Royal Thai Air Force Base, Bridger's F-4 Phantom fighter plane was disabled over North Vietnam. Forced to eject, he was taken prisoner by the North Vietnamese and soon found himself in the infamous Hỏa Lò prison, known among its American prisoners as the Hanoi Hilton. Thus began an ordeal of 2,232 days as a prisoner of war (POW), which would end with his repatriation on March 4, 1973. His character, forged by his parents and loving community as a youth, now faced a test.

Conditions at the Hanoi Hilton were horrible. Bridger and his fellow prisoners were chronically underfed. Poorly clothed, even in the relatively mild weather of the dry season, they were often cold. Things were worse during the monsoon season, when the mean high temperature in Hanoi exceeds ninety degrees Fahrenheit and lows often drop only to the low eighties. Worse was the humidity, averaging 85 percent during the monsoon, resulting in a heat index exceeding 130 degrees on many days. Rodents, insects, and even snakes were common. It was the perfect recipe for illness, and many of the prisoners suffered continually from intestinal distress and other chronic diseases. Hard enough for a healthy person to endure, these ailments were potentially deadly for the POWs.

The prisoners were subjected to frequent torture and physical abuse, sometimes so extreme that it crippled them for weeks or months at a time. The guards could come get them at any time, without warning. There was no safe time to relax, to heal, and to get their heads together. And there was no end in sight. By the time Bridger was released, he had been a POW for six years and forty days. Others endured for even longer. Army captain Floyd James Thompson was captured on March 26, 1964, after his observation airplane was shot down. Thompson has the dubious distinction of being the longest-held American POW during the Vietnam War, spending nearly nine years (3,278 days) in captivity, the last six years of which were in the Hanoi Hilton. The uncertainty of when, or even if, they would ever be released added to the horror of their situation and, for some, led to despair and hopelessness.

Years later, long retired from the Air Force as a lieutenant colonel, Bridger recalled his experience:

> If you were captured by the North Vietnamese, you were placed into a concrete box. You had no idea what was about to happen. You were all alone with your thoughts and values. Eventually you were taken to an interrogation and given two choices. Cooperate fully with the North Vietnamese camp authority, or go to the torture chamber.[2]

Bridger received numerous awards and medals for his experience and service to his country. One was the Silver Star, which is the third-highest award that the US Air Force bestows for valor (the highest being the Medal of Honor). His Silver Star citation illustrates what he endured while recognizing his character strength of devotion to duty to enable him to persevere under such conditions:

This officer distinguished himself by gallantry and intrepidity in action in connection with military operations against an opposing armed force while a Prisoner of War in North Vietnam. Ignoring international agreements on treatment of prisoners of war, the enemy resorted to mental and physical cruelties to obtain information, confessions and propaganda materials. This American resisted their demands by calling upon his deepest inner strengths in a manner which reflected his devotion to duty and great credit upon himself and the United States Air Force.[3]

We conclude Barry Bridger's story with something he said on his return to the United States after more than six years as a POW. His statement summarizes his character and his honorable service as a prisoner of war: "Now I've come home with the satisfaction of knowing I served with honor."

UNPACKING COURAGE

Most of us, thankfully, will never have to fly a combat mission over enemy territory. By virtue of being human, each of us inevitably faces situations requiring moral courage, grit, or integrity and—perhaps when you least expect it—physical courage as well. It takes moral courage to deal with a life-threatening illness. Equally important are integrity and honesty. In many ways, doing something that is physically brave is easier than being consistently honest and of high integrity. A police officer chasing an armed suspect must have physical bravery. The brave act is over, and you move on. But we face challenges to our integrity and honesty daily. You can't let your defenses down. Foul up just once and it may take years to regain trust and confidence among others.

In this spirit, West Point cadets are taught to choose "the harder right" over "the easier wrong."[4]

For Bridger and his fellow POWs, moral courage—standing up for what is right even when it may cause you harm—enabled them to persevere and endure. These values came from their upbringing, their spiritual beliefs, and from values of honor and integrity inculcated in them from their military training and culture. Their focus was on others, not themselves. It is difficult to imagine the resolve it took to sustain this focus for the long months and years of captivity. As Bridger observed:

> For America's Vietnam POWs, the depravity and evil of our existence ravaged our minds and bodies; but the values of a good heart, the strength of our spirit was empowered by each selfless act to rally around those in greater need than ourselves. It was a point of honor, therefore, to remain in the torture chamber as long as possible to deny its use for a fellow POW.[5]

There is more to understanding the strengths of the gut than simply recognizing the distinction between physical and moral courage. Psychologists Paul Lester and Cynthia Pury point out three factors that must be present for an act to be considered courageous.[6]

FREE CHOICE (VOLITION)

The courageous act must involve a conscious and deliberate decision. Captain Bridger volunteered to serve in the Air Force and chose to be a fighter pilot. He put himself, by conscious choice, into harm's way. This applies equally well to moral courage. Martin Luther King, Jr., stood by his values, risking personal harm and ruin, for the betterment of others. Certainly, he showed remarkable physical courage. But his moral courage was what inspired his generation and generations to come.

History is full of such iconic figures. Some are household names such as Florence Nightingale or more recently, Mother Teresa. Others are less well known, such as Sophie Scholl. Scholl's story is both inspiring and illustrative of the power of moral courage. Scholl was a Munich university student who joined her brother and friends to set up an underground resistance movement in World War II. Arrested by the Nazis in 1943, she was executed by guillotine on February 22, 1943. Like all youths of that period, Scholl was indoctrinated with Nazi propaganda, but she quickly identified with the anti-Nazi views of her father and her older brother, Hans. Outraged after learning of the mass execution of Russian prisoners of war on the eastern front and the mass murder of Jews, Scholl and a small group of dissenters began writing and distributing pamphlets calling for passive resistance of the Nazi regime. Scholl was arrested for distributing these pamphlets, found guilty of treason, and executed, along with her brother Hans and another student, Christoph Probst. Sophie's words, reflecting her utter devotion to fighting the evils of the Nazi regime, echo to this day: "What does my death matter if, through us, thousands of people are awakened and stirred to action."[7]

Daily, moral courage makes a tremendous impact on the quality of our lives. The actions of the student who stands up against bullies in school may not make the headlines or the history books, but is essential nonetheless, as the foundation of a civil society.

NOBLE OR WORTHY GOAL

To be considered courageous, the act must be done in pursuit of a goal that is valued by society. Captain Bridger's physical and moral courage was motivated by his love of his fellow POWs and for his country, not by personal gain. In contrast, some people engage in foolish and dangerous behaviors that serve no higher purpose. Watch *America's Funniest Home Videos* or spend some time watching YouTube videos. A fad among teens is the Bird Box challenge—driving while blindfolded and livestreaming it or putting it on social media. Driving while blindfolded is not courageous; it is simply foolish!

SIGNIFICANT PERSONAL RISK

True courage requires you to have some skin in the game. This may be physical, moral, or both. Captain Bridger refused to cooperate with his captors' demands to divulge sensitive military information or to make statements that would sully the reputation of his country. He could cooperate with the enemy and compromise his oath to support and defend the Constitution of the United States, or he could refuse and go to the torture chamber. He chose torture or even the prospect of death rather than sacrificing his values.

Another exemplar of courage is Chiune Sugihara, a Japanese diplomat assigned to a Lithuanian consulate in 1939. Recognizing the peril they faced under Nazi rule, many Jews fled to Lithuania in hopes of finding refuge there or as a waypoint to other destinations. To travel legally without a visa was nearly impossible, especially for Jews. Seeing the persecution of Jewish people, and anticipating even more draconian actions, Sugihara repeatedly asked his superiors for permission to grant individual Jews and Jewish families transit visas so they could escape. Each time he asked, he was denied.

So, by his own choice, at great personal risk, and for a noble cause, Sugihara defied his superiors and issued transit visas to Jews as fast as he could write them (a task done by hand in those days). In every spare moment, day and night, he wrote visas. He did this from July 31 until September 4, 1940, when the consulate closed and he was forced to leave. As he left, he gave his visa stamp to a refugee, so more visas could be issued. Sugihara's actions are estimated to have allowed six thousand Jews to escape the Nazis. An estimated forty thousand descendants of these Jewish families came into the world because of his selfless actions.

Why did Sugihara do this? He could have faced imprisonment or even execution from his own government for defying orders. His family could have suffered as well. When asked why he did this, he replied simply, "We had thousands of people hanging out the windows of our residence, there was no other way." Nine years before his death in 1986, he said, "I told the ministry of foreign affairs it was a matter of humanity. I did not care if I lost my job. Anyone else would have done the same thing if they were in my place."[8] Others see his courage in a different light. In 1984, Yad Vashem, Israel's official memorial to the Holocaust, recognized Mr. Sugihara as a Righteous Among the Nations, an honor bestowed to non-Jews who risked their lives during World War II to save Jews from extermination by the Nazis. To this day, he remains the only Japanese citizen to receive this honor.

The three attributes of the moral virtue of courage are indeed important considerations, but we think there are several more.

PERSONAL COURAGE IS MORE THAN A ONETIME RESPONSE TO AN ISOLATED SITUATION

Consider the case of Brendan Marrocco. One of the deadliest threats to American soldiers in Iraq was the explosive-formed projectile (EFP), a shaped charge designed to penetrate armor by deforming a metal plate into an armor slug. It is used along with other roadside bombs, called improvised explosive devices (IEDs).

On the evening of April 11, 2009, the night before Easter Sunday, a patrol in Salah ad Din province was returning to their base when the second vehicle in the convoy triggered an EFP, which immediately penetrated the door of a mine-resistant, ambush-protected vehicle (known as an MRAP). These vehicles are armored to protect occupants against many of the IEDs. As the war progressed, the enemy developed the EFP into a roadside IED, designed to penetrate the MRAP's door and create a deadly metal spray inside the vehicle. This EFP tore into the driver's arms and legs and severely wounded both the gunner and vehicle commander.

The driver was Private First Class Brendan Marrocco, from Staten Island, New York. Brendan's injuries were significant. Both of his arms and both of his legs were mangled, and the artery in his neck was severed. He suffered significant injuries to his face, including a broken eye socket and broken nose, the loss of eight teeth, shrapnel in his eye and face, severe lacerations, and burns to his neck and face. His left eardrum was pierced.

When the attack occurred, the unit immediately called for a medevac to Tikrit, where the combat support hospital (CSH) was located. Unfortunately, the initial weather call, during a dust storm, would not allow a helicopter to fly to the attack site. Medevac pilots take the weather call as a recommendation, but they knew the severity of the attack and that three lives depended on getting these soldiers to the proper medical care as soon as possible. So, without hesitation, knowing the risks of flying at night in the middle of a dust storm, the pilots cranked up a helicopter for the forty-five-minute flight to the attack site, loaded all the injured soldiers, including Brendan, and evacuated them to the CSH in Tikrit.

Upon arrival at the hospital, one soldier had already died, and the medical team did all they could to save the life of the driver—Brendan Marrocco. Word spread across the base that the wounded soldiers needed blood transfusions, and more than 150 soldiers lined up to donate blood to keep their brothers-in-arms alive. The medical experts worked feverishly to save Brendan's life. A couple hours later, they rolled Brendan into the recovery room. He was alive, but the drastic measures needed to save his life left Brendan with no arms and no legs. His head was wrapped in gauze, and he was covered by a blanket to keep him warm. Brendan would not wake up until a few days later, when he finally got to the Walter Reed National Military Medical Center, but the care and compassion from the CSH medical team were overwhelming. Throughout the night Brendan received fifty-nine pints of blood donated by his teammates.

While he was still in the recovery room, the medical team determined he needed upgraded care at another hospital, in Balad, located outside Baghdad. With the dust storm ongoing and visibility zero, air control would not give a green light for the flight to Balad. Nonetheless, the medevac team and in-flight nurse loaded Brendan into the helicopter and flew him to Balad, where he received another eighteen pints of blood and additional care. Brendan was shortly moved to Landstuhl, Germany, then to Walter Reed, where he finally regained consciousness.

Fast-forward to November 2009. Caslen received word that Brendan and his family were flying to Hawaii to participate in the Twenty-Fifth Division's homecoming activities. Brendan's platoon arrived home a couple days before his scheduled flight, and instead of Brendan meeting the platoon on their arrival, the platoon decided to meet Brendan when he arrived in Hawaii from Walter Reed. The platoon (about twenty-five soldiers) all received gate passes at the Honolulu airport and were able to walk to the arrival gate for Brendan's plane. When the airplane arrived, the last passenger off the plane was Brendan. With the entire platoon waiting, arms outstretched, everyone yelling and cheering, there came Brendan with two prosthetic legs and two prosthetic arms, walking unassisted down the jetway into the arms of his platoon. There was not a dry eye anywhere, and against all odds, the platoon celebrated the reunion with their wounded brother-in-arms.

In December 2012, Brendan underwent a thirteen-hour operation to transplant two arms from a cadaver donor, and today he has partial use of both arms, where before he had only two stumps. His mental and physical toughness are examples of the tenacity needed to overcome adversity and to persevere in the direst situations life has to offer.

Brendan's story is a great example of strengths of the gut. Men and women who in the direst circumstances persevere over long periods draw strength as they continue to move forward. Despite what life has thrown at them, with mental and physical toughness and grit, they see their way through the challenges and overcome obstacles.

Courage is not a flash in the pan. As with Brendan, your character strengths of courage play out over the long haul. We hope you never have to endure challenges like Brendan's, but the day-to-day courage needed to persevere and succeed in life is no less an exemplar of what is meant by the moral virtue of courage.

TRUE COURAGE IS SELFLESS

At the end of *Band of Brothers*—the book by Stephen E. Ambrose—the grandson of Sergeant Mike Ranney asks him if he was a hero in the war. In a poignant reply, Sergeant Ranney said, "No, but I served in a company of heroes."[9] While most of us would have disagreed with his assessment (Sergeant Ranney was clearly a hero himself), his response was typical of people who have displayed great courage.

Other examples come to mind. Captain Sullenberger, after landing US Airways Flight 1549 on the Hudson River when his Airbus A 320 lost its engines following a bird strike, was the last person off the aircraft as he helped passengers and crew onto life rafts and rescue boats. Afterward, the Guild of Air Pilots and Air Navigators awarded Captain Sullenberger and the entire crew the Master's Medal. New York City mayor Michael Bloomberg gave them the keys to the city, and they received high praise from both New York governor David Paterson and President

Barack Obama. In 2016, Tom Hanks starred in the movie *Sully: Miracle on the Hudson*. Directed by Hollywood legend Clint Eastwood, the movie was a huge box-office success. And what did Captain Sullenberger have to say about his actions that day? Downplaying his personal courage of that moment, he said, "We all have heard about ordinary people who find themselves in extraordinary situations. They act courageously or responsibly, and their efforts are described as if they opted to act that way on the spur of the moment. . . . I believe many people in those situations actually have made decisions years before."[10] That is, he attributes his heroism that day to years of training and experience, not some sudden rush of personal courage.

The US military confers its highest award for valor, the Medal of Honor, to soldiers, sailors, marines, or airmen who display great courage on the battlefield. A citation describing the heroic actions that resulted in the award accompanies each Medal of Honor. Psychologist Nansook Park analyzed the content of these citations for 123 Medal of Honor recipients, from World War I to the current conflicts. She identified a number of character strengths that were consistently mentioned in these citations, including bravery (not surprisingly), self-regulation, perseverance (grit), leadership, teamwork, creativity, and kindness. More than anything else, Park found that humility was the character strength infused throughout the narratives. Like Sergeant Ranney from *Band of Brothers*, Medal of Honor recipients will deny being a hero and will always point to the men and women serving with them as the true heroes.

Humility is a strikingly consistent trait among the courageous. They readily admit that training helped them in their moment of truth and that their love of others motivated their actions. If you meet someone who self-proclaims to be a hero or highly courageous, think again. The person probably is not.

GRIT—A SPECIAL KIND OF COURAGE

When beginning her doctoral studies in psychology at the University of Pennsylvania under the direction of the eminent psychologist Martin Seligman, Angela Duckworth asked herself why highly talented people often failed to rise to the very top of their fields, and why others with perhaps less talent achieved great things. Reflecting on her time as a Marshall scholar, she observed, "All of the Marshall fellows were really smart, but not all of them go on to achieve exceptional things."[11] As Duckworth describes in her bestselling book *Grit: The Power of Passion and Perseverance*, she turned this simple question into a years-long quest to unpack the relationship between talent and grit, which she defines as the passionate pursuit of long-term goals.

Duckworth's first task was to develop a reliable measure of grit. With scores ranging from very low (1 on a 5-point scale) to very high (5 on a 5-point scale), she began testing different types of people to see how grit contributed to completing difficult tasks. You can take the grit test yourself by answering ten simple questions at angeladuckworth.com/grit-scale. Before reading further, go ahead and take the test. You will get instant results, showing your rank among the hundreds of thousands of people of all ages and descriptions who have taken the test.

Grit is a special form of the moral virtue of courage. Like the other forms of courage we have discussed, it plays out over the long haul. Grit applies best to tasks that take months or years to complete, such as completing college or medical school (and doing your best), sticking with the long hours of practice needed to excel in music or sports, or overcoming lengthy situations that are physically or emotionally challenging. Barry Bridger showed grit in not just surviving more than six years of confinement and torture at the Hanoi Hilton, but also by helping his fellow POWs endure captivity. Brendan Marrocco showed incredible grit by enduring years of surgeries and other medical treatments to recover from his wounds and to adapt to his "new normal."

In her original studies of grit Duckworth first looked at the relationship between grit and education.[12] Who would be grittier, high school graduates or college graduates? That is, do gritty people tend to advance further in education than their less gritty peers? Duckworth examined the grit scores of more than fifteen hundred adults age twenty-five and older. She then computed the grit score for the following levels of educational attainment: some high school, high school graduate, some college, associate's degree, bachelor's degree, and postgraduate degree (master's, PhD, MD, etc.). What is your prediction of the results? Would there be a stair-step increase in grit as a function of educational attainment? The answer is a definitive *almost*! With every increase in educational attainment grit scores rose significantly, with one exception. People with an associate's degree not only showed higher grit than those with less education, but they were also higher than those who had completed bachelor's degrees and were equal to those who had completed postgraduate degrees.

This finding gets to the core of what grit means. Maybe you have an associate's degree. Or maybe you are a college teacher who has taught in associate-degree programs. If so, you will note a big difference between associate-degree students and traditional college students. They are generally older, some have families, and many work full-time while pursuing their degree. Being able to raise children and work forty or more hours per week *and* make steady progress toward a degree takes a lot more than a high IQ. It takes a passion for the subject and perseverance to undertake a task that often takes more than two years to complete. If you have an associate's degree, you may be the grittiest person in your circle of friends!

Next, Duckworth wanted to know if grit was related to age. Using the same sample, she calculated the mean grit scores for people aged 25–34, 35–44, 45–54, 55–64, and 65 and older. Here, she did find a stair-step relationship with higher grit scores for each increasing age category. The biggest step, interestingly, was from 55–64 to 65 and older. In this analysis, Duckworth also looked at the relationship between grit and frequency of career changes. Those with the highest grit scores were substantially less likely than their less gritty counterparts to change careers frequently. This is important because it takes time and consistency of effort to achieve great things, and frequently changing careers hits the reset button to zero. In contrast, people who stay in one career or make few changes are able to better use grit to achieve their long-term goals.

Okay, so being older and in general being better educated is associated with higher grit. But so what? Does grit matter in predicting success in difficult tasks? More than a decade of psychological research indicates that it does. For example, among students enrolled in an undergraduate psychology course at the University of Pennsylvania, students high in grit made better grades. Grit did even better than SAT scores in predicting grades.[13] More interesting, students with lower SAT scores tended to have higher grit scores, suggesting that smarter students at an elite Ivy League school might be less gritty than those lower in talent. Maybe those with less talent rely on dogged perseverance (grit!) to achieve their goals, rather than simply relying on raw intellectual horsepower.[14]

A fascinating finding is that among children participating in the Scripps National Spelling Bee, gritty contestants were more likely to advance to higher rounds of the competition. Spelling Bee kids are smart, but among them grit and IQ were not related. That is to say, knowing a contestant's IQ score gave no information about his or her grit score. Surveys done with the contestants suggested that grittier kids studied more for the Spelling Bee than less gritty contestants. Being smart helped, but the kids who worked harder tended to come out on top.[15]

Duckworth also looked at a completely different group of people and a task quite different from an academic course or a spelling bee. In July of 2004, she administered the grit test to all incoming members of the West Point class of 2008. West Point is consistently ranked as one of the best colleges in America, but it is much more. New cadets quickly learn about the "much more" part because their first summer is devoted to a challenging and at times grueling program called Cadet Basic Training, better known by cadets as Beast Barracks, or simply Beast. For six weeks they make the transition from civilian to soldier. They are awakened at five in the morning (if you have teenagers, you can imagine the pain inflicted by this change in sleep schedule!), learn military customs and courtesies, and participate in rigorous field training. The weather in upstate New York in the summer seems to always be too hot, too cold, or too wet. Away from their friends and family and cell phones for the first time, many find Beast one of the most challenging situations they have ever undertaken. Most are successful and complete Beast and begin their four years of top-drawer academic study, military and leader development, and physical training. But some don't make it. Duckworth wanted to know if grit makes a difference in who makes it through Beast. She found that grit was the *only* factor that predicted who would complete Beast. Grit and SAT scores were not correlated. Being smart didn't matter when it comes to completing the gut check that Beast represents.

The West Point study (later replicated many times) is telling about just what grit predicts. Adapting to military training and surviving Beast has little to do with strengths of the head (intelligence), but almost everything to do with strengths of the gut. Having a high IQ doesn't help when you are cold, tired, and wet. But having the tenacity and determination to complete a long and difficult task by simply *never giving up* captures the essence of grit. And grit doesn't just matter among West Point cadets. Subsequent research with Army Green Berets shows that grit matters in other extremely difficult training situations.[16]

Before we leave the topic of grit, let's see where your grit score stacks up. You learned your grit score when you completed the grit questionnaire. But you may be interested in how you compare to the groups of people that Duckworth studied. Here are some comparison points taken from her original grit research:

ADULTS 25 AND OVER (STUDY 1)   3.65
ADULTS 25 AND OVER (STUDY 2)   3.41
IVY LEAGUE UNDERGRADUATES   3.46
WEST POINT CLASS OF 2008   3.78
NATIONAL SPELLING BEE FINALISTS   3.50

So what is the takeaway? Simply this. Grit provides a character edge in completing daunting tasks. The best combination is to be smart *and* gritty. One can't help thinking here of a famous saying attributed to Thomas Edison: "Genius is 1 percent inspiration and 99 percent perspiration."[17] For evidence, see Spelling Bee contestants or West Point cadets!

BUILDING THE GUT STRENGTHS

You can build your strengths of the gut and learn to better apply existing strengths. Here are some suggestions.

1. *Know yourself.* First, assess yourself; you may find you are already strong in physical or moral courage, integrity, and/or grit. Look back at your self-ratings of the twenty-four character strengths introduced in chapter 1, and also look at your grit score. Do any of your signature strengths come from the moral virtue of courage? How does your grit compare to college students, West Point cadets, and others? Reflect on your experiences. Where, when, and under what conditions have you been brave (physical courage), stood up for what is right (moral courage and integrity), or worked

hard for months or years to attain a goal (grit)? Once you have self-evaluated your courage virtue, systematically find situations where you can employ one or more of these strengths to succeed in something difficult. It may be hard to anticipate a situation requiring physical bravery, but you can think of situations where you can use your integrity and honesty, your grit, or your zest and vitality. Considering this scenario, develop a plan that allows you to use one or more of these strengths. Doing so will help you succeed in the task and also give you practice being courageous and strengthening those skills, and it will even make you feel better for having done so.[18]

2. *Practice courage.* Make it a habit, when faced with a difficult task, to develop a plan to use these strengths in completing the task. What challenges intimidate you? Do this for a variety of tasks. You can do this physically through actions or mentally through imagination and rehearsal. Using these strengths repeatedly and in different situations will make it easier to invoke them when an unanticipated challenge occurs. Psychologists Lester and Pury tell us to practice "hands on courage."[19]

3. *Look for and be a role model.* Who in your family, workplace, or school are exemplars of the virtue of courage? Study their actions and their words; try to emulate what they do. You can learn vicariously by reading about the brave and courageous. The famous psychologist Albert Bandura taught us that learning by observation is one of the most common and powerful ways that we change our own behavior, beliefs, attitudes, and character.[20]

4. *Use social persuasion and feedback.* Find others who are in a position to observe and evaluate your behavior and provide you with feedback. Be constructive but honest in feedback you give to others. Maybe you aren't making any progress on that book you are writing because you are doing email or other tasks. You need feedback from others, or honest insights about yourself, to stay on task. Perhaps your child wants to excel at the violin but only goes through the motions of practice and is easily distracted. Feedback, gently and honestly applied, may motivate him or her to persist in practice.

5. *Embrace stressful conditions.* By framing stress as something that goes hand in hand with opportunity, rather than something that is inherently damaging and harmful, you can better maintain the attention and motivation needed to do hard things. By learning to work effectively under conditions of physical and emotional stress, you will strengthen your ability to persevere under duress, a hallmark of courage. Soldiers call this *embracing the suck.*

6. *Surround yourself with courageous people.* Nansook Park's study of Medal of Honor recipients showed that social bonds are critical in demonstrating courageous behavior. You will often live up to, or down from, the standards set by the people you associate with. You can't change your family, but you can choose your friends. If you have friends who fail in important aspects of the moral virtue of courage, maybe it is time to forge new friendships. If others in your workplace fail in these characteristics, it may be time to change jobs.

LEADERS CAN BUILD COURAGE IN OTHERS

As leaders, we can engage in practices that build the virtue of courage in others. We close this chapter with a story of how a losing football program at West Point was transformed into one of the best college programs in America. Strengths of the gut made the difference. This transformation depended on honing these strengths among players and coaches. As you read this, see if you can identify how West Point leaders and the Army football coaching staff built a culture of courage.

THE TRANSFORMATION OF THE WEST POINT FOOTBALL PROGRAM

When Lieutenant General Bob Caslen assumed command as superintendent of West Point, his boss, General Ray Odierno, the chief of staff of the Army, publicly directed him, during the assumption-of-command ceremony, "Beat Navy." In 2013 when Caslen took over, Army had lost the famed Army-Navy game for twelve straight years and had suffered losing records for sixteen of the previous seventeen seasons under five different coaches. General Odierno, a West Point football player himself, knew the importance of transforming the Army football program back to the winning tradition it once had.

When the nation puts its Army in harm's way, it does not expect its Army to look good or to do their best. It expects them to accomplish the mission and win. But it does not expect them to win at all costs; it expects them to win in accordance with national and Army values. When 25 million people tune in to the Army-Navy football game in December, they do not just see collegiate athletes playing a game, they see the future leaders of our military and our nation. They expect their future military leaders to fight with grit, tenacity, discipline, and mental and physical toughness. As chief of staff of the Army, responsible for the trust relationship between the Army and the American people, General Odierno understood what America expected of its Army and its future leaders.

During the 2013 Army-Navy football game Caslen had an enlightening observation on why the team was mediocre and did not demonstrate the level of character our nation expects of its future Army leaders. The game was played in Philadelphia on a cold, snowy December afternoon. During the game numerous Army players huddled around heater blowers on the sideline, more concerned about keeping themselves warm than staying abreast of the action on the field. General Odierno watched the game from the sidelines as well and noticed the same thing.

At halftime Army was losing 17–0. A television reporter interviewed each coach as he returned from the locker room. She asked Navy coach Ken Niumatalolo if the weather was having an impact on his players or on the game plan. He answered that the weather was of no impact whatsoever. He knew the weather forecast was for a cold, sloppy game day and had made the team practice outside in the elements all the week before. The difference between the future leaders of the Navy, the Navy football team, and the future leaders of the Army, the Army football team, as witnessed by about 25 million Americans, could not have been more different and distinct. The Army players huddled around a heater not paying attention to what was happening on the field, while the Navy players were fully prepared for the elements and were engaged in the game. Guess what the final score was and who won? Navy extended their winning streak another year, 34–7.

Caslen recognized that the Army football team had to transform from a culture of mediocrity to a culture of excellence. To make that happen West Point needed to—as Jim Collins says in his book *Good to Great*—get the right people on the bus.[21]

To achieve this, Caslen hired a coach who was familiar with the military academy and had a proven record of building winning programs—Jeff Monken. Because of the military-disciplined life of a cadet, and the five-year obligation to serve after graduation, the nation's best football recruits are normally more drawn toward universities without these demands. Although Army may play some of the best teams in the country, Army is unlikely to get the best recruits in the country. As a result, Academy players will most likely be a few pounds lighter and a few tenths of a second slower than the players on most of the teams they play. But winning and excellence are not just about being heavier and faster. It is about possessing the character traits of the gut—discipline, mental and physical toughness, tenacity, and the relentless pursuit of excellence.

A team gets the ball on offense eight to ten times a game, and to win, you normally need to put about 30 points on the scoreboard. That means you need to score—either a field goal or a touchdown—on about half of the possessions. An undisciplined team that turns the ball over frequently has fewer opportunities to put points on the board. Fumbling the ball or throwing interceptions are mistakes indicative of a lack of discipline. Additionally, a penalty, which is truly a lack of discipline, can stop an offensive drive in its tracks. But you can coach and teach discipline. Doing so increases your opportunities to score. Playing with discipline reduces common mistakes, is critical to winning, and is a sure sign of excellence.

To measure the toughness of your team, look at the score in

the last quarter of each game. In the fourth quarter, the most tenacious, tough, and physically fit players will persevere and dominate when this is needed most. To be more mentally and physically fit than your opponent is a game changer. At the end of the game, regardless of your opponent's weight or speed, mental and physical toughness are the great equalizers.

To create a culture of excellence, the Army team had to start with character traits of the gut—toughness, conditioning, and discipline. A culture of excellence also depends on learning to play to the upper level of your potential. Think of your performance as a bell-shaped curve. Sometimes you play above your average, and sometimes you play below your average. But most of the plays are average. Average does not enable improvement. Excellence occurs when you play to the upper level of your ability, not only during the game, but also in practice, in the classroom, in study hall at night, and in your private life as well as your public life. Excellence is playing to the upper part of that bell-shaped curve. And guess what? When you perform consistently in the upper part of the curve, that becomes the new average and you find yourself in a zone of excellence. Mike Krzyzewski, Duke basketball coach and West Point graduate, says it best: "My hunger is not for success, it is for excellence. Because when you attain excellence, success just naturally follows."[22]

As the new Army football coach, Jeff Monken first walked into the team locker room and inspected each player's equipment. Any player whose equipment was not laid out exactly in accordance with team standards had to report to Monken and learn why disciplined attention to detail in everything was critical to winning. A couple weeks before spring practice, Monken ran a mat drill in the stadium at 5:30 A.M. A mat drill is one of the most intense physical drills and requires 100 percent effort by 100 percent of the team, every minute and every second. If any player was observed not giving 100 percent, the entire team had to repeat the entire exercise. The team quickly learned mental and physical toughness and the importance of discipline. And they learned the importance of selflessness to the success of the team. The team was learning the character strengths of the gut; traits such as discipline, toughness, selflessness, loyalty, and teamwork took on new meaning and importance.

In his first year, Monken's team won 4 games and lost 8. Each loss was devastating, but Monken ensured that each player learned from these losses. The following year was a 2-and-10 season, but you could tell the Army team was tougher and more competitive, as seven of those losses were of 7 points or fewer, including a 4-point loss to Navy, decided on the last play of the game. Then in 2016, Army went 8 and 5, including a win over Navy—for the first time in fifteen years—followed by a bowl-game victory. In 2017, Army had a 10-win season, including another victory over Navy and another last-play victory in their bowl game against a Top 25 team. They were even better in 2018, with an 11-win season, the most in Army's storied history. They beat Navy again, extending their winning streak to three years, and won the Armed Forces Bowl, defeating Houston 70–14.

During the 2018 football season, Army's annual game against Air Force had special significance. The victor would win the coveted Commander-in-Chief's Trophy, which meant a presentation by the president in the White House Rose Garden. Near the end of the fourth quarter, Army led by 3 points. With the ball on the 50-yard line, fourth down, needing 1 yard for a first down, and with about forty-five seconds left in the game, Army had a critical decision to make. They could go for the first down and run out the clock, or they could punt, giving Air Force the ball with the chance to tie the game with a field goal or win outright with a touchdown. Failing to get the first down would give Air Force good field position and an even better chance of winning the game.

Most coaches would punt the ball. Going for the first down would be too risky. But not for Monken. He went for the first down and got it by a yard, thus enabling Army to run out the clock and win the game. His decision to go for the first down is indicative of the culture of excellence and grit that is necessary to build a winning program. When asked in a postgame interview why he went for the first down, his reply was simple: "If we can't get one yard on fourth down and one, then we don't deserve to win."[23]

Coach Monken's approach to winning and winning honorably are proven and time-tested. They provide a model for how teams and other organizations may transform themselves into a culture of excellence.

Leaders at the highest levels played a role in this amazing transformation. General Odierno, the Army chief of staff, clearly communicated to the incoming superintendent of West Point, Lieutenant General Robert Caslen, that mediocrity on the football field was unacceptable, and that it had a negative impact on the development of West Point cadets—both for the football players and for the rest of the corps. General Caslen assessed the situation, made winning a priority, and hired a coach who had the skills to create a culture of grit, determination, and tenacity. In his first year as head coach, Coach Monken saw players who were anything but gritty. They were sloppy with their equipment. They were more interested in staying warm and avoiding physical discomfort than they were in winning a game. So Monken created situations where players had to follow rules and adhere to strict standards and so increased their grit. He created challenging physical drills that were tied to everyone on the team giving it their best and so built perseverance. Monken developed a team culture that focused on being a good teammate, not in being well liked and friendly, but in all knowing they could depend on each other to practice and play at peak effort.

If this story only mattered to West Point football, it would not be worth telling. Other organizations need to win, too. Corporations must excel to survive. Law enforcement agencies must build a similar culture of courage to serve their communities bravely, but also honorably and with integrity. Schools and universities are no different. Teachers and administrators who possess the moral virtue of courage produce students who have the same traits.

The lesson here is simple. Through effective leadership, improving strengths of the gut is possible. Clear standards, high expectations, rewards for high performance, and, yes, punishing those who fail enable courage in all its forms. These allow individuals, teams, and organizations of all types to win the right way.

STRENGTHS OF THE HEAD

Authority without wisdom is like a heavy axe without an edge,
fitter to bruise than polish.

—ANNE BRADSTREET[1]

Strengths of the head are character traits that compose the moral virtue of knowledge and wisdom. By strengths of the head, we mean more than IQ. For psychologists Martin Seligman and Christopher Peterson, the moral virtue of knowledge and wisdom refers to "cognitive strengths that entail the acquisition and use of knowledge."[2] Individual character strengths that contribute to knowledge and wisdom are creativity, curiosity, open-mindedness, love of learning, and perspective. Whether your IQ is 110 or 140, you can possess, nurture, and display these strengths. Many of the problems we face in life require us to do just that.

THE DILAPIDATED TOMATO-PASTE FACTORY

One of the more contentious areas in Iraq during the well-known surge was north of Baghdad in Salah ad Din province, which was heavily Sunni and the home province of the former

Iraq dictator Saddam Hussein. The Sunni sect was at war with itself, as the radical wing, led by Jordanian-born al-Qaeda-in-Iraq leader Abu Musab al-Zarqawi, bombed and destroyed the holy Shi'ite Al-Askari Mosque in the city of Samarra. The mosque, built in 944, is one of the most important Shia shrines in the world, and its bombing was designed to create a violent sectarian conflict between the Sunni and Shia sects. Samarra is just outside the US base called Balad, and besides the ongoing conflicts among the sects, US forces also became the target of this outbreak of violence, making this region one of the most volatile areas in all of Iraq.

Given that background, Lieutenant Colonel Dave Hodne, a capable and intelligent battalion commander of the Third Squadron, Fourth US Calvary Regiment, was assigned the mission of defeating the insurgent elements, enabling and supporting Iraqi security forces, and assisting the fledgling local government build its legitimacy among the local population. A daunting mission for sure, but Hodne used his intellect to think his way out of the quagmire that had plagued this part of Iraq for several years.

Hodne's approach was different. Previous commanders in Iraq prosecuted the war with a heavy hand. Their main effort was to mass combat power at what the commanders felt was the decisive point. This created significant collateral damage and unintended consequences that polarized the Iraqi population, resulting in attacks on coalition forces.

Rather than using raw combat power to achieve his mission, Hodne began thinking of novel ways to address this problem. He built relationships with two wealthy Iraqis and convinced them to pool their money to create an Iraqi bank. This bank could loan money to small local businesses, providing them with much-needed capital to build or rebuild their businesses. This was a risky strategy because under Saddam Hussein's regime banks did not exist in the Iraqi economy. Hodne had to overcome a lot of doubt and build a lot of trust to make this work. But Hodne was not an ordinary commander. He had great interpersonal skills and built the trust necessary to get the bank started.

One of the first loans went to a dilapidated tomato-paste factory that had been inoperable for several years. The loan allowed the owner to purchase replacement parts and get his factory running again. This was important because now that the factory was working, farmers had a market for their products. This part of Iraq is agrarian, and farming in Mesopotamian Iraq requires irrigation from the Tigris and Euphrates Rivers. To get water from the river, you have to first get it into canals, then out of the canals and into the fields. This requires an operational irrigation infrastructure. After four years of war, the electrical grid that ran the pumps was inoperable, and the canals were broken and full of silt.

In Iraq, running and maintaining the irrigation infrastructure is the state's responsibility, and the local farmers put pressure on the government to get the canals repaired and the electrical grid operational. The government responded and began to make the necessary repairs. With the pumps functional, the water flowed out of the river and into the canals, and from the canals into the fields. And the farmers started growing tomatoes again.

This was important for another reason. Repairing the infrastructure and allowing the farmers to grow tomatoes restored the local population's confidence in their government's ability to provide the essential services the population demanded. In fighting an insurgency, establishing the legitimacy of the local government in the eyes of the population is critical for success.

Now that the farmers were growing the tomatoes, they were putting them in their pickup trucks and bringing them to the tomato-paste factory. The factory was adjacent to the main highway between Baghdad and Mosul, which traversed downtown Balad. With so many trucks waiting to drop off tomatoes, they created a traffic jam on the highway, causing another problem that demanded a solution.

An entrepreneurial Iraqi solved that problem by building a parking lot adjacent to the factory. Because the trucks were waiting awhile, another entrepreneurial Iraqi built a snack bar to sell food to the farmers, and another built a small hotel for those that were waiting overnight. Soon another entrepreneurial Iraqi started making the cans for the tomato paste, and yet another started a factory to make labels for the cans. Before you know it, an industry was reborn. Young men, many who were previously part of the insurgency, were now employed, and the government had gained the confidence of the population. But more important, Balad, which had previously been one of the most volatile areas in Iraq, was now one of the more peaceful. It became a model for other cities in dealing with their insurgencies.

The US military was criticized in the beginning of Operation Iraqi Freedom for using a heavy hand in dealing with insurgent elements, indigenous Iraqi security services, and the local population. Rather than breaking their will, in many cases it hardened the resistance, making it all the more difficult to achieve mission objectives. It took time to realize that dealing effectively with this insurgency required building relationships among diverse stakeholders in the region, including indigenous forces and their leaders and other coalition elements. Building these relationships required understanding the local culture and the second, third, and fourth order of effects of the decisions made. The battlefield was complex, and the greatest weapons on the battlefield were not rifles and tanks, but the six inches between the ears—the intellectual understanding of the complexity of this battlefield.[3]

The case of the dilapidated tomato-paste factory illustrates what can happen when a leader invokes character strengths that make up knowledge and wisdom to solve a complex problem. Hodne could have followed the lead of previous commanders in the region and tried to defeat the enemy by brute force. Instead, he demonstrated at least three strengths of the head to attain his military objective. He used *creativity* in developing a plan to obtain the cooperation of local Iraqi leaders by giving them a loan. Hodne showed *perspective* by understanding the culture and history of that part of Iraq and its people. And he employed *open-mindedness* in working with others—Americans and local Iraqis alike—to implement this program. The result, attributable in no small measure to Hodne's intellect—was a significant reduction of hostilities and loss of life, and the empowerment of the local government.

The case of the dilapidated tomato-paste factory offers another important lesson: Hodne's chain of command allowed him to exercise his creativity, perspective, and open-mindedness to achieve the mission. Too often, in the military and other organizations, leaders do not empower their subordinates to capitalize on their strengths of the head. In 2019, Hodne, now a brigadier general, reflected, "I am incredibly thankful for the opportunity to have served with General Caslen during that experience. Precisely because he afforded subordinates the room to operate within his intent, he leveraged the intellect, talent, and character throughout his formation."[4]

INTELLIGENCE HAS MANY DIMENSIONS
TRADITIONAL INTELLIGENCE, IQ

Psychologists who study intelligence make a distinction between general intelligence (a single, overall measure of one's intellectual capacity, measured by IQ) and specific subtypes of intelligence. For good reasons, most of us do not spend much time thinking about our overall IQ. We are too busy putting it to use to be concerned about its specific value. But being aware of different aspects of intelligence may allow us to learn to apply these specific intellectual skills to solve problems.

Psychologist Robert Sternberg discovered an interesting thing about intelligence. He found that overall intelligence breaks down into three subtypes: analytical, creative, and practical. This triarchic theory, as Sternberg calls it, suggests that people differ in the strength and balance among these three components. Analytic intelligence—the ability to analyze, compare, and evaluate—is useful in sizing up a problem. Creative intelligence brings innovation and inventiveness to design a solution to the problem. With practical intelligence a person applies the analytic and creative components of intelligence to implement the solution.[5]

Some of us are better at one form of intelligence than another. Some are eggheads (high analytic intelligence) who cannot put brilliant ideas to practical use or think of creative ways to address a problem. Others can take that brilliant plan and creative solution and use their practical intelligence to make it work. Hodne showed all three aspects of intelligence and also identified others in his command and among local Iraqis who could use their own practical intelligence and make the plan work.

Another psychologist, Howard Gardner, identified eight types of intelligence: linguistic, logical-mathematical, spatial, musical, bodily-kinesthetic, interpersonal, intrapersonal, and naturalistic. A college professor might be strong in linguistic and logical-mathematical intelligence, a police officer in interpersonal intelligence, and an athlete might excel at bodily-kinesthetic intelligence. Charles Darwin was off the charts in naturalistic intelligence, being able to see patterns in nature that were invisible to others.[6]

In understanding strengths of the head, our message here is simple. The traditional idea of IQ is complex. Each of us has a unique pattern of intellectual skills. Some of them may be average, but some may be exceptional. For you to fully employ strengths of the head to flourish in school, the workplace, or socially, you must know what types of intelligence you are good at. A great leader recognizes his or her intellectual strengths and limitations. These leaders then build a team around them that complements their own intellectual skills and so enables success for the entire organization.

CREATIVITY

Creativity provides innovative and novel ways of solving problems. It is sometimes called thinking outside of the box. Creativity is the ability to see things in a different way from others, such as seeing uses for objects other than what they were designed for. Dr. Matthews's father had a knack for this. He had purchased a well-used 1950 Chevy (for $50) for his sixteen-year old son, Glen, to drive. One day while Glen was driving the car, he depressed the accelerator and it stuck on full throttle. The motor raced at its highest RPM, but fortunately Glen shifted the transmission into neutral and pulled over before causing a wreck. After Glen pushed the car back to his home driveway, his father needed a quick interim solution to get the car roadworthy again. Having been raised in the Great Depression, he was frugal. So he examined the car and found that the spring that controls the accelerator pedal had broken. With a sudden smile, he retreated to his storage shed and emerged with a mousetrap. He attached the mousetrap to the accelerator pedal, and (for a while at least) the car worked again. Not many people would have come up with that solution. The mousetrap car is long gone, but its legend is testimony to the power of creativity.

Psychologists have learned interesting things about creativity and creative people. Creative people use divergent thinking—the ability to generate multiple solutions to a given problem.[7] The late comedian Jonathan Winters once had a network television show. In one of his regular routines someone would throw him a common object, then he would rattle off as many non-traditional uses for the object as possible. For Mr. Winters, a yardstick quickly became a fishing pole, a rifle, or one of a dozen other things. Creative people are good at this kind of task.

Creative people also share certain personality traits. They tend to be high in grit; once committed to solving a problem, they do not give up easily. They are open-minded, accepting of other people regardless of race, religion, or culture. They are motivated by the work itself, rather than by extrinsic rewards such as money or fame. They are self-assured and self-accepting. On the downside, they may be ambitious, dominant, and sometimes hostile and impatient with others. Many had demanding parents and showed passion for their chosen field at an early age. Most had supportive and influential mentors along the way.[8]

CURIOSITY

Curiosity is the trait of finding pleasure in exploring new ideas and possibilities. You may have an intuitive sense of your level of curiosity just based on the breadth of your interests and your daily behaviors. Do you like to stay in your own lane (not so high in curiosity)? Or do you enjoy reading about and experiencing new ideas and activities? Maybe you do not have much artistic talent but enjoy visiting museums or viewing art simply for enjoyment. Or you join a book club because you find discussing ideas from different books, authors, and genres rewarding and enriching. For a more systematic evaluation of your curiosity, look at your curiosity score from the Values-in-Action Inventory of Strengths test (VIA-IS). Where does your curiosity strength fall with respect to your other twenty-three character strengths?

Curiosity is linked to a variety of positive outcomes. Highly curious people tend to enjoy more positive moods and feelings.[9] They are less bored and prefer challenging tasks at work, school, or recreation. Curiosity and complex decision-making are linked. Highly curious people tend to form closer and more meaningful relationships with others. One study even showed that among a sample of geriatric people, those higher in curiosity had a higher survival rate over five years than those lower in curiosity.[10]

OPEN-MINDEDNESS

Open-minded people listen to and consider ideas and perspectives that differ from their own. They use sound judgment in making decisions. They display good critical thinking. Instead of clinging to long-held beliefs in the face of contradictory evidence, open-minded people change their minds to adapt their attitudes and beliefs to accommodate new information.

Open-mindedness has positive consequences. Open-minded students outperform others on a variety of cognitive tests, including the SAT. Leaders who keep an open mind make better decisions than those tied to a specific belief or ideology. A good leader will include among his or her staff people who have opposing views and empower them to express ideas that are at odds with his or her own. [11]

Open-mindedness allows diverse thought to be considered, and by allowing diverse thought, we broaden our understanding, become more empathetic, and arrive at better solutions. Narrow-minded thinking creates narrow-minded solutions. They may be sufficient solutions, but they can block alternative and perhaps better solutions. Allowing diverse thought will bring a better range of solutions to the table.

The failure to exercise open-mindedness may have widespread effects. Some people believe the US moon landings were an elaborate hoax. Others believe the world is flat. Scientific evidence strongly supports the idea of global climate change. But for a host of reasons, some politicians and others discount and disregard this evidence. Because it is a global issue, nations must come together to form international agreements to address the problem. When a country that is responsible for a substantial portion of greenhouse gas emissions denies the problem and refuses to help solve this global problem, then everyone suffers.

How open-minded are you? Look at your VIA-IS score for open-mindedness. Or reflect on your own behaviors, attitudes, and beliefs. Better yet, ask close friends whether they consider you to be open-minded, and why they think this. Be honest with yourself. Most of us may be open-minded on some things, but resistant to change in others. The irony is that people who are not open-minded probably will not follow this advice. The flip side is that if you do evaluate your open-mindedness, that may be good evidence that you are indeed just that!

LOVE OF LEARNING

Love of learning means enjoying the learning of new skills and knowledge, whether formally or on your own. Love of learning may manifest itself in a passion for a particular topic, motivating one to continue to build an ever-deeper knowledge of the subject, or in learning a variety of new things. You can usually spot people who have a love of learning. They will be excited to talk about a new book they have read, a course they are taking, or a novel approach to a common problem. They prefer to engage in active learning versus passive activities such as watching television.

Psychologists identify multiple benefits associated with a love of learning. These include positive feelings about learning new things, increased ability to persevere in the face of obstacles, an enhanced sense of autonomy, better problem-solving strategies, and a sense of self-efficacy.[12] The underlying theme is that love of learning is related to general well-being, both mental and physical. Evidence even suggests that love of learning may help protect against age-related cognitive decline.[13]

How are you doing in love of learning? Again, look at your VIA-IS score and then reflect on your behaviors. Do you attend educational events or visit a museum to see the works of an artist you have developed an interest in? Do you read—a lot? Both fiction and nonfiction? Do you get excited about new things you have learned and enjoy discussing them with friends? These are all solid indicators of a passion and love for learning.

PERSPECTIVE

Perspective is equivalent to wisdom. In many ways, it is a product of the other strengths of the head. Creativity, curiosity, open-mindedness, and love of learning all contribute to perspective. Perspective is not arrived at overnight. It takes time to build and is a lifelong process. One can have perspective in a given domain but not others. An experienced teacher can make sense of what good education means, both for him- or herself and for others, but may lack insight on other issues. Perspective grows with depth and breadth of experience, but it does not do so inevitably. It depends on other character strengths and the ability to contemplate and reflect upon what is important. Perspective is not the same thing as intelligence. You do not have to be a genius to be wise. And knowledge alone does not equate to perspective.

Perspective is essential to deriving meaning from life. When faced with what at the time seemed to be a major, anxiety-causing issue, a biologist friend reflected, "None of this will matter in a million years!" He was trying to be funny, but the ability to put one's trials and tribulations into a larger picture does help in managing the worry that accompanies the daily aggravations of life. Perhaps this is why psychologists have found that among older adults those high in perspective have a higher sense of well-being, despite challenging health, financial, and other issues. Whether successful aging builds perspective, or whether perspective leads to successful aging, is not known. But psychologists do know that perspective is positively related to successful adjustment throughout a person's life span.[14]

Once again consider your VIA-IS score for perspective. But self-reflection is especially important for this trait. When you encounter a setback, can you place it into context? Do others turn to you for advice? Think about this last question. If you are older and more experienced, when did people begin to more frequently seek your advice? A new assistant professor may work mostly with students, but over time colleagues may increasingly turn to him or her for guidance. Who are your mentors? You probably do not choose a mentor just because he or she is highly knowledgeable on a topic. Facts can be found elsewhere, usually with a mouse click or two. Instead, you choose a mentor because he or she helps you frame things better and aids you in developing your own perspective on large issues. Thus, a good indicator that you have gained perspective is when others seek you out for your opinions, views, and ideas.

SECOND LIEUTENANT SAM KETCHENS

Coupled with the surge in 2007 was an internal movement within Sunni Iraq. Moderate Sunnis felt their future was best aligned with an Iraqi representative government, even though the senior leadership in this government would come from the Shia majority. The sectarian conflict between the Shia and the Sunni was generational, but moderate Sunnis felt that a future based on the radical extremist wing of their sect was not in their best interest. So they sided with the American-backed Shia representative government. This was called the Awakening, and the transition of moderate Sunni support from the insurgents to the legitimate government was sensitive and risky. Included in this transition was the switch of Sunni insurgent foot soldiers from fighting US and coalition forces to now joining with US forces in fighting their former allies, the radical Sunni insurgent forces. Bringing these new partners on board was risky, and even more challenging was gaining their trust and confidence. How would you feel if your previous enemy was now supposed to be your trusted partner?

The former insurgents now supporting the government were called Sons of Iraq. The challenge was to integrate them into the Iraqi forces and to gain their acceptance by the Iraqi military leadership, most of whom were from the Shia sect. Given the historical mistrust between the Sunni and the Shia, integrating the Sons of Iraq would require a lot of time to build the necessary trust. The US forces were eager to bring them on board and worked hard to facilitate their integration into the Iraqi security forces. It took a lot of dedicated work at Caslen's level as a major general (at the time), and in addition the junior officers and NCOs had their work cut out for them.

One officer with oversight of about three hundred Sons of Iraq was a former West Point cadet and now a second lieutenant, Sam Ketchens. Sam had played rugby at West Point and was a scrappy, tough, hard-nosed officer. He served in the infantry, became a Ranger, and was one of the best young officers in his battalion. Caslen knew Sam from his days at West Point and watched with great interest as Sam worked with the Sons of Iraq.

Sam was given the mission to integrate the Sons of Iraq into the Iraqi Army, and to operationally deploy them to interdict the flow of foreign fighters from the Syrian border through the Jazira Desert. Gaining the support of the Iraqi Army leadership to accept these former Sunni fighters was the tough part. But Sam was great. He negotiated, reasoned, and won the support of his Iraqi Army counterparts and got these former insurgents the support, equipment, and rations they needed. In their operational mission, Sam led them to successfully block the access of foreign fighters from Syria.

Caslen recalls meeting with Sam in one of the towns in his area of operation. While Caslen was talking with him about the mission, Sam's cell phone rang, and without an interpreter he carried on a five-minute conversation in the native Iraqi Arabic dialect with one of the sheikhs of the Sons of Iraq. When Sam was done, Caslen asked him where he learned to speak Arabic so well, and Sam said he picked it up while in Iraq. Later in the mission, Sam held a meeting with about fifteen sheikhs who were the tribal leaders of Sam's three hundred Sons of Iraq. It was a great meeting, and Caslen departed, admiring how one twenty-three-year-old US Army lieutenant had pulled this off.

Wisdom is the ability to draw on one's knowledge and experience to make well-informed judgments.[15] Sam was a natural at this. His strengths of the head set him apart from his peers. His interpersonal skills enabled him to build functional relationships between former enemies, making him an effective leader. His innovative approach to building relationships enabled his unit to be successful.

STRENGTHS OF THE HEAD IN AN INSTITUTIONAL CONTEXT

Philosophers talk about "wicked" problems—those that are so complex that they seemingly defy solution.[16] Climate change, world hunger, war, and political instability are examples. Similarly, when a large, complex organization suffers a major failure, fixing the problem can be daunting, just as wicked as any other large-scale problem. When an organization fails, it is up to the leader of that organization to fix the problem. While strengths of the gut such as grit and determination help, finding solutions most often comes from strengths of the head.

SECRETARY ROBERT MCDONALD AND THE TRANSFORMATION OF THE US DEPARTMENT OF VETERANS AFFAIRS

How do you change the culture of your organization, whether it is a thirty-person small business or the largest department in the US government? If you became the leader of an organization of more than three hundred thousand people with a bureaucratic culture that had lost sight of its purpose, how would you change its direction? Changing a culture is not easy. It must start with the senior person in charge, driven by that leader's character and values.

In 2015, an elderly veteran broke his foot and drove himself to the Puget Sound Veterans Affairs (VA) emergency room in Seattle. His foot swelled so badly while driving that when he arrived, he was unable to walk the ten feet from his car to the emergency room. He called the emergency room for help. Unfortunately, the VA representative who answered the phone refused to assist him and instructed him to call 911. Soon the fire department arrived and carried the veteran the ten feet from his car to the emergency room door.

When the story went viral in the news and on social media, the VA defended their actions, quoting regulations stating that they were only allowed to treat a veteran once the veteran was inside the medical center's building. Clearly the bureaucratic, rules-based culture caused this organization to fail this veteran, resulting in widespread distrust among the entire veteran community.

This occurred on the heels of another embarrassing incident. A year earlier, in 2014, the Phoenix VA center manipulated its appointment process to give the impression they were remaining within the fourteen-day timeline standard for veterans to get an appointment. Rather than scheduling the appointment when the veteran requested it, they waited until they entered the fourteen-day window, to give the appearance that they were meeting the regulated minimums. A whistle-blower reported a veteran who died while waiting for an appointment that had not yet been scheduled despite his request having been made almost twenty weeks earlier. A follow-up investigation by the inspector general found "widespread data manipulation intended to obscure the Phoenix VA's poor performance." Altogether, the inspector general received 225 allegations of wait-time manipulations at the

Phoenix VA facility, and 445 additional allegations of wait-time manipulations at other VA facilities. A vociferous public outcry had significant repercussions within the VA leadership. Ultimately this crisis led to the resignation of the secretary of veterans affairs, a criminal investigation by the Federal Bureau of Investigation, and the eventual replacement of thirteen of the VA's top seventeen leaders.[17]

President Obama knew that the VA had to be transformed and to change how they cared for veterans. To lead this transformation, the president selected Robert McDonald, who was the retired chairman, president, and CEO of Procter & Gamble (P&G). McDonald was a West Point graduate who served in the Army for five years, then served thirty-three years at P&G. His career included leading P&G businesses across North America, Asia, and Europe, and he also led several major corporate transformation efforts.[18]

Secretary McDonald had an immediate impact when he employed a High Performance Organization Model, designed to frame the issues at the VA and focus on transforming the organization. "It starts with purpose, values, and principles, which, to me, is the bedrock of every organization," McDonald said. "What happened in 2014 was a violation of purpose, values, and principles."[19]

Once in charge, Secretary McDonald began an intense study of the entire organization. He and his senior leaders met with veterans, veteran-service organizations, the VA workforce, and congressional members and their staffs. They wanted to see the VA from all perspectives, but principally from the veteran's perspective. They sought meetings with critics of the VA to understand their concerns and issues. This initial assessment revealed a department in disarray that needed quick, forceful, and ethical leadership to build trust between the institution and its veterans, and between the institution and its employees and stakeholders.

One immediate and effective initiative McDonald put in place was the MyVA initiative, with the purpose of empowering employees to deliver excellent customer service to improve the veteran's experience.[20] The initiative achieved some immediate practical successes, but more important, it began rebuilding trust.

McDonald also realized that lasting transformation required buy-in from the entire department and the ability to connect VA employees at all levels. To help connect employees, McDonald introduced an internal training program called Leaders Developing Leaders (LDL), an ambitious program that also had an immediate impact. The objective was to have every employee identify with the VA's vision and mission—from the custodian cleaning the floors at night to the high-level managers—knowing his or her work enables the VA to provide the service needed for every veteran who uses their facilities. The overarching goal was for the VA to become the number one customer-service organization in the federal government.[21]

Bob McDonald is a leader who lives and exemplifies character in everything he does. Character is the foundation of how he leads, how he engages with people, and how he drives the principles of any organization of which he is a part. In a paper titled "What I Believe In," McDonald lists ten principles that "drive my behavior everyday."[22] His first principle is "Living a life driven by purpose is more meaningful and rewarding than meandering through life without direction," and his life's purpose "is to improve lives." Given that purpose alone, President Obama could not have selected a more fitting candidate to transform the VA from a rules-based to a principle-based organization.

Another of McDonald's principles is "Character is the most important trait of a leader."[23] He defines character as "always putting the needs of the organization above your own." This definition goes to the heart of why character in a leader is so important. He followed this principle his entire career. As an Army captain he placed the needs of his soldiers above his own. At Procter & Gamble, he ensured every leader took personal responsibility for the results of their organization.

McDonald developed his leadership philosophy at West Point, where, as a freshman, he was allowed to reply with only one of four responses: "yes, no, no excuse, and I do not understand." These four responses put him as a soon-to-be-leader in a position that is perfectly in line with his definition of character—to put the needs of others above your own. There is no equivocation or excuse in these answers; there is no "but." He also learned at West Point to "choose the harder right over the easier wrong." As McDonald says, "A leader who lives by his or her word can be counted on to do the unpopular thing when it is right. To always follow 'the harder right,' a leader must truly believe that a life directed by moral guidelines promises deeper and richer satisfaction than a self-serving, self-absorbed life. Living up to this ideal of character requires courage, determination, integrity, and self-discipline. You must live by your word and actions and know that is the most powerful demonstration of leadership."[24]

As P&G CEO, McDonald also demonstrated the values of wisdom and perspective needed to understand local cultures when doing business in Asia. He could not do business in Japan the way he did in Belgium. Similar to Lieutenant Sam Ketchens's learning Arabic in Iraq, P&G paid for language lessons for their employees working in foreign countries. Their goal was not fluency. McDonald recognized that even a rudimentary learning of the native language fosters cultural understanding, creates bridges, and builds trust.

If you need an example of a leader of character who leads not only from the heart and the gut, but also from the strengths of the head, Bob McDonald is a good place to start.

BUILDING THE HEAD STRENGTHS

1. *Know your best talents and use them systematically.* We saw there are different sorts of mental abilities. You may not have had a formal assessment of your intelligence since high school, and it could be worth your time and money to make an appointment with a mental-skills coach for an assessment and discussion of your mental abilities profile. Review again the eight mental abilities that Gardner defines. Reflect on your past successes and failures, then rank order your strengths from highest to lowest, or just note your top three or four abilities. Identify your strengths and mindfully apply them to solve problems. Lieutenant Sam Ketchens did this, using his proficiency with languages to build trust with the Iraqi people with whom he worked.

2. *Practice creativity.* Build a creativity phase into the problem-solving approach you typically employ. Brainstorm different solutions. If you are a manager or a leader, form

small teams to assist you in deriving multiple solutions to a problem. The more complex the problem, the more important this stage may be. You may also observe creative people directly and note some of the ways they go about problem-solving. Reading biographies of creative people is useful, too.

3. *Rediscover your innate curiosity.* Children are curious by nature. As we mature, many of us become locked into narrower lanes of interest. Adults often find it challenging to find free time to explore new ideas and ways of thinking, but successful individuals and organizations thrive on curiosity. Engage in behaviors that require curiosity. Visit a museum. Spend time reading about art or science. Keep a journal and each day write down new things that you find interesting and would like to know more about, then follow up and learn about them.

4. *Open-mindedness.* People can become more open-minded by intentionally entertaining views that are counter to their initial way of thinking. Someone who deeply holds to the view that global climate change is occurring should systematically explore counterfactual arguments, and vice versa for climate-change deniers. People who thoughtfully engage in counterfactual thinking develop a deeper understanding of other points of view. This may be particularly important in social attitudes and beliefs. Sometimes just exposing yourself to people with views different from your own may have a profound impact on your tolerance and acceptance of the beliefs and attitudes of others. Psychologists also point to the positive impact of additional education on instilling a more open-minded worldview. You may already have a college degree or even an advanced degree, but taking a class in philosophy or social science may be fun and rewarding. Develop that habit of exploring different sides of issues with others. Join a book club and learn different viewpoints from both books and others in the club (an activity enhanced and fortified by wine and cheese).

5. *Love of learning*. Engaging in learning may be done for learning's sake alone. But you may also learn new things that will aid you in your job, as a leader, or in your family and social relationships. The military is a big believer in the importance of lifelong learning. It may surprise you to learn that the US Army is the largest education and training organization in the world. All soldiers, whether enlisted or officers, are required to attend professional military education and training courses throughout their careers. West Point cadets graduate with a bachelor's degree and immediately go to a Basic Officer Leader Course, where they learn the specific skills needed to lead others in whatever branch they will serve. They may also take shorter qualification courses in a variety of skills, such as learning to make combat parachute jumps (known as airborne training). Four years later, they attend the Captain's Career Course. After promotion to major, Command and General Staff College follows. Those who are ultimately selected for even higher ranks may attend the Army War College. Lifelong learning is seen as vital and essential in the profession of arms, and all branches of the military devote significant time and resources toward this end.

Take the initiative to see what training opportunities your organization may have. If you are self-employed or work for a small firm that does not have the resources to support education and training opportunities, then you may seek out these opportunities on your own. Take a computer course or two, work toward a degree in management, or learn a new language that will aid you in working with a wider variety of customers.

Not all learning needs to be job related. Some of the most rewarding new things you may learn will have nothing at all to do with your job. Learning a new recreational skill may yield many benefits. Learning to ski is fun, and you will also make new friends along the way and visit new places. Taking up bridge will do the same thing. Learn to paint or write poetry. Travel to unfamiliar places. Doing these things will expand your horizons and fuel the desire for even more learning.

6. *Perspective and wisdom.* These strengths build through the complexity and richness of personal experience. They are also based on the other strengths of the head, so following the advice already presented is helpful. You can be intelligent and knowledgeable but not possess perspective and wisdom. There is no easy path to perspective and wisdom, and aging alone won't necessarily imbue you with these capacities. High social intelligence helps. Learn to use your other strengths of the head, be considerate of others and their opinions, and take time to reflect on important matters in your personal and work life. Consider things in the larger context. Doing so will set the stage for building both your perspective and your wisdom.

4

STRENGTHS OF THE HEART

Kindness in words creates confidence. Kindness in thinking
promotes profoundness. Kindness in giving creates love.

—LAO-TZU

FIRST LIEUTENANT DANIEL B. HYDE

On March 7, 2009, General Caslen was sitting in a meeting with the senior US forces commander General Ray Odierno and the director of a key oil refinery in northern Iraq, in Baiji, Salah ad Din province. Baiji was not far from Balad, where Lieutenant Colonel Dave Hodne was dealing with the dilapidated tomato-paste factory and shared many of the same radical-versus-moderate-Sunni issues Balad was experiencing. The oil refinery was a key facility in the area because it provided a steady source of energy for the fragile community and economy. But its ability to operate was contingent on its ability to remain secure. If it failed to operate, it would be a source of discontent between the population and the central government, and it would show the failure of US efforts to build a secure and stable economy and government, an outcome critical in winning the support of the Iraqi population.

While sitting in the meeting, Caslen's aide passed him a note informing him that one of his infantry platoons was in a fight in the town of Samarra, which was about a twenty-minute helicopter flight from his current location. The report noted that a soldier was gravely wounded. Knowing that Dan Hyde was a platoon leader in Samarra, Caslen's heart jumped into his throat, thinking that possibly the injured man was him. Caslen asked his aide to keep him informed of the situation and to obtain the name of the injured soldier, while secretly praying for Dan and his troops.

Caslen knew Dan Hyde well from Caslen's previous assignment as commandant of cadets at West Point. The commandant, a brigadier general position, is subordinate to the superintendent (a job Caslen would have later on) and is responsible for cadet military, character, and athletic development at West Point. As commandant, Caslen would regularly engage with the cadet leaders, and they frequently sought his advice and guidance. In Caslen's first summer as commandant, Cadet Hyde was the senior cadet in charge of new-cadet training. During the spring of his junior year, Hyde had competed against all other cadets in his class to be the senior cadet commander that summer. During the academic year, Dan was the leader of his regiment, commanding more than eleven hundred cadets. Caslen came to know all of the senior cadets and was particularly impressed with Dan. He had impeccable values with unsurpassed competence and energy. An intellectual and physical paragon, he excelled at every task within the cadet program. Graduating near the top of his class, he could have chosen any Army specialty in which to serve as an officer and elected to serve in the infantry, regarded as the Army's "tip of the spear." Following graduation from West Point and from the Infantry Basic Officer Leader Course, Hyde reported to the Twenty-Fifth Infantry Division in Hawaii, his first choice for assignment. With the war raging, it didn't matter what division he chose because everyone would rotate through Iraq or Afghanistan.

Dan graduated high school in Modesto, California, in 2003, just two years after the 9/11 terrorist attack on the United States. As with many of his peers, he was deeply moved by the events of 9/11 and chose to attend West Point from the many civilian and other military academy options he had. He did so knowing that when he graduated, he would find himself in the crucible of ground combat. You have to wonder where you find such incredible men and women who, despite so many options available to them, choose to place themselves in harm's way for the benefit of their nation.

Caslen left his commandant position in April 2008 to become the commander of the Twenty-Fifth "Tropic Lightning" Division in Schofield Barracks, Hawaii. The division deployed to northern Iraq in November 2008. Dan Hyde, by now a member of that division, was also a part of that deployment.

Once in Iraq, Caslen made a point to stay in contact with and encourage the former cadets he had known as commandant, including Dan Hyde. Caslen recalls visiting Hyde while touring the battlefield and awarding him the Combat Infantry Badge. Caslen encouraged Hyde and told him to stay safe.

Dan was assigned to the town of Samarra, the location of the holy Shi'ite Al-Askari Mosque. Built in 944, the mosque is one of the most important Shia shrines in the world and was the target of an earlier attack by the Sunni radical leader Abu Musab al-Zarqawi, which destroyed the mosque and created a violent sectarian conflict between Sunni and Shia sects. Dan found himself in the middle of this conflict.

While on patrol on March 7, 2009, Dan's vehicle was attacked by an insurgent who threw a grenade that created a copper spall that penetrated Dan's armor-plated door. After receiving the initial report of the attack, the staff kept Caslen updated on the progress of the fight. Despite his hopes and prayers, the next report revealed that the injured soldier was Lieutenant Dan Hyde. Tragically, despite great efforts to keep him alive, Hyde passed away.

As soon as possible, Caslen flew to where Dan was and asked to be alone with him for a few moments. It was one of the hardest moments of Caslen's life. But he held Dan and told him how much he loved him and cared for him, and how sorry he was for what had happened. Caslen's pain and sorrow brought him even closer to Dan and his family and to the other men and women in his command. Times like that cement the importance of character traits of love, compassion, caring, commitment, and loyalty.

When the division returned from deployment, the families were present to welcome their soldiers home. The ceremonies included the families of those soldiers who had been killed during the deployment. This was no doubt tough for them, being present while seeing other families welcome their loved ones home. But the division wanted them to know they were still part of the family, and that the division would be there for them for whatever support was needed.

Dan Hyde's mom and dad flew out for the ceremonies, and Caslen spent time with them. They were incredibly brave and courageous to be there. Caslen and the other soldiers expressed their love for Dan and the family and assured them that the division would forever be indebted for Dan's sacrifice.

Caslen continues to stay in touch with Dan's parents to this day. He spoke at Dan's high school, telling the students what an incredible man, leader, and officer Dan was. Caslen visited Dan in his final resting place in Modesto. Although it was hard, it gave Caslen closure and comfort to be with Dan again, while offering comfort to Dan's family and friends. West Point honored Dan by naming one of its summer training events after him. The entire West Point class of 2019 was called Task Force Hyde, and Dan's father spoke to them when they completed their training.

Dan and the many others who have sacrificed for their country should never be forgotten. Dan was an incredibly talented and gifted officer with tremendous potential. We will never know why he was taken from us, but his story is important, and it remains inspiring to the generations of leaders who will follow. Since Dan's death, Caslen has worn a bracelet bearing his name and the date he was killed. Many do the same for other fallen soldiers. This is strength of the heart. This is the compassion and love felt for Dan and his family, even years after his passing. We never want to forget Dan Hyde and what he sacrificed in defense of his nation.

STRENGTHS OF THE HEART: KEY TO EFFECTIVE LEADERSHIP

As a division commander, Caslen was responsible for planning and executing a vital wartime mission and leading and caring for the welfare of twenty-three thousand soldiers. In a large corporation or other civilian organization, a lieutenant would be equivalent to an entry-level management position. Scores of lieutenants were under Caslen's command, and he could be excused if he did not take time to engage with Hyde and his family. After all, Caslen had a war to fight. But he did take the time, and the impact on Hyde's family and the other soldiers in the division was immeasurable. Here you can see the link between strengths of the heart and leadership. A genuine caring for Hyde, his family, and his fellow soldiers show how strengths of the heart make a technically proficient leader into a transformative leader who is trusted and respected by his subordinates.

Strengths of the heart are vital in all domains of life. Strengths of the gut and the head help us in many ways, but these strengths of the heart enable us to be a trusted leader, friend, parent, or teammate. Capacity to love, kindness, forgiveness, and gratitude matter for everyone. These strengths transcend culture, context, and time and represent what it means to be human.

Effective leaders understand this. Think about different places you have worked. You can probably recall examples of leaders who possessed strengths of the heart and overtly demonstrated this understanding—and leaders who did not. Effective leaders demonstrate these character strengths in a variety of ways. Many are simple actions. Sending birthday cards to employees, arranging social activities so that members of the work group can share experiences outside the workplace, or showing a genuine interest in employees' families or personal interests all contribute to a high-functioning work environment. Formally recognizing achievements is another way to demonstrate caring and concern for others in the workplace. When you think about that "boss from hell," you probably aren't thinking about his or her technical competence. Rather, you probably are reacting to a leader or a supervisor who lacked these strengths of the heart. This type of leader is selfish and only cares about your technical job performance and demonstrates no concern about you as an individual.

St. Louis Cardinals manager Mike Shildt gets it. Although he did not play professional baseball, he rose through the ranks of the St. Louis Cardinals farm system and managed winning teams at every level. An outsider might think that a better choice for manager would be someone with extensive experience playing baseball at the major league level. After all, they would have both the experience and the street cred to manage a team. But baseball is filled with examples of great players who did not excel as managers. Home-run king Barry Bonds is not a manager. Babe Ruth wanted to manage but never did. So why did the Cardinals hire Shildt as the new manager midway through the 2018 season?

It is because Shildt's genuine caring and love for his players allow them to coalesce into a cohesive team and to work together to achieve excellence on and off the field. Shildt is beloved by many of the current Cardinals, who gush about his pregame "ball talk" meetings and his mantra of "I'm not here to judge you, I'm here to love you."[1] Shildt was recognized for his leadership when he was named National League Manager of the Year following the 2019 season.

Shildt's case is a great example of the power of character strengths of the heart in leadership. He no doubt has considerable technical expertise in baseball, but the difference maker is his ability to connect with players and create a cohesive team. Interestingly, in baseball the on-field leader is called a *manager*, not *head coach* as is common in football or basketball. Baseball managers employ a host of technical experts such as hitting and pitching instructors who work daily with players to improve skills or correct bad habits. The manager's job includes technical expertise, but much more. Shildt and other successful baseball managers succeed in no small way due to heart-based character strengths. Again, we encourage you to think of situations in your own life where these strengths are critical in individual or group success.

SPECIFIC STRENGTHS

The Values-in-Action Inventory of Strengths (VIA-IS) includes several character strengths from the six moral virtues that may be thought of as strengths of the heart. These strengths have in common a positive focus on others and a genuine concern for their well-being. These strengths are capacity to love, kindness, forgiveness, and gratitude. Alone and in combination with other character strengths, they are important to how individuals interact with and relate to others, and how leaders inspire others to attain organizational goals.

Capacity to love. Psychologists make a distinction between passionate love and companionate love. When you experience passionate love, you know it! It includes an overwhelming preoccupation with another person, typically in the early stages of romantic relationships. Think about your first experiences with romantic love, and you will have an idea of what passionate love means. Companionate love, on the other hand, is a more enduring and stable form of love. It is characterized by a lasting and strong positive emotional bond for others but lacks the emotional intensity of passionate love. The love of a parent for a child, or vice versa, is a good example.

Another and important sort of love is not as well recognized by psychological science. This is the love that leaders have for their subordinates, and teammates have for each other. General Caslen's caring for Dan Hyde and Cardinal manager Shildt's feelings for his players are not uncommon and represent an essential ingredient to effective leadership and team performance. This is a powerful type of companionate love.

A tragic event near Springfield, Missouri, provides a profound example of this type of love. During the night of September 7, 2018, Deputy Aaron Roberts of the Greene County Sheriff's Office responded to a call for service in a remote corner of the county. After completing the call, Deputy Roberts continued his patrol duties. On this stormy night it had been raining hard for several hours. Shortly after radioing headquarters that he was back in service, Deputy Roberts called again and told the dispatcher that his patrol car had been swept off a low-water crossing and into rushing water. Despite repeated attempts to recontact him, there was no further word from Deputy Roberts. After an intense search, Deputy Roberts was found deceased in his patrol car, having drowned after being swept away by the swift water.

Deputy Roberts's death was a shock to his fellow officers and the entire community. The Sheriff's Office and other local law enforcement agencies rallied to support Deputy Roberts's wife, Kim, and their family. The outpouring of love from the community was significant. But the actions of Greene County sheriff Jim Arnott and his deputies over the months that followed showed the deepest form of companionate love. Sheriff Arnott helped Kim clean out her garage in the days following her husband's untimely death. He noticed a 1995 Mitsubishi Eclipse sitting on blocks in the garage. Kim said this car was what had caught her attention when she first met Aaron. But something about Aaron also caught her eye. "I ended up calling my best friend that night and telling her that I was going to marry him. The joke was I married him for his car. I dated him for his car, I know that."

Recognizing the importance of the car to Kim, Arnott asked her if he could rebuild the car and restore it to running order. With the help of other deputies and members of the local community, on March 19, 2019, Sheriff Arnott presented the restored car to Kim. It cost more than $7,000 and hundreds of hours of labor to restore, but the car was now in mint condition. Kim was deeply touched and told a reporter for the local newspaper, "There were so many hands on this car it just blows my mind. My mind can't even wrap around how many people helped on this."[2]

This expression of love impacted others in addition to Kim. By overtly showing their love and concern for Deputy Roberts and Kim, everyone who contributed to the restoration also benefited. "I think it's a proud moment and I'm proud of my community—that's the big thing," Arnott said.

All forms of love are important to the good life and represent a character trait that enables us to derive meaning and purpose in life. If you are high in this trait, you will have close positive relationships with others, and your feelings of love for them will be reciprocated. What is your score for capacity to love from the VIA-IS? Peterson and Seligman give several examples of capacity to love.[3] Individuals high in this trait will answer yes to the questions of whether there is someone with whom they

- feel free to be themselves
- feel trusted and supported by
- hate to be away from for long
- would do almost anything for
- find the person's happiness matters as much as or more than their own
- are committed to the person's welfare
- are physically affectionate
- feel deep commitment in the person's company
- are passionate about

Kindness. To tout kindness as a character trait that is central to optimal human functioning seems like stating the obvious. Scouts are inculcated with the idea of the "good turn," which says they should do good deeds or favors for others daily.[4] Growing up, we are told to "do unto others as you would have them do unto you."[5]

But understanding that kindness is a positive trait of the heart is one thing, and being kind is another. Bullying is rampant among schoolchildren. On social media people demean and demonize those who disagree with their own political or social views. Politicians feed these views to energize their political base. Simply put, the world seems full of hate and anger, and all too often it spills out into hateful speech and violence. Strangers call a woman names because she wears a burka. A terrorist kills people in response to his or her ideologically based hatred of people with a different faith or political view. A radio talk show hosts denies that twenty children were murdered by a deranged gunman in Newtown, Connecticut, and thousands believe him, adding to the pain of those who lost a child or loved one there. Members of a Christian church picket the funerals of fallen soldiers, screaming insults at their families and loved ones. It goes on and on.

You can't be blamed if, in the face of the constant barrage of stories about people behaving in markedly unkind ways toward others, you conclude that kindness has eroded in today's society. But in concluding this, you are succumbing to what psychologists call the availability heuristic, a common decision-making failure. The availability heuristic occurs when you make a decision or reach a conclusion—in this case that kindness is a lost art—based on information that is most easily retrieved from memory. For example, many older Americans fear home invasions or other forms of violence. This is because when an elderly person is attacked in his or her home or elsewhere, the media frequently make it a headline story. In truth, young males are and have always been the most common victims (and perpetrators) of violent crime. But because of the "if it bleeds, it leads" approach of news media, older people come to believe they are more vulnerable than they actually are.

The availability heuristic contributes to our perceptions about kindness in similar ways. Kind acts rarely make the news. But with a bit of reflection, many instances of kind acts will likely come to mind. Following a snowstorm, a woman with a snowblower clears the driveways of her elderly neighbors without being asked and without expectation of compensation. One student helps another understand a calculus problem. A work group organizes meals for the family of a coworker who just had a baby. These daily acts of kindness just don't make the news.

Volunteerism represents another form of kindness. Many small towns are protected by volunteer fire departments. A quarter of all Americans volunteer, averaging fifty hours per year in donated time and effort. Organizations such as Meals on Wheels could not achieve their mission without volunteers. Following a natural disaster, people stand in lines to donate blood to the Red Cross. The economic impact of volunteering is substantial, reaching $184 billion a year in the United States alone.[6]

Psychologists report that kindness is just as good, or better, for the person doing the good deed as for its recipient. Those who do kind acts may enjoy better emotional and physical health than nonvolunteers. Although not extensively studied scientifically, anecdotes and cultural traditions as expressed in religious writings and secular literature abound with the notion that deliberately doing kind acts may transform and improve a person's personality and well-being. Richard McKinney provides an example. Once a hateful white supremacist who plotted to bomb a mosque, he decided one day to visit his next-door neighbor, who was Muslim, and confront him with all that McKinney thought was evil and wrong with Islam. But the neighbor kindly listened, and over time McKinney lost his hatred, converted to Islam, and is now an imam at a local mosque, where he teaches others the message of peace and kindness.[7]

The Jewish custom of *tikkun olam* represents another ancient recognition of the importance of kindness as a component of civil society. *Tikkun olam* is the concept of behaving in a constructive, pro-social manner. It means engaging in acts that promote the welfare of others. *Tikkun olam* is a complex concept but at its heart is an expression of basic human kindness coupled with the understanding that practicing it makes the world a better place.

Yale professor Nicholas Christakis considers kindness a central human trait. In his recent book, *Blueprint,* he uses evolutionary biology to argue that kindness is a form of altruism that enables large groups of people to work cooperatively.[8] The soldier who sacrifices his life so that others may live represents a dramatic example of altruism. Army staff sergeant Travis Atkins did this on June 1, 2007, when he tackled an enemy insurgent wearing a suicide vest. The bomb exploded, killing Atkins, but his actions saved the lives of three fellow soldiers.[9]

The mundane acts of day-to-day kindness promote successful group life. Humans, according to Christakis, are genetically wired for such selfless behavior. We are not alone in this. Jane Goodall observed similar behaviors in her studies of chimpanzees. Wild rats will even work to free other rats that are caged.[10]

We argue that kindness is not a lost art. Rather, it continues to be a central strength of the heart and promotes positive social relationships as well as builds your own sense of well-being and self-worth.

Forgiveness. On March 15, 2019, during Friday Prayer, a gunman attacked the Al Noor Mosque and the Linwood Islamic Centre in Christchurch, New Zealand. Within minutes, fifty people were killed and another fifty were wounded, some severely. The suspect in the shootings was Brenton Harrison Tarrant, a twenty-eight-year-old Australian. Motivated by ethnic hatred, Tarrant had planned such an attack for years. A gun-club member, he purchased his weapons legally. Australia has restrictive gun laws requiring a clean criminal record and a justification for possessing a weapon. None of the weapons used were "military-style" assault rifles.

One can only imagine the pain and suffering of surviving loved ones. But not everyone responded to this brutal and hateful act with a demand for vengeance. Instead, Farid Ahmed, whose wife, Husna, was among the fifty people killed, called for forgiveness. At a service held in Christchurch to commemorate those who died in the attacks, Ahmed said, "I don't want to have a heart that is boiling like a volcano. A volcano has anger, fury, rage. It doesn't have peace. It has hatred. It burns itself within, and also it burns the surroundings. I don't want to have a heart like this."[11]

Ahmed's response to this unthinkable act represents the heart strength of forgiveness. The virtue of forgiveness is fundamental across time, culture, and religious and philosophical thought. Peterson and Seligman point out that forgiveness is a formal part of Judaism, Christianity, Islam, Buddhism, and Hinduism.[12] Ahmed's Islamic faith instructed him that Tarrant was his brother, and although he had to be held responsible for his hideous act, he had to be forgiven. Christians learn in their Lord's Prayer to "forgive our trespasses, as we forgive those who trespass against us." Forgiveness may range from the dramatic, such as in Ahmed's case, to more mundane forgiveness for the daily transgressions we all experience.

History provides many other examples of forgiveness. Imprisoned under apartheid in South Africa from 1962 to 1990,

Nelson Mandela rose to become the first black president of the country. For many of us, the pain and anger of imprisonment and subjugation would be overwhelming. But Mandela rose above these feelings to become the greatest unifying force in his country's history. His name is synonymous worldwide with forgiveness. Cultural anthropologist Janice Harper writes, "If a man tortured and imprisoned for nearly three decades could find in himself forgiveness, what lessons might we take from him on how to respond to acts of aggression and cruelty in our ordinary lives? Ought we forgive those who are not sorry for their cruelty and the pain and suffering it produced?"[13]

Psychologists find that forgiveness diminishes negative emotions such as anger, hostility, depression, and anxiety.[14] This makes sense. Hatred requires a lot of energy and detracts from positive engagement. Adaptive people learn to channel negative emotions into socially constructive ones. After the February 14, 2018, shooting that took the lives of seventeen students and staff at Stoneman Douglas High School in Parkland, Florida, many survivors helped establish a movement to prevent future mass murders. This included a student-led demonstration on March 24, 2018, called the March for Our Lives in Washington, D.C., and 880 other locations, that called for a reexamination of gun laws in the United States.

Turn again to your VIA-IS scores and reflect on where forgiveness lies in your hierarchy of strengths. If it is among your top five or six strengths, good! If it is lower than you prefer, think about small ways that you may routinely practice forgiveness. Thankfully, most of us will not share Farid Ahmed's experience, but all of us must deal with the transgressions of daily life. Practicing forgiveness for small transgressions may help you build the capacity to forgive larger ones.

Gratitude. One of the most powerful strengths of the heart is the capacity to give and receive thanks in life. The greatest thing about gratitude is that practicing it may bring greater positive benefits for you than it does for the recipient of thanks. Positive psychologists recommend a simple exercise—called the gratitude visit—to reduce negative feelings, such as depression, while simultaneously increasing positive ones, such as happiness and life satisfaction.[15] With gratitude, it may indeed be better to give than to receive.

Receiving gratitude is good, too. Teachers know the good feeling and sense of reward that follows receiving a genuine compliment from a student. This may be a word of thanks or encouragement or a more systematic expression.

Dr. Matthews experienced this recently. For more than a year, he had mentored a cadet who had been arrested for driving while intoxicated. Matthews had come to know this cadet a year earlier and they had mutual trust, so the cadet naturally turned to Matthews as a mentor. While violations of the code of conduct of this serious nature often result in separation from the academy, this cadet had a good track record at West Point and, aside from this incident, showed great potential as an Army officer. So instead of being expelled, he was placed in a formal and rigorous mentorship program. His graduation and commissioning were delayed for a year and were contingent upon his successful completion of this program.

Over the next year, this cadet admitted to himself that he was an alcoholic and not only enrolled in substance-abuse counseling but also established a cadet-run support group to help other cadets struggling with substance abuse. Matthews and the cadet met frequently to discuss self-understanding, social relationships, academic success, and what it means to be an Army officer. After successfully completing the mentorship program the cadet graduated with the West Point class of 2019 and received his Army commission as a second lieutenant.

A few days before the cadet's graduation, Dr. Matthews received the following note from his young protégé:

> I wanted to personally thank you for your mentorship over the past three years. I never thought I would meet someone as caring, brilliant, and understanding as you. Although I made a mistake, a serious one, you went to bat for me and helped me continually after that. You believed in me when no one else did and for that I am extraordinarily grateful. You showed me more respect than anyone at West Point when I was at my lowest. You also continued to mentor me following my poor decision into my fifth year at West Point. While I am certain I am lucky to be where I am today, it would not be possible without the help, motivation, and inspiration from you. As I continue on to my next duty station, I wanted to formally thank you for all you have done for me over the past three years. I hope to see you again soon, but I know you will be one of the people I will always remember at West Point for all of the positive experiences and learning I received from you. Thank you again, sir, for all you are. It has truly been an honor and a privilege working with you.

Experiencing adversity and deprivations may cause you to be more grateful for the good things in life. For example, among

Army combat leaders at the height of the Iraq and Afghanistan Wars, gratitude (along with capacity to love) increased substantially following their combat experiences. The captains had led soldiers in ground combat. Some had experienced the death of comrades. All of them had endured difficult conditions and long periods of isolation from their families. Upon return from their combat deployments, they were more appreciative of their families and a safe home and for the other elements of day-to-day life.[16]

Gratitude may be found in everyday circumstances. Check your gratitude score and, as with forgiveness, think about ways you can overtly express your gratitude to others. Whether it is thanking a former teacher for his or her impact on your life, or simply thanking your spouse for a kind deed he or she did that day, doing so will boost your mood.

STRENGTHS OF THE HEART AND ADVERSITY

Strengths of the heart matter a great deal in day-to-day living. Taking time to show and receive love, to be kind to and forgiving of others, and to express gratitude vastly improves the quality of everyday life. These ordinary expressions of the strengths of the heart are the foundation of social relationships, and in return we feel valued and that we, ourselves, indeed matter.

Strengths of the heart may seem more poignant and impactful in times of adversity. Soldiers rally around a wounded or lost comrade, or law enforcement officers support the family of a fallen officer. Those who lead others in such in extremis situations must possess strengths of the heart to be trusted and must be trusted by their subordinates, peers, and supervisors to be effective.

Henry V knew something about strengths of the heart. King of England from 1413 to 1422, Henry reigned at a critical period during the Hundred Years' War between England and France, a war waged from 1337 to 1453 over the right to rule France. On October 25, a day that the Christian community honors Saint Crispin (martyred in 286), in 1415, Henry faced the French Army in a fight known as the Battle of Agincourt. Tremendously outnumbered, the English soldiers were nervous and fearful of the pending battle.

Recognizing the degraded morale, Henry delivered his famous Saint Crispin speech, motivating his soldiers, who would go on to defeat the French and enjoy the ensuing victory. In William Shakespeare's play *Henry V,* written 180 years after the battle, this speech appears in act 4. In Shakespeare's version, the speech contains a phrase that relates to military combatants today and illustrates the camaraderie, love, loyalty, and commitment between warriors who share the hardships of war. Also known as the "Band of Brothers" speech, it continues to resonate with today's soldiers who experience similar challenges, failures, and successes in the crucible of combat.

Imagine seeing your king in the miserable conditions of combat, sharing the same hardships and dangers you experience. You would do everything within your power to never let him down. The Band of Brothers speech resonates timelessly with soldiers, particularly the phrase "we few, we happy few, we band of brothers, for he today that sheds his blood with me shall be my brother."

Although armies in the fifteenth century consisted principally of male warriors, today's gender-integrated forces find both men and women experiencing these challenges together. So, although the term *band of brothers* was applicable to an all-male force, today's military will more commonly use the term *band of brothers and sisters,* which portrays the composition of today's battlefields. Whichever version is used, it accurately captures the strength of the heart and the loyalty and bonds that exist among these men and women.

This concept of a band of brothers and sisters may be found in other situations where groups of individuals come together to overcome challenges and adversity. *USA Today* writer Monica Rhor describes a group of school-aged African immigrants residing in Houston, Texas. Freed from the horrendous conditions of refugee camps in Africa, these young immigrants face new challenges in the United States. Learning a new language and a new culture, struggling to succeed in school, being the target of bullying and racial taunts, and doing so in an era of palpable anti-immigrant prejudice was their new normal.[17]

Enter Charles Rotramel, the head of reVision, a nonprofit that works with youths in the Houston area who become involved with the juvenile justice system. Sensing a need for these young immigrants to be part of something larger than themselves, something that would impart a sense of meaning and purpose to their lives, he formed a soccer team called reVision FC and recruited these kids to form the team. In the team's locker room is a large sign with a single word—FAMILY. A band of brothers was born. The team members look out for each other, on and off the pitch. If a member struggles with a personal issue or money problems, his teammates step up. "They are like my brothers," one player says. "When I don't have something, they give it to me. When they don't have, I give it to them."[18]

Another soccer team that exemplifies this team bond is the US Women's National Team. The champions of the Women's World Cup embody the idea of sisterhood in achievement. To win a World Cup takes more than raw athletic talent and motivation. Success hinges on cohesion. Team cocaptain Megan Rapinoe says, "Everyone always talks about with a team that you want camaraderie, but we really do have a tight team. Whoever needs to be leaned on, the whole team is comfortable leaning on that person." Adds teammate Kelley O'Hara, "It's refreshing to be part of a group where, what we show on the field, having each other's backing and taking care of each other and winning for each other, is really felt off the field as well."[19]

From the loyalty of this brotherhood and sisterhood, you will find love, passion, and the commitment to never, ever leave your brother or sister in a fight without fully committing yourself to stand by him or her, shoulder to shoulder, even if it means that you will die in doing so. This character trait is born from shared hardships but creates a commitment to your teammate that is perhaps stronger than a commitment you would ever have with your own blood brother or sister.

BUILDING THE STRENGTHS OF THE HEART

Psychologists have not much studied ways to enhance strengths of the heart. But one theory seems especially relevant to nurturing these strengths, and this theory has implications for improving daily interactions and leadership. Psychologist Carl Rogers's theory of human development was based on years of therapy he conducted with individuals suffering from psychological and emotional distress. His insights into the strengths of the heart provide guidance on how you may better develop these capacities in yourself and others.

Rogers believed that human adjustment is developed during childhood. His most important concept was that of unconditional positive regard. Parents should love their children without what he called conditions of worth. Consider two different children, each raised in a different family. Both children misbehaved at times, as all children will do, and as they matured, they sometimes struggled to succeed in school. One set of parents, although they would say they loved their child, imposed conditions of worth upon her. When the child behaved and was successful, these parents showered her with love and attention. But when she fell short, they became cold and distant. The parents of the second child consistently and genuinely expressed unconditional love for their child. When the child fell short, these parents corrected the behavior and offered strategies to improve his behavior. They made a distinction between the undesirable behavior or action, which needed to be corrected, and their love for their child, which was unconditional. Rogers observed that children who developed under conditions of worth were often anxious, depressed, and otherwise poorly adjusted as adults.

You can take Rogers's ideas and apply them to your own social interactions to sharpen your strengths of the heart. In your interactions with family or others, keep the distinction between conditions of worth and unconditional positive regard in mind. As a leader, when a subordinate fails at a task, focus on helping him or her do better the next time. Don't automatically label the offender a bad person. By practicing unconditional positive regard, you can strengthen social relationships and still be an effective spouse, teammate, or leader.

Most people have strengths of the heart, but some are not good at expressing them. People vary a great deal with how comfortable they are in expressing their feelings. One can both give and receive love without talking a great deal about it. Parents who make sacrifices to provide for their children are expressing love, even without continually verbalizing it. The same goes for adults who care for their aging parent. Actions matter a great deal. We suggest that you think of ways that either through actions or words enable you to regularly and intentionally express love, kindness, forgiveness, and gratitude. Make it a habit to do this. But be genuine in your words and actions. Spouses who verbalize love but act in hurtful ways toward each other are not truly showing these character strengths. Focus on those who matter in your life, and regularly think of ways to express these strengths of the heart through words and deeds. As with the gratitude letter, you will benefit more than those who receive your positive feelings and actions.

5

TRUST: THE STRAW THAT STIRS THE DRINK

I came to believe that a leader isn't good because they are right;
they're good because they're willing to learn and to trust.

—STANLEY MCCHRYSTAL[1]

During preparations for the US-led coalition attack into Iraq in February 1991, then lieutenant general Fred Franks, the Seventh Corps commander, launched into a detailed and passionate explanation of the corps' attack plan to one of the units assigned to his command. General Franks felt it was imperative that everyone understand the mission and why he had chosen this concept of operation. As he wrapped up the presentation, Franks asked if there were questions. A noncommissioned officer (NCO) jumped in and said these simple words: "Don't worry, General, we trust you."

In that brief instant, that NCO illustrated the essence of what we seek when we are in command or in a leadership position. This soldier placed unwavering confidence in his commander from the essential trust built and fostered over time, and without that trust, the mission would crumble.

From years of leadership experience, we assert that trust is the most important element of effective leadership. The soldiers' trust of their commander, General Franks, facilitated a historic victory for Seventh Corps during the ground war of Desert Storm.

It may seem obvious that trust is essential in war. But think about your best supervisor or manager and your worst supervisor or manager in your work experience. How would you describe your trust of each? How important is trust in your working relationships? If you are a supervisor or manager, do you think your subordinates trust you? What is trust, exactly? What happens when a bond of trust is broken? And can it be restored? Can I learn to be more trustworthy by understanding the elements of trust?

Psychologists have studied trust extensively, and leaders have learned a great deal about trust based on their experiences in leading and influencing others in military, corporate, and other settings. We believe that trust is an essential personal and leader attribute. It is hard to imagine any setting where humans may operate effectively without trust. Nevertheless, it seems that trust is under assault by politicians and others who believe they can achieve their goals by undermining trust in the media, the justice system, education, and other institutions. Social media does not help. People are prone to believe what they see, read, or hear on social media. News that does not support one's views is dismissed as "fake news." People do not vaccinate their children because they believe (without supporting evidence) that vaccinations cause autism or are a government plot to control their minds. Intentionally or not, once esteemed institutions are under attack with the net effect of an erosion of trust.

Former chairman of the Joint Chiefs of Staff General Martin Dempsey, in his book *Radical Inclusion,* discusses what he calls the "digital echo." He maintains that social media have enabled anyone to post an idea regardless of how true it is. What matters is not the truth, but rather how many views or "likes" the post generates. And if views and "likes" are more important than truth, then truth no longer matters. When truth is distorted, then trust evaporates. This occurs daily and is a threat to trust that we should guard against.[2]

What may be the long-term impact of this erosion of trust? If law enforcement and the court system are not trusted and are viewed as illegitimate, people may not feel compelled to obey the law. If all news is fake news, then people make decisions on their personal biases and prejudices rather than on an analysis of facts. The movement to not vaccinate children is especially troubling. Measles, essentially eradicated, is once again on the rise. In Rockland County, New York, just outside New York City, 25 percent of children are unvaccinated.[3] The result has been a resurgence of the disease, so bad that the county issued a ban against unvaccinated children visiting public places. If people don't trust measles vaccinations, what about polio?

WHAT IS TRUST?

Trust is a relationship between two or more individuals characterized by the expectation that the other will behave in ways that are mutually beneficial. Digging in a bit more deeply, trust has two elements. First, trust requires predictability, that each person in the relationship will behave in consistent ways. Trust evaporates when predictability and consistency disappear. The spouse who cheats on his or her partner, even once, may never be trusted again. Second, trust involves risk. You expect the trusted person to do the right thing, but if the person does not, negative consequences may follow. A police officer trusts her partner to cover her while she conducts a vehicle search. If the partner fails to do so, the suspect may assault the officer or flee. Violations of trust have a cost.[4]

Trust is especially critical in dangerous contexts such as the military and law enforcement. Studying and understanding trust in these contexts not only aids in educating, training, and developing better soldiers and law enforcement officers, but also informs us how trust works in other contexts.

An especially intriguing field study of trust was conducted by military psychologist Patrick J. Sweeney. Sweeney (a lieutenant colonel at the time) was in graduate school pursuing his doctorate in social psychology when the United States invaded Iraq in 2003. Although Sweeney was slated for assignment to West Point to teach psychology and leadership upon completion of his doctoral studies, General David Petraeus (a major general at the time) asked him to suspend his graduate studies and assist in the initial military operations in Iraq in March of 2003. After agreeing to this request, Sweeney quickly designed a study that allowed him to conduct research on trust among soldiers in combat.

Sweeney devised a set of surveys and administered them to officers, noncommissioned officers, and enlisted soldiers during combat operations. It is an understatement to say that this methodology had high external validity. Following his stint in the war, Sweeney returned to his graduate studies, spent several months analyzing the data he had collected in Iraq, and successfully completed and defended his dissertation. We suspect that the University of North Carolina, where Sweeney obtained his doctorate in social psychology, had never seen a dissertation of this sort!

The results of Sweeney's research were enlightening. He found three factors central to trust by soldiers in their leaders. Sweeney calls these factors the three C's of trust: competence, character, and caring.[5] First and foremost, to be trusted, leaders must be viewed by their soldiers as competent. The leaders had to demonstrate to their subordinates that they possessed the knowledge and skills needed to get the job done. Incompetence could result in unnecessary deaths or injury to soldiers.

The second C, character, is also necessary to form bonds of trust. The Army espouses seven basic values that it believes are the essential ingredients of character. These are loyalty, duty, respect, selfless service, honor, integrity, and personal courage. Stemming from hundreds of years of military experience and culture, these values map directly to the strengths of the head, heart, and gut discussed already in this book. Sweeney found that competence is necessary but is not sufficient to engender trust. High character is also critical. A skilled and competent leader who is disloyal, shirks duty, is disrespectful, and so forth is simply not trusted by his or her soldiers. If you fail in character, you fail in leadership because you lose the trust of your subordinates and your superiors.

Sweeney's third C of trust is a sense of genuine caring for the welfare of soldiers. Caring does not mean blindly catering to the whims of individuals, but rather a clear and heartfelt commitment to doing the right thing for the soldiers, under trying circumstances. A caring leader shows empathy, shares risk with his or her soldiers, and stands with his or her soldiers in the face of daunting challenges. In the direst case, the caring leader ensures that a soldier killed in action is treated with utmost respect, his or her remains retrieved and sent home, and the soldier's family supported and consoled.

Sweeney emphasizes that each of the three C's is necessary for trust, but none by itself is sufficient. Soldiers assigned to units led by officers and senior noncommissioned officers who exemplified competence, character, and caring were ultimately more effective. Morale was higher, and soldiers were more willing to give their all to complete assigned missions.

A significant engagement during the Battle of Gettysburg illustrates the timeless nature of the three C's. As you read about this engagement, think to yourself how and where competence, character, and caring contributed to the successful completion of the battle. Also consider how these characteristics might apply in your own situation.

THE BATTLE OF GETTYSBURG

On July 1, 2, and 3, 1863, in the Battle of Gettysburg the Union persevered, defeating for the first time in two years a seemingly invincible Confederate Army. Among the units in the battle was the well-ordered Minnesota regiment commanded by Colonel William Colvill. Colvill's corps commander, General Winfield Scott Hancock, saw that a massed Confederate attack toward the center of the Union line was gaining momentum, forcing a retreat by the Union line. Recognizing the potential disaster, Hancock ordered William Colvill to attack the Confederate line, knowing the deadly outcome that faced the Minnesotans. Colvill, fully aware of his impending fate and that of his men, complied with the order. The soldiers, knowing what was about to happen to them, dutifully obeyed the orders of their commander and attacked the Confederates, buying the time necessary to reorder the Union line. Although successful, the Minnesotans suffered catastrophic losses, with more than 80 percent of the regiment killed in the attack. This costly but successful move was an incredible example of duty, loyalty, and trust.

Neither side during these three days of battle showed any shortage of valor and courage. One of the more renowned and historic engagements occurred on the afternoon of the second day at Little Round Top, which was the leftmost flank of the Union line.

Confederate general Robert E. Lee ordered his corps commander James Longstreet to attack the Union forces on the left flank, directly in the path of Little Round Top. Adding to the complexity of the battle, Union general Daniel Sickles, who was in a mutually supporting position to the right of Little Round Top, had moved his forces forward in an attempt to occupy higher ground, leaving the forces on the Union left flank on their own and defenseless.

As Longstreet prepared to attack, the Union's senior engineer, Brigadier General Gouverneur Warren, was sent to reconnoiter the key terrain on the left flank of the Union line. Recognizing Longstreet's impending attack, and seeing no Union forces on this critical terrain, he immediately summoned troops to defend Little Round Top. Union brigade commander Colonel Strong

Vincent ordered his forces to occupy Little Round Top, with the Twentieth Maine Regiment on the extreme left of the line. He ordered the Twentieth, "Hold that ground at all hazards."

The Twentieth was commanded by Colonel Joshua Chamberlain, a former professor from Bowdoin College, who was revered and loved by his troops. Chamberlain moved his men into position just in time to repel General Longstreet's attack, led by the Fifteenth Alabama Regiment. The Confederates attacked again and again and were repelled again and again.

As the Fifteenth regrouped to prepare for one more attack, Chamberlain gathered his leaders to assess his own regiment's situation. He found significant casualties, with the regiment nearly out of ammunition. Under these conditions almost any other commander would have ordered a withdrawal. But Chamberlain, remembering Colonel Vincent's order to "Hold that ground at all hazards," refused to consider withdrawing at such a critical time. Instead, Chamberlain ordered the remaining men in the regiment to "fix bayonets" and prepare to assault the Confederates down the hill.

The order to "fix bayonets" meant hand-to-hand combat, and certain injury and death. One can only imagine what went through the soldiers' minds when they received the order. This is where trust between commander and soldiers truly mattered. Disregarding their own safety, they prepared to execute the commander's order. In the absence of such trust, they would never have followed such a life-threatening command.

How did Chamberlain create such a trusting relationship with his troops? Chamberlain was always with his men, regardless of the conditions. He shared hardships and always led from the front. Before Gettysburg, he was given the remnants of another Maine regiment, in which a number of the troops had been arrested for mutiny, and ordered to shoot the mutineers if necessary. Rather than treating them as "excess baggage," Chamberlain talked to them, reasoned with them, cared for them, and convinced them to fight with the Twentieth Maine. Given a leader of his caliber, you can see why his men revered and trusted him. That trust made the Twentieth Maine victorious against tremendous odds, helping the Union persevere through day two of Gettysburg and to fight and ultimately win at the end of day three. Chamberlain's competence, his irreproachable character, and his genuine caring love for his soldiers enabled him to win the day.

Most of us work in jobs that are important, stressful, and demanding. It may be useful to reflect, from your own experience, on the validity of Sweeney's three C's in your own work experience. Do your leaders or managers possess and exemplify competence, character, and caring? What is the effect on your performance or morale if one or more of the C's is absent? Were you satisfied to work for a leader who was competent, but who lacked character and/or did not express genuine concern for your well-being? Perhaps most important, what can you do to build your own three C's?

A FOURTH C

Another factor critical to trust is communication—it may be thought of as the fourth C. Effective communication is a prerequisite for building and sustaining trust. And it is not one-directional. Lasting and rewarding relationships of all types depend on regular and honest communication. Marriages are hinged on lateral communication. Each partner must communicate with the other and listen to the other as well. One-way communication is a recipe for divorce court.

When Chamberlain was given the remnants of the other Maine regiment consisting of mutinous soldiers with morale as low as one can imagine, he communicated genuine respect, love, and purpose. Because of his communication skills, these men went from mutinous, disobedient soldiers, to men who agreed to put their lives at risk fighting with their fellow Mainers. Their morale and commitment were transforming and only occurred when their leader, Chamberlain, demonstrated caring leadership and did so by communicating respect and purpose.

In organizational settings, vertical communication is also critical. Workers must communicate clearly with coworkers and also with their managers and subordinates. This is particularly true in high-risk occupations, where members of a team must be clear and timely in their verbal interactions with team members in tactical situations. Watch a few episodes of *Live PD* and observe how law enforcement officers communicate with each other as well as with suspects in dangerous situations. In less dramatic work settings, written communication helps employees form a common operating picture of the work to be done.

General Caslen once watched a team-building activity called the mousetrap exercise, in which one person was blindfolded and had to navigate his hand through a minefield of mousetraps on a tabletop via the voice commands of his teammate. Knowing the pain of responding to a bad or misunderstood verbal command, the blindfolded teammate had to place complete trust in his teammate's communication skills. Successful verbal commands resulted in a safe and nonpainful completion of the task. The goal of this exercise was to convey the importance of communication in building trust.

Failure to communicate may have immediate negative impacts on task and mission and, in the long run, erodes trust. Perhaps this fourth C may be considered part of competence, one of the three C's identified by Sweeney. Wherever you classify it, a member of a team who does not communicate clearly both laterally and vertically puts others at risk and over time becomes less trusted.

General Caslen also observed the importance of communication on building trust while serving as an observer-controller at the Army's Joint Readiness Training Center (JRTC), near Leesville, Louisiana, at Fort Polk. The mission of JRTC is to allow units that are about to deploy to combat zones the opportunity to practice skills in a realistic setting. The training is designed to resemble actual combat conditions.

JRTC training is stressful and tough. The three-week exercises are conducted against a formidable foe that is highly skilled and familiar with the terrain. It is as close to real combat as the Army can make it. Veteran soldiers often say that they prefer actual combat over the JRTC training exercises.

Caslen's role was to observe the brigade combat team. He had free rein to go wherever he wanted on the battlefield and to attend any of the team's meetings, engagements, operations, or activities. JRTC is a laboratory of leadership. Of the many commanders who had gone through the exercise, Caslen observed both incredibly gifted leaders and others who did not deserve to be in command. He came to recognize traits of outstanding leaders and could likewise recognize bad traits of poor, ineffective leaders.

Caslen recalls walking into an exercise unit's command head-quarters and recognizing right away if it was going to be a successful exercise, where learning would occur at all levels. Entering the headquarters, you immediately notice a buzz of activity, with formal and informal communication. Junior leaders engage senior leaders, and senior leaders stop and listen to them. When the staff updated the commander at the end of the day, staff officers clamored to be the one to brief the commander. They were proud of their work and accomplishments and wanted to show off their skills to the boss. The culture of learning, growth, and teamwork was tangible. People exercised initiative and were stretching, making mistakes and learning from them. Supervisors underwrote mistakes as opportunities to learn and grow. As a result, the staff, commander, and entire unit improved with every operation. The staff trusted the boss; the boss trusted the staff; and everyone within the staff trusted each other.

But it was not that way with every unit. When you entered the headquarters of a unit that did not do well, it was quiet, cold as ice, with all sitting staring at their computers without engaging with one another. The dynamic engagement that was evident in the strong learning units was absent. When it came time to brief the commander at the end of the day, no one within the staff volunteered, leaving it to the senior staff officer to conduct the briefing. As soon as the commander opened his mouth, you knew right away why no one wanted to brief him. Rather than being uplifting and edifying, he would criticize and ridicule, in front of a soldier's peers. No one exercised any initiative. People did only what they were told to do, fearing criticism for exercising initiative and risking a mistake. There was no learning and no growth. Overall the exercise was a terrible experience for the soldiers.

You may be thinking about your own workplace as you read this. What kind of work climate does your boss prepare? How does it measure up in communication? What is the impact on trust? If you are a supervisor or manager, maybe you can do some things to improve communication within your work unit. Make communication a priority and set aside time each day to reflect on whether you have communicated to your team—both laterally and vertically—the information they need to maximize effectiveness. You should also practice your listening skills. Doing so will increase vertical communication. Simply put, communication is critical to trust, so make it a priority.

THE IMPACT OF LOST TRUST ON ORGANIZATIONS

The culture of an organization is critical to its growth, values, morale, learning, development, and mission success. The person responsible for that culture is the commander, the CEO, or the leader. Critical to that culture is its character as defined by the values it embraces. Trust is critical to effective leadership.

Failures of trust may come in many ways. Leaders may be incompetent, of questionable character, or fail to demonstrate caring for those in their organization. Or followers may, for a host of reasons, fail to do the same. Let's look at three case studies and see the impact on an organization of a failure of trust.

Our first example comes from the world of business. In 2017, Kate McClure and her boyfriend, Mark D'Amico, set up a GoFundMe page seeking donations to assist a homeless veteran living in Philadelphia, Johnny Bobbitt. They pitched a story about the terrible plight Bobbitt was in and, via social media, solicited donations to help provide for Bobbitt's needs. Kindhearted people from around the world responded generously, eventually donating $400,000. This seemingly kind effort by McClure and D'Amico received wide attention in both traditional and social media, no doubt adding to the amount of the donations. It was a feel-good story at its best, two Americans helping a veteran who had served his country in war. What is not to like?

There was much not to like. McClure and D'Amico did purchase a camper for Bobbitt and gave him $25,000, but they pocketed most of the rest of the money and used it for personal purchases and vacations. In 2019, Bobbitt pleaded guilty to conspiring with McClure and D'Amico to defraud donors. McClure also pleaded guilty to wire fraud.[6]

As reprehensible as this fraud case is for the individuals involved, the impact on GoFundMe was significant. A crowdfunding enterprise, GoFundMe is a for-profit website designed to help people raise money for a variety of reasons. GoFundMe campaigns often help people pay for medical costs, replace or repair damaged homes or property, or, as in the Bobbitt case, assist those in need. But trust is an essential piece of the GoFundMe enterprise. When the site is used to defraud donors, and especially when it is as widely publicized as the Bobbitt case, trust in the company may be eroded. This may result in a decrease in contributions, thus adversely affecting the many cases where a true need exists.

How did GoFundMe respond to this crisis? They had to address the three C's. First, they needed to affirm their competence. Company officials publicly asserted their efforts to identify fraudulent campaigns.[7] By establishing a policy that defrauded donors would receive a full refund, the company bolstered its character by showing its commitment to honesty and integrity. Addressing the third C, caring, the company continues to regularly assert the positive impact its services have for those in need. Based on Sweeney's model of trust, GoFundMe is taking the right actions to restore the public's perception of their corporate three C's.

Our second example, from another major social institution, is the child-abuse crisis facing the Catholic Church. Reports of sexual abuse of children by priests are widespread. This has resulted in a host of criminal and civil investigations. In October of 2018, for example, former priest David Poulson pleaded guilty to sexually abusing two boys from his church in Pennsylvania.[8] In January of 2019 he was sentenced to up to fourteen years in prison. The abuse spanned an eight-year period. Poulson, who began work at the church in 1979, was defrocked in 2018.[9]

Unfortunately, this is just one of many well-publicized cases facing the Catholic Church, nor are they just a recent phenomenon. Allegations of sexual abuse of children by priests, and sometimes nuns, have been widespread for decades.[10] Numerous media stories have documented these cases, which have been reported across the globe. The failure, in the eyes of many, of the Church to address this crisis has led to an erosion of trust among parishioners. It may even have contributed to a decrease in belief of Catholic doctrine. In the United States, for example, a Gallup poll in 2019 indicated that more than a third of American Catholics questioned their Church membership because of its continued inaction on addressing the abuse openly and effectively.[11] The impact may extend beyond the Catholic Church. A CNN report in April of 2019 summarizing results from the General Social Survey revealed that as many Americans identify as having "no religion" as do those who say they are Catholic or evangelical, with all three representing just fewer than a fourth of all Americans.[12] The number of nonbelievers began to spike in the early 1990s, when child sex abuse in the Catholic Church began surfacing.

An analysis based on the three C's model suggests that besides the perception of failing in character, the Church may be perceived as failing in competence and caring. A failure in competence is manifested by the inability of Church leadership to effectively address the child sex abuse scandal over a long period. And in its failure to take meaningful and effective action, the Church may be perceived by many as uncaring. When it comes to trust, "three strikes and you're out" may apply. Fail at competence, character, and caring, and a price will be paid.

The Catholic Church could take a lesson from the GoFundMe case. Although occurring in a different social institution (religion versus business) and on a global scale, the Church could base its response to the child sex abuse crisis on the three C's. If it could demonstrate competence, character, and caring in a genuine and consistent way, over time the negative impacts of the scandal could be overcome. After all, religion plays a central role in the well-being and sense of meaning and purpose of many people, and a systematic effort to address the scandal following the three C's model would likely be well received by alienated Church members. Thus, restoring faith in the Church is very much a matter of restoring trust in the Church, and the three C's supply a framework for doing just that.

Our final example of organizational failure in trust comes from a third major social institution, education. Between 1992 and 2005 Michigan State University sports-medicine physician Larry G. Nassar abused as many as 250 girls, some reportedly as young as six years of age.[13] From 1996 to 2014, Nassar also served as the national medical coordinator for USA Gymnastics, a position in which he had regular contact with young, aspiring female gymnasts. Following an investigation stemming from widely publicized reports from former gymnasts, Nassar was eventually charged with twenty-two counts of criminal sexual misconduct with minors. He was also charged with receiving child pornography. Nassar pleaded guilty to these charges and was sentenced to up to 175 years in prison.

Nassar's actions had impacts not only on those victimized by him, and on his own status and reputation. In the months following the revelation of the charges against him, dozens of lawsuits were filed against Michigan State University, the United States Olympic Committee, and USA Gymnastics. These organizations stand accused of not doing enough to police their own ranks, of not heeding signs of abuse, and of not listening to and following up on complaints of misconduct. Besides the obvious monetary consequences (Michigan State has agreed to pay $500 million to the victims), the damage to the reputation of these institutions is significant. Michigan State University's president, Lou Anna K. Simon, resigned in January of 2018 following severe criticism of her stewardship of the university in the face of the crisis. Former Michigan governor John M. Engler was then appointed interim president and resigned under pressure just a year later.[14] The consequences of the scandal were not confined to Michigan State University. Besides civil action, USA Gymnastics faced severe public scrutiny, and all of its board members resigned.[15] The overall impact on the reputation of these institutions is difficult to assess but continues to be substantial. And the impact on the organizations pales in comparison to the lasting effects of Nassar's criminal behavior on his many victims and their families. As in the case of the Catholic Church, the institutions involved here failed in all three of the C's.

These cases, in diverse types of institutions, underscore the impact of loss of trust on an organization's reputation. If an organization such as the Catholic Church, with centuries of efforts of doing good in the world, can be damaged by the loss of institutional trust, then all organizations are equally vulnerable. Similarly, Michigan State University, founded in 1855 as a land-grant university, must now fight hard to regain lost trust. No matter how venerable the institution, the loss of trust resulting from character failures among its members (or in the case of GoFundMe, its customers) is a clear and present danger to the institution's reputation and viability.

HIGH-PERFORMING TRUSTED ORGANIZATIONS

What can organizations do to guard themselves against character failures? An important first step is recognizing that organizations have attributes, positive or negative, just like individuals. Sweeney's notion of the three C's can therefore be looked at both as attributes of individuals and as attributes of organizations. Organizations that are high in competence, character, and caring tend to promote these same attributes among their individual members.

Sports teams provide an interesting case study of organizational excellence. Matthews consults with professional sports franchises on how to achieve this continuity of excellence in the face of regular turnover among players and senior leadership. Professional sports teams bear many similarities to the military. Both are highly competitive, the pressure to win is immense, and separation from family and friends is frequent. Players are traded or sign as free agents with new teams. Senior management and sometimes ownership changes. Despite this, a few select teams are successful year in and year out.

A big part of Matthews's message to professional sports teams is to educate them about the three C's. Teams that are owned and managed by leaders who are competent, who are of high character, and who care about the welfare of players tend to succeed. Perennially successful teams take an active role in promoting high performance and character by establishing an organizational culture that embraces the three C's. They have clear mission and vision statements. They communicate clearly with players and other staff. These successful teams have high standards of conduct and character, model and reward adherence to these standards, and punish deviations from these common values. The outcome is an organization that is robust and capable of maintaining continuity across the inevitable changes in leadership, management, and players.

Successfully sustaining achievement in the military, sports, or other institutional settings requires that organizations take a proactive role in promoting the three C's and establishing a culture that nurtures and supports competence, character, and caring. Even individuals of high character may find it challenging to consistently behave in an ethical manner if the organization in which they work does not adhere to positive values and practices. To have a successful team one must begin with an organizational commitment to provide a consistent, positive work environment. In such organizations, newly arriving members learn these values, which in turn motivate and guide exemplary character, thus allowing a continuity of excellence in the face of personnel change. B. F. Skinner's widely quoted adage "The rat is always right" captures this idea. Before blaming the rat, look to the organization in which the rat is behaving. Good organizations breed and sustain excellence, and organizations with poorly articulated or practiced values sustain failure.

BUILDING TRUST AND LEADERSHIP

Managers and leaders may build trust within their teams and organizations by assessing where they stand on the three C's. Consider how intimidating it must be to a West Point cadet, knowing he or she will become a platoon leader soon after graduation and receiving a commission as an officer in the US Army. Platoon leaders are in charge of about thirty soldiers. This includes an experienced NCO who serves as the platoon sergeant, and three junior NCOs who serve as squad leaders. The platoon leader is responsible for training the platoon and preparing it for combat and other duties. The platoon sergeant may have ten or more years of experience in the Army, much of it in combat. Except for the most junior enlisted privates, the platoon leader is usually the least experienced member of his or her team.

As graduation draws near, this looming responsibility begins to weigh heavily on the minds of cadets. The authors of this book, like everyone else at West Point, spend considerable time mentoring cadets to prepare them for what lies ahead. In our mentoring, we discuss the three C's and what new lieutenants can do to ensure they meet standards on all three.

In the months preceding graduation, West Point brings in lieutenants and sergeants from operational units across the Army to spend time mentoring the soon-to-graduate seniors. These lieutenants and NCOs tell stories of how they took command, and the issues they faced. The cadets are eager to soak up every lesson. And what do they hear from these experienced lieutenants and NCOs? Mostly stories of the three C's.

Competence may be the easiest challenge. A new infantry lieutenant will benefit immensely by knowing the skills required by subordinate soldiers. It is not the job of the platoon leader to operate a machine gun in combat. But when a junior soldier is learning how to use the weapon, the lieutenant may gain instant credibility by showing the soldier how to properly operate it. The Army builds the new lieutenant's competence by sending the officer to a series of schools before he or she arrives at his or her first unit. Soldiers have high expectations for the new lieutenant. They will expect their lieutenant to be a skilled and competent leader because their lives may depend on the lieutenant's competence. For the new lieutenant it is a great way to quickly build trust. But a lack of competence is an equally quick way to lose trust.

The second C, character, is less tangible. We discuss with our future lieutenants how members of their platoon will look to them to set the standard. We explain how seemingly minor words or actions may affect judgments of character, either positively or negatively. Our cadets listen intently, hungry to learn from our experiences and to think about how they will respond when assigned to lead a platoon.

Caring, the third C, may seem like a quality that one either naturally has or not. You may not consider yourself to be the most caring person in the world, but you can behave in ways that reassure others that you do care for their well-being. Simple actions such as remembering birthdays or knowing about a challenge a soldier is facing in his or her personal life and offering support and assistance do a lot to establish a caring relationship. Spend time with soldiers, we tell our cadets. Make an effort each day to make each one feel special.

Caring does not mean that you will baby your subordinates. It means that you will develop them to meet the highest standards and that you will take the time to personally get them there. It means that their training will be tough, realistic, and well resourced. It means that you will prepare them physically to operate in the harshest of environments, and that those who cannot meet these standards will be given remedial programs to help them do so. It means you walk through their barracks during off-duty hours to ensure they have acceptable living conditions. It means listening to their opinion of how things are going. It is amazing what a soldier will tell you on his or her time and turf. When you see something that is not right, you must take the time and energy to fix it. Instead of babying your subordinates you hold them to a high standard, personally help them develop their skills, and spend time listening to them so that you know as much about their personal lives as you do their professional lives. When subordinates know you will do whatever you can for them, they will want to never let you down. Said another way, they will trust you with their lives.

SWIFT TRUST

In the military, turnover of both leaders and followers is a constant. Commanders and other leaders remain in their positions for short periods—eighteen months to two years as a rule—before being reassigned to other duties. Similarly, subordinates remain in specific jobs for periods of four years or fewer. This organizational churn gives soldiers and their leaders opportunities to develop greater technical and leadership skills by moving them to new positions with greater responsibilities. Frequently, by the time an Army colonel assumes the command of a brigade, he or she will have had half a dozen or more prior commands and assignments. Senior enlisted personnel experience the same sequence of new jobs, promotions, and frequent relocations.

Frequent reassignments also have negative consequences. In some ways, military members become "jacks of all trades, and masters of none." About the time they feel competent and comfortable in a particular position, it is time to move again. The incoming, replacement leader will have had a variety of previous command and leadership positions, but will be a novice at the level of their new appointment. For subordinates, losing a competent and experienced leader increases stress, requiring them to "train another commander" and get used to new ways of doing things. Enlisted soldiers carry their basic skills with them to new assignments, but must also experience a period of integration before being ready to perform at their best capacity in their new unit. But sometimes a poor commander is replaced by a competent one. Even so, both the leader and his or her subordinates require a period of adjustment.

Because of this regular inflow and outflow of personnel, the military has developed strategies to both speed up and to ease the transition between leaders, and among new personnel. Military psychologist Paul Lester talks about "swift trust."[16] Military awards and decorations, besides honoring members for exemplary performance, publicly display a military member's assignment history. You can tell at a glance that a newly arrived commander has completed Ranger School, served in combat, and/or has been assigned previously to elite units. Military units also have explicit mission and organizational vision statements that allow new commanders and soldiers to adapt more quickly to their new job.

Swift trust is not just a military thing. Civilian institutions may experience similar challenges from personnel churn. The new school principal or a newly hired manager won't be wearing a uniform, but the need for swift trust may exist. The organization may make efforts to establish trust by properly introducing the leader to the organization. New leaders may facilitate trust by quickly demonstrating the three C's and getting to know others in the organization with whom they will interact daily.

A TRUST CRISIS?

It is one thing when bad actors behave in ways that undermine trust in an institution. It is yet another when legitimately elected or appointed individuals do so. We are bombarded with accusations of "fake news," and government officials and other "leaders" portray long-standing and reputable institutions such as law enforcement and the judicial system as incompetent or worse. Individuals in these institutions do, and always have, failed, but the institutions themselves have been resilient. In today's 24/7/365 news and social media environment, it seems the extent and impact of these failures are magnified. Acts or events that would barely make it into print in traditional newspapers now jump out at us as "breaking news!"

The institutions of the judiciary, law enforcement, journalism, education, business, religion, and the military are the foundation upon which a functional democracy depends. This erosion of trust undermines the legitimacy of these institutions. These accusations are often made to bolster a particular political point of view or to rally voters behind a candidate. The immediate gain of more votes is weighted more heavily than the long-term consequences from a loss of trust in major social institutions. Braying "witch hunt" or "fake news" at every institution or person that presents a view inconsistent with one's own can only, in the long run, reduce trust in our long-valued institutions.

We maintain that human nature with all of its imperfections has not changed over the millennia. What has changed is the instant access to all manner of information and, yes, misinformation. Until recent times public figures kept their thoughts private and only revealed them to others with due deliberation.

But social media enable people to share these thoughts in 280 characters or fewer, instantly with everyone in the world who has a smartphone. We have not learned how to separate the wheat from the chaff in social media. And there is a lot more chaff than wheat. This is the essence of General Dempsey's concept of digital echoes.

To preserve trust in the major social institutions, it is incumbent upon individuals to become wiser and more selective interpreters of the media storm we face every day. Perhaps more important, leaders must assume responsibility for what they portray in the news and social media. Leaders must also better understand the potentially devastating second- and third-order effects of irresponsible messaging. The cost to our institutions and therefore our way of life is too great to do otherwise.

THE BANK OF PUBLIC TRUST

Can you imagine a leader being effective if his or her subordinates do not trust him or her? Or can you imagine a leader trying to lead if his or her boss does not trust him or her? If you work in a hostile environment where you are constantly belittled and demeaned, even in front of your peers, can you have a trusting relationship with your boss? If I'm working for you and you're my boss, and I don't trust you, finding the motivation to work for you will be difficult. Likewise, if I'm your subordinate, and you as my boss do not trust me, then for you to sustain an effective relationship with me will be difficult. You would obviously refrain from assigning me any tasks of importance if you do not trust me. The likely outcome is that I'll be looking for another job.[17]

In any profession, a unique service is afforded the clients of the profession. In the profession of arms, the unique service the military provides is the ethical application of lethal force wherein service members are prepared to give their lives. The client in the profession of arms is the nation, because the use of ethical lethal force is for its security and protection. As with any profession, developing a relationship with your client is critical, and that relationship is built on trust.

Reflecting on his time as a West Point cadet in the 1970s, General Caslen recalls:

> When I was a cadet at West Point during the Vietnam era, anytime I wore my uniform off post, I would find myself ridiculed, spit on, and harassed, simply because I was in the Army. I also recall some of my high school teachers who found ways to not go to Vietnam encouraged me not to go to West Point because I would be a "baby killer." It is a terrible indictment to have a relationship with your client when the client fails to trust you and fails to trust your institution as was the case during the Vietnam era. We never want to go back to something like that again. Trust is a critical component of leadership, and it is worth studying what creates trust and what destroys trust.
>
> A critical element of our profession is our commitment to it. In our profession, we choose to hold ourselves accountable. If we do not, then someone will, whether it is Congress, other agencies, or even the American people. If one within our profession exhibits behavior that is outside our values and norms, and that person's behavior goes uncorrected, it will usually catch up with the soldier. However, the damage that can occur between our client, the American people, and our profession goes much further than the damage to the individual leader. I call this the Bank of Public Trust.

Our relationship with the American people is built on trust. If a member of our profession, especially a senior officer with high visibility, commits egregious acts outside our values, it not only brings harm to himself or herself, but to the entire profession. It also puts a chink into the trust between our client and our profession. Continued bad behavior can ultimately drain the trust, where eventually the American people no longer have any trust or confidence in our profession. Those of us who served in the Army during Vietnam know all too well what it feels like to serve in an Army that is not trusted by the American people.

It is hard to earn America's trust. It takes consistent behavior and performance of the highest values and standards, always meeting the expectations of the American people. Even when we do, it will almost always go unnoticed. But hundreds of valued acts will slowly increase that trust. Unfortunately, one egregious act by a senior leader, or even a misaligned junior soldier, can and will eradicate the entire trust deposit within the Bank of Public Trust. How this works has a funny dynamic, but it is tremendously important for all of us to realize the potential damage and consequences in public trust created by the misaligned acts of a single soldier or officer. It is a terrible indictment to lose the trust of our client. We never want to go back to that again.

This underscores the importance of holding ourselves accountable. If we see our teammates conducting themselves in a substandard way, our responsibility is to hold them to standard. If we fail to do so, we will have set a new standard, which is now lower than the first. And if we again fail to correct substandard behavior, we continue to set a lower standard, and as this occurs, discipline erodes, thus forfeiting the glue that holds our organization together.

In the same way, individuals and organizations in other walks of life also build banks of trust. Students will more surely place their trust in the teacher who is competent, has higher character, and genuinely cares about students. This same principle is behind the concept of community policing, where individual officers are assigned to beats and told to get out of their patrol cars and get to know the people they serve. The idea is to build trust, and the hope is that as citizens come to personally know the officers patrolling their neighborhood, they will build trust not just in those particular officers but in the law enforcement agency itself. Indeed, the Police Officer's Creed concludes with "I recognize the badge of my office as a symbol of public faith, and I accept it as a public trust to be held so long as I am true to the ethics of the police service. I will constantly strive to achieve these objectives and ideals, dedicating myself to my chosen profession . . . law enforcement."[18]

The trust account builds incrementally with deposits of competence, character, and caring. When an individual or an organization violates the bonds of trust, essentially making a withdrawal from the trust bank, restoring the account to its original value is a long and difficult task—and in some cases impossible. Trust is the straw that stirs the drink in human interactions, small and large. It should be nurtured and treasured above all else.

6

IT IS NOT JUST ABOUT YOU

Culture does not change because we desire to change it. Culture
changes when the organization is transformed; the culture
reflects the realities of people working together every day.

—FRANCES HESSELBEIN, FORMER CEO OF THE GIRL SCOUTS OF THE USA[1]

Your parents may have told you, when you were growing up, how important it was for you to associate with the right kind of friends. They meant that you are judged by the company you keep, good or bad. But there is more to it than that. Who you are is more influenced by your social environment than by any other factor. When it comes to character, this is especially true. Our focus thus far has been on individual character. Strengths of the gut, head, and heart determine who we are as a person and to no small degree how successful we are in school, work, and family and social relationships. Here we explore the powerful role organizations have on these strengths of character. High-character organizations promote and sustain positive individual character. How do they do this? What can leaders do to ensure their organization has a culture that achieves this goal?

JOHNSON & JOHNSON: A CASE STUDY

A crisis can come your way as a result of a leader's misjudgment, misconduct, or negligence, or for reasons beyond his or her control. It can be expected, or it can come totally without warning. A true measure of character is not that the crisis appeared, but how the leader and the organization react to it.

An example of a company that suddenly found itself in the middle of a crisis is Johnson & Johnson, the world's largest diversified health-products company. In 1982, seven people died from cyanide poisoning while taking one of Johnson & Johnson's most popular over-the-counter drugs—Tylenol. Tylenol had 35 percent of the over-the-counter analgesic market in the United States and contributed 15 percent of Johnson & Johnson's profits. Although the crisis was caused by only one person, who deliberately and criminally tampered with on-the-shelf bottles, consumers associated Johnson & Johnson with this incident. The company's market value fell by more than $1 billion, and fear rose about the safety and reliability of every other Johnson & Johnson over-the-counter product.[2] Suddenly and with no warning, Johnson & Johnson was in a crisis they did not cause, one they were totally unprepared to deal with, and one that could cause irreparable damage to the company.

We interviewed the current chairman of the board and CEO of Johnson & Johnson, Alex Gorsky. Mr. Gorsky, a West Point graduate who served in the US Army, entered Johnson & Johnson at the bottom ranks, working his way up. We asked him what drove Johnson & Johnson's response to the Tylenol crisis, especially knowing the company was at risk of losing significant profit and inventory, and also of losing customer trust in their entire product line. Today, Johnson & Johnson touches more than one billion people every day with their products. That is a lot of customer value that was at huge risk when this crisis occurred.

Gorsky's answer was immediate, unequivocal, and laced with honor and character: "Nothing is more important than not compromising your integrity to the people who trust and depend on you." He said the leadership in 1982 never asked about the financial impact. They knew that overcoming the crisis meant taking responsibility for the incident and restoring the trust of their customers and their employees. The public expected this answer, but it does not come easily if you are focused on the financial results. A company of high values and integrity will place its organizational values above the bottom line and not think twice about the cost of what it will take to maintain trust with its customers and workforce. Where did these values come from for Johnson & Johnson?

The answer is their Credo. Johnson & Johnson's Credo was created by Robert Wood Johnson II, who joined the family business at the age of seventeen and worked his way up to become the company president and eventually became chairman of the board in 1938. When World War II broke out, he was commissioned as a brigadier general in the US Army Reserves, helping to ensure the Army was supplied with necessary military goods and provisions. In 1943, Johnson reassumed the chairmanship of Johnson & Johnson and wrote the Credo, a set of business principles that captured the company's commitment to integrity and character. The Credo was so important to Johnson that he had it carved into the wall of the company headquarters.

The Credo has stood the test of time with few modifications since its inception. Gorsky feels the Credo is not just a "moral compass" but also a "recipe for business success." In our interview, Gorsky reflected on the current business environment, in which managers and executives frequently move from one company to another. At Johnson & Johnson, he said, all of the senior leaders have been with the company for twenty-five years or more, and many employees at all levels expect to spend their entire career with the company. This loyalty to the company is taken as proof that Johnson & Johnson is one of only a few corporations that have flourished through a century of change and innovation. Gorsky declared, "Johnson and Johnson is a career, not just a job. It [the company] becomes like family."[3]

THE JOHNSON & JOHNSON CREDO

We believe our first responsibility is to the patients, doctors and nurses, to mothers and fathers and all others who use our products and services. In meeting their needs everything we do must be of high quality. We must constantly strive to provide value, reduce our costs and maintain reasonable prices. Customers' orders must be serviced promptly and accurately. Our business partners must have an opportunity to make a fair profit.

We are responsible to our employees who work with us throughout the world. We must provide an inclusive work environment where each person must be considered as an individual. We must respect their diversity and dignity and recognize their merit. They must have a sense of security, fulfillment and purpose in their jobs. Compensation must be fair and adequate and working conditions clean, orderly and safe. We must support the health and well-being of our employees and help them fulfill their family and other personal responsibilities. Employees must feel free to make suggestions and complaints. There must be equal opportunity for employment, development and advancement for those qualified. We must provide highly capable leaders and their actions must be just and ethical.

We are responsible to the communities in which we live and work and to the world community as well. We must help people be healthier by supporting better access and care in more places around the world. We must be good citizens—support good works and charities, better health and education, and bear our fair share of taxes. We must maintain in good order the property we are privileged to use, protecting the environment and natural resources.

Our final responsibility is to our stockholders. Business must make a sound profit. We must experiment with new ideas. Research must be carried on, innovative programs developed, investments made for the future and mistakes paid for. New equipment must be purchased, new facilities provided and new products launched. Reserves must be created to provide for adverse times. When we operate according to these principles, the stockholders should realize a fair return.[4]

When you read this, Johnson & Johnson's values and principles are immediately apparent. Gorsky told us he goes back to the Credo quite often; it is important not only to him as the CEO, but also to the entire corporation because "it defines our purpose." He feels the organization must lead the effort to develop personal traits defined by the values articulated within the Credo. He believes "the most important characteristic in Johnson and Johnson is espousing the values in the Credo."

To drive this ethic throughout the entire organization and through all levels of management, Gorsky looks for opportunities to talk about the Credo, to demonstrate its principles, and to ensure that his management team is doing the same. "Senior leaders are the role models, and they must live the Credo every day." According to Gorsky, the Credo is talked about at the beginning and end of every meeting.

During their performance assessments, employees are asked to sit down with their manager and read the Credo line by line and explain what it means to them. Then the employee signs it and is asked to display it in a prominent place at his or her workplace. The employee's Credo assessment becomes one of the key factors management considers for developing their future leaders. "Character and values are part and parcel to our [leadership] development process. It is everything we do."

Strengths of the head—curiosity, love of learning, creativity, open-mindedness, and perspective—are especially important to a company such as Johnson & Johnson. Innovation is essential to success. "With new ideas, we are pleased but never satisfied," Gorsky commented. "Diplomas have a short half-life—your diploma is nothing more than a license to learn." Emerging developments in cell-based therapies, genomics, and robotic surgery are topics the company must be smart about. "It is not just about biology and chemistry anymore. Just as new cars have advanced technologies, such technologies will be deployed in surgery within the next ten years."

Does it make a difference when the leader of a corporation drives values-based character throughout the entire organization? In the 1982 Tylenol crisis, it certainly did. The company won praise for its quick and immediate actions, and within five months the company recovered 70 percent of its market share of this drug with continued improvement over the following years. They put solid measures in place to ensure no recurrence.

Through their competence, character, and caring, they reestablished trust with their customers. Evidence even suggested that some consumers switched from other brands to Tylenol because of Johnson & Johnson's transparent, authentic, and values-based response to this crisis.[5]

A GUIDE TO DEVELOPING HIGH-CHARACTER ORGANIZATIONS

Excellence does not happen by chance, and building and sustaining a high-character organization is no exception. It takes deliberate and systematic efforts and requires leaders to embrace the importance of character within an organization. Johnson & Johnson's Credo and their focus on it at every level throughout the organization shows how, even in a large corporation, such a positive culture can be instilled. The result of the Credo is "360-degree trust"—confidence that all in the organization will do their best to do the right thing and in the right way to achieve the company's goals.

Values-based trust is the foundation upon which high-character organizations rest. We have explored the three C's of trust—competence, character, and caring. These are prerequisite traits and skills individuals must possess to be trusted by their peers, subordinates, and leaders. But what can an organization do to inculcate and encourage its members to excel in the three C's?

Patrick Sweeney, retired from the Army and now the director of Wake Forest University's Allegacy Center for Leadership & Character, created a conceptual model that captures how high-performing organizations maintain excellence in the face of personnel turbulence and character failures. The Individual-Relationship-Organization-Context (IROC) model describes the complex relationships among organizations, individuals, and the context in which they operate, and how these relationships influence trust and sustained high performance. The following chart summarizes the IROC model.

INDIVIDUAL CREDIBILITY

- Competence
- Character
- Caring

RELATIONSHIPS MATTER

- Respect and concern
- Open communications
- Cooperative interdependence
- Trust and empower others

ORGANIZATION SETS THE CLIMATE

- Shared values, beliefs, norms, and goals (culture)
- Structure, practices, policies, and procedures

CONTEXT INFLUENCES ALL

- Dependencies and needs
- Organization systems

INDIVIDUAL CREDIBILITY

Almost all organizations understand and value the importance of competence among individual employees. Universities evaluate the potential of prospective students using a variety of competence indicators, including standardized test scores such as the SAT or ACT and high school grades.[6] The armed forces use the Armed Services Vocational Aptitude Battery (ASVAB) to screen and classify hundreds of thousands of recruits every year. The development of the first large-scale aptitude tests resulted from the need during World War I for the services to screen their recruits, allowing them to assign new members to jobs for which they possessed the aptitude and competence to succeed.[7]

Organizations differ on what defines competence. Most jobs require intelligence, but some may have additional requirements. Law enforcement agencies, for example, typically require applicants to pass both a medical examination and tests of physical strength and agility.

Smaller organizations may not be able to afford formal testing. So they often employ proxies for competence. Completion of a college degree is commonly held to be a reliable indicator of mental ability. Except for specialized jobs such as accounting or finance, employers typically do not select an applicant based on the subject of his or her college degree. Completing a two- or four-year degree in any subject is generally proof of sufficient intelligence to do the job.

Other organizations may focus primarily on physical skills. Professional sports teams carefully evaluate future players on this domain. To be a great player, the other two C's are critical, but physical competence comes first. Basketball teams systematically evaluate past performance in high school or college and also look at a variety of specific skills and attributes. Speed, leaping ability, arm reach (many top professional basketball players have a "wingspan" longer than typical of others their same height), hand size, and aerobic capacity are evaluated. Baseball scouts seek the "five-tool player," who possesses speed, can hit for power, hit for average, field well, and has a strong throwing arm. With the advent of advanced metrics, these five tools are supplemented by measurements such as exit velocity and launch angle for batted balls.

Once an employee is selected into an organization, efforts follow to take the basic aptitude and skills to a higher level. Universities hone the intellectual skills of students with four or more years of academic courses. Law enforcement agencies spend months training specific skills needed to be an effective officer. Once drafted by a major league team, most baseball players spend several years in the minor leagues further sharpening the skills needed to excel in "the show" (baseball slang for the major leagues). The military probably takes the prize in skill development. An officer who retires at the rank of colonel will likely have attended four or more specialized courses in his or her career, some of which last a full year.

The bottom line is this: organizations must carefully define the set of skills they need within their organization, select people into the organization who possesses these skills, assign them to jobs that match their talents, then continue to train and develop each employee throughout his or her tenure within the organization.

This leads to competence. But it is not enough.

Character is the second component of *individual credibility.* While many organizations understand and value the importance of character, they are less sure of how either to select high-character individuals or to further develop character once the individuals join the organization. Unlike for competence, no widely accepted standardized tests for character exist. The Values-in-Action Inventory of Strengths (VIA-IS) is useful for personal feedback and reflection but was not designed for screening and selection. Potential employees could easily "game" the VIA-IS by providing what they think are the right answers. The same holds true for other questionnaire-based character assessments.

Consequently, organizations turn to indirect indicators of character. West Point selects high school students who were team captains or class presidents. Baseball teams look at a player's "makeup," by which they mean past actions and behavior consistent with team values. Law enforcement agencies do extensive background checks on potential officers, interview them, talk with neighbors and others that know the applicant well, and conduct a criminal-history check to screen out applicants with a prior history of violating the law.

The following case study underscores the importance of character among a group of the most competent basketball players in the world.

In the early summer of 2008, the leadership of the Twenty-Fifth Infantry Division participated in a program designed to prepare them to build an effective team for their upcoming Iraq deployment. Their deployment would occur toward the end of the now-infamous surge, and the division would have responsibility for some of the most contentious areas in all of Iraq—the northern Sunni provinces and the three Kurdish provinces. The mission included interdicting foreign fighter flow across the Syrian border, interrupting Iranian weapons and fighters across the Iranian border along Diyala province, countering the remnant Baathist nationalism in Saddam Hussein's home province of Salah ad Din, integrating the former radical Sunni insurgents (now called the Sons of Iraq) into the Iraqi Army, defeating the remaining radical Sunni insurgents (who later evolved into the Islamic State fighters, or ISIS), and building a relationship between the Kurdish and the Iraqi central governments. It was a complex security environment to be sure.

In addition, the Twenty-Fifth Division would not deploy with all of its own subordinate commands. It was being assigned units from other US Army divisions, thus making the challenge of building a team even more problematic.

The assistant division commander, Brigadier General Bob Brown, a former West Point basketball player and team captain, was fortunate to have a strong relationship with Duke basketball coach Mike Krzyzewski, who had been Brown's coach at West Point. To assist the Twenty-Fifth Infantry Division in team building, Brown reached out to Krzyzewski (commonly known as Coach K), asking him to talk with division leaders before the deployment. Coach K was busy preparing the USA Men's Olympic basketball team for the 2008 Olympic Games in Beijing, China. But he made time to spend an evening with the division. In that single evening, he taught the leaders of the division a lesson on leadership; one that he later used to completely turn around the fortunes of the USA basketball team (they won the 2008 gold medal after an embarrassing showing in the 2004 Olympics); one that taught the division leaders lifelong lessons on team building and leadership that played out significantly during combat operations in northern Iraq once the division deployed.

Coach K's turnaround of the fortunes of the USA basketball team is nothing short of amazing. Contrary to the winning traditions of USA basketball over many years, and contrary to its tremendous talent compared to that of all the other teams, the 2004 team lost three games and ended up settling for an embarrassing bronze medal. An average person would think that an Olympic bronze medal is a great achievement, but looking at the talent, the circumstances, and the tradition of excellence over many years, fans in the United States and across the globe knew that the 2004 team had the potential to repeat a USA gold medal performance but failed to do so. Numerous articles and opinions have been written about why the team did not win, but clearly this group of All-Stars failed to become a cohesive unit; individual players were more concerned with their own performance than with what was good for the team, and the coaching style failed to optimize the talent on the court. The result: a lackluster performance and great disappointment for both the players and the American sports world.

To change this culture and prepare for the 2008 Olympics, the USA basketball director brought in Krzyzewski, who emphasized team unity. Coach K recognized the huge athleticism advantages of the NBA players and learned how to exploit these gifts without too much focus on a stricter set of offensive sets and defensive rules. His players were not only playing for the team, but were also allowed to showcase their athletic prowess.[8]

What was not discussed in any analysis or articles written about the transformation Coach K achieved is what he shared with the Twenty-Fifth Division leadership at their team-building session. He revealed the principal criteria he used to determine who would be a member of the USA basketball team.

Keeping in mind the lessons of the past teams, Coach K

decided that character was the most important criterion for his 2008 team selection. To personally assess the character of each team member, he talked with each player in the player's living room or kitchen with the player's family present. While discussing the prospect of playing on Team USA, he also watched how the players interacted with their family. Coach K felt that how the players treated their own family was a crucial indicator to how they would treat the other members of the Olympic team, and how they would balance the importance of the team with their individual ego. The most important criterion to a team's winning performance was the team's character. Would they be out there playing only for themselves? Or would they play for the good of the team? What was most important? Me? Or team?

This incredible lesson is applicable not only to athletic sports teams at the highest level, but in all other aspects of leadership as well. The Twenty-Fifth Division hung on to that lesson throughout their entire deployment. All of America was proud to see how well that culture took hold within the 2008 USA Olympic men's basketball team, as they were undefeated in the tournament, leading once again to a gold medal.

Krzyzewski was also asked to coach the USA basketball team from 2013 to 2016. Coach K asked Caslen if he could bring the team to West Point, engage with cadets both informally and in scrimmage basketball, and schedule a guided tour of the West Point cemetery. The West Point cemetery is hallowed ground—the final resting place of West Point graduates who have served their country and given their lives. It includes notables like General Norman Schwarzkopf, commander of coalition forces in the 1991 Gulf War; Lieutenant Laura Walker, the first female West Point graduate to die in combat, during Operation Enduring Freedom in Afghanistan in 2005; Lieutenant Emily Perez, the first female graduate of West Point to die during Operation Iraqi Freedom, in 2006; General William Westmoreland, who served as US Army Chief of Staff, superintendent of the US Military Academy, and commanded US forces in Vietnam from 1964 to 1968; and Lieutenant Colonel Ed White, the first American to walk in space, who was killed in the Apollo 1 fire on January 27, 1967.

Caslen asked Coach K why he wanted the basketball players to visit the cemetery. His reply was that these well-known NBA players would be playing for their country, and he wanted them to know the meaning of sacrifice and duty to country. At the West Point cemetery, they would visit the graves of men and women of all ranks who gave their lives in defense of our country's values. He wanted the players to reflect on that sacrifice and to know that playing for your country is nothing compared to giving your life for your country.

The attribute of caring is like character in that no simple tests exist to identify individuals with a genuine concern for others. Organizations can use strategies to identify potential employees who care about others, such as looking in interviews and background checks for evidence of behaviors that signal caring. Look for a pattern of volunteering to help others, for example. Interviews with previous employers and coworkers may be revealing.

Once an individual is accepted into the organization, this third C can be nurtured and developed, similar to character and competence. Community service is an expectation for West Point faculty (and for members of many other organizations). Most professional sports teams embrace community service and assist players and other personnel in doing good works in their communities. Doing so reinforces the attribute of caring and ingrains it into the organization's culture.

Leaders should engage in deliberate strategies to demonstrate caring. For decades, the San Antonio Spurs have been a winning organization. In no small measure, this is because they embrace the three C's model. They recruit and develop top-notch talent, make character a core focus for all team members, and through their leadership demonstrate and build caring among the players, coaches, and staff.

R. C. Buford, the long time Spurs general manager, now CEO for Spurs Sports & Entertainment, told Dr. Matthews a story that demonstrates how the Spurs create a caring culture. One of their players, Patty Mills, is an Australian with Aboriginal roots. Growing up, he heard many racist taunts, similar to what African Americans experience in the United States. One of Mills's heroes is Eddie Mabo, who is often described as the Martin Luther King , Jr., of Australia. Australia celebrates Mabo Day on June 3. Little known outside Australia, this observance is of major significance especially to Australians with Aboriginal heritage.[9]

On June 3, 2014, the Spurs were preparing for an important playoff game. Legendary coach Gregg Popovich ("Pop" to his players and fans) gathered the players during the last practice before this critical game. Most coaches might have reviewed game strategy or offered a "win one for the Gipper" pep talk. But Popovich chose a different approach. He asked Mills to tell the rest of the team who Eddie Mabo was and why he was so important to Mills. The players listened with rapt attention, setting aside their thoughts about the upcoming game to hear

Mills tell Mabo's story. Hearing this story on Mabo Day was riveting.

What did Mills and the other Spurs players learn from this? More than anything else, they learned that Coach Popovich genuinely cares about his players. By asking Mills to share the story of Eddie Mabo, Pop put the game of basketball into proper perspective. The other players, many who had experienced racism themselves, forged an even stronger emotional bond with their Australian teammate. In this simple act, Popovich demonstrated decisively the caring that the Spurs organization has for its players.

Leaders in all types of organizations and at all levels can learn from this example. There is no simple method for establishing a climate of caring. Leaders must first realize how important caring is to organizational excellence and, second, think of ways to demonstrate caring. Like Popovich, take time to know each employee. Learn about what matters to him or her. Send a thank-you note when he or she does something well. Spend a little one-on-one time each day with your immediate subordinates and set the expectation that they will, in turn, do the same with their own subordinates. The key is to be consistent and genuine. Caring cannot be faked. Employees sense fakery immediately. Thus, a major responsibility for senior leaders is not just to be caring themselves, but to make caring a key attribute for those they promote to management and leadership positions.

RELATIONSHIPS MATTER

The late psychologist and pioneer of positive psychology Christopher Peterson summed up his life philosophy in three simple words: "Other people matter."[10] This is the crux of high character and of high-performing organizations as well. When leaders show respect and concern for their employees, communicate with them frequently and openly, and trust and empower workers at all levels, good things follow. These factors enable what Sweeney calls cooperative interdependence. It is more than a case of "I will scratch your back if you scratch mine." Instead, cooperative interdependence refers to an organizational culture in which leaders and followers share a common vision and goals and recognize that success hinges on working together to achieve that mission and those goals.

Observe any high-performing organization and you will see these relationship principles playing out. We have already discussed the San Antonio Spurs, which is hands down the most successful National Basketball Association franchise for the past quarter of a century. The Spurs have built their success in no small measure around valuing positive relationships. Positive relationships build and sustain good character. And good character, coupled with competence and caring, allows the team to win year in and year out.

Dr. Matthews observed the Spurs practice the day before the first NBA playoff game in April 2017. R. C. Buford sat with him on courtside folding chairs and talked with some awe about how Coach Popovich nurtures positive relationships with and among players. Buford instructed Matthews to watch closely how Pop interacted with each of his players during the practice session. He said that Pop would, during the practice, approach every player on the team and literally place his hands on him, look him in the eye, and engage personally. Pop did just that.

It didn't matter if you were the top star on the team or the last player on the bench, Pop engaged with everyone.

This touching and engaging with players is just one ingredient in a veritable cocktail of positivity that Pop immerses his team in, day in and day out. His team dinners are legendary. A wine connoisseur and gourmet foodie, Coach Popovich frequently treats his team to dinner, especially while on the road. He sees meals as an opportunity to build relationships. He doesn't do this in a haphazard way. Players come into the league with vastly different experiences and backgrounds, and team dinners help the team form and reinforce its own positive culture. Coach Popovich thinks of every detail. Buford says that Pop enlists the aid of experienced and more socially adept players to sit with and encourage new players to feel part of the team. These dinners address all components of Sweeney's relationships factor. They set the occasion for open communication and show respect and concern; they also empower players, build trust, and establish conditions for cooperative interdependence. [11]

How does your organization rate on this relationship factor? Make a list of things your leaders have done to build relationships. Chart a plan for what you can do at your level in the organization, whether you are the CEO, a midlevel manager, or a team leader. When leaders and managers make relationships a priority, workers follow suit.

ORGANIZATIONS SET THE CLIMATE

Leaders make their greatest impact by establishing an organizational climate that embraces character and positive relationships.

Johnson & Johnson's Credo is a stellar example of how a large company makes its values, beliefs, norms, and goals public. High-character organizations support these values, beliefs, norms, and goals with structures, practices, policies, and procedures that ensure that they are met.

CONTEXT INFLUENCES ALL

Organizations differ in mission and structure. The organizational chart of a university is not the same as that of an infantry combat brigade. Even within a given organization, the context changes. The infantry brigade deployed in combat faces different contingencies than when in garrison. Specific goals and strategies must adjust to account for these contextual changes. But an organization's core values remain the same. Johnson & Johnson did not change their Credo in response to the Tylenol crisis, nor was it changed in response to fluctuations in the economy. The focus of the San Antonio Spurs on IROC principles remains constant in the face of changing players and team success.

When we say that context influences all, we mean that specific tactics, techniques, and procedures must change as we adapt to different conditions. For example, Sweeney tells us that in a dangerous context, such as combat, followers naturally depend more on leaders to provide for their physical safety and emotional well-being. His study of soldiers showed that in combat they placed their highest reliance on their leader's "competence, loyalty, integrity, and leadership by example." From the leader's perspective, the importance of empowering and trusting subordinate soldiers to accomplish the mission was highlighted. In these conditions, successful leaders "place great importance on follower characteristics of competence, honesty, and initiative, which help ensure mission completion."[12]

CASE STUDIES OF ORGANIZATIONAL EXCELLENCE AND FAILURE
SAINT THOMAS HOSPITAL

A good example of the pivotal role that leaders play in setting a positive organizational climate comes from Dr. Deborah German at Saint Thomas Hospital. German is a second-generation Italian American who grew up aspiring to be a medical doctor. Because of her talent and potential, not only did she graduate from Harvard Medical School and become a fellow in rheumatic and genetic diseases at Duke University in Durham, North Carolina, but she was also a brilliant hospital administrator and is currently serving as the founding dean of the University of Central Florida College of Medicine and vice president for health affairs. How did she catapult from being a medical doctor to a proven leader of large organizations? Simply because she is a compassionate and caring leader with incredible competence and character. And one with an amazing talent to create a character-laden organization.

In 1988, Dr. German joined Vanderbilt University in Nashville as associate dean for students and later senior associate dean of medical education. After thirteen years at Vanderbilt, Dr. German was selected to serve as president and CEO at Saint Thomas Hospital in Nashville. This hospital is part of a system that overspent its budget. At the time, the hospital budget needed to gain an additional $2 million a month but was losing $2 million instead. The crisis was so bad that the system CEO's guidance to Dr. German was to immediately cut the workforce by 10 percent—or said another way, to fire 350 employees. How would you like to face a situation where you are told to fire 10 percent of the work-force? Who would want to work in an environment such as that?[13]

Dr. German knew the catastrophic outcome these actions would have on the morale of the remaining employees. She knew this because she was a hands-on CEO, and because she cared for each of them. She worked closely with the employees and knew the pressure and burdens they were already under. If anything, she felt she needed to increase the workforce by 10 percent, not fire 10 percent.

To deal with this dilemma, she brought the leadership to-gether. She recognized that institutional expertise resided with the department heads. They were the hospital's experts, dealing with the organization's problems every day. She believed that if she could collectively unleash this body of intelligence, together they would fix this problem.

By bringing everyone together, she shared their thoughts on the problem and solicited feedback on how to address it. She brought in both administrators and doctors. At the first meeting, to demonstrate her trust in her leadership to solve this problem, she stated that the first person to be fired would be her own daughter (who worked in the hospital), then herself. After explaining the problem, she asked each of her leaders to present this briefing to their subordinates with the goal that every per-son in the hospital would not only share knowledge of the issue and concern, but each person would also have the opportunity to offer ideas on a solution.

For the next two weeks, the leadership team met every day from 6:00 A.M. to 8:00 A.M., to discuss the incoming ideas. The intent was to encourage everyone to get involved, and to think of ways to solve this problem, both innovative and traditional. During the meetings, the entire team would drill down on every proposed solution and see how it could be implemented.

Dr. German told her leadership that if you take one stick and bend it, it will easily break. But if you take a couple dozen sticks together and try to break them, it is nearly impossible. By ourselves, we will lose. But with all of us together, we will win. And win they did.

A great idea came from one of the assistants whose job was to push newly discharged patients in their wheelchairs out the front door to their waiting ride home. The hospital would put a pillow or two in the wheelchair for comfort, and naturally the patient would want the pillows in the car to provide comfort on the ride home. The hospital had been doing this for years, and when the administration examined its cost, they found it was nearly $1 million a year. The assistant suggested encouraging new in-patients and their families to bring to the hospital the patient's pillow from home. It would not only provide the comfort and security of using one's own pillow but also would comfort the patient on discharge and the ride home. This grassroots solution not only saved the hospital nearly a million dollars a year, but also provided more comfort and appeal to patients. It was a win-win!

Dr. German was brilliant in approaching her hospital's financial problems, but her compassion, empathy, and caring for every person in her workforce steered her toward solutions. By involving every employee, she unleashed the potential of every doctor, administrator, and staff member. Dr. German demonstrated personal responsibility and a sense of urgency and priority.

Because of this initiative, within three to four months the hospital eliminated the $2 million monthly deficit and was saving more than $4 million a month without firing a single person. That was the tangible outcome, but intangible outcomes included long-term benefits such as an increase in morale, greater trust and cohesion within the team, and, probably most important, the trust and confidence the entire organization had in their president and CEO, Dr. Deb German.

Is caring an important criterion in a leader with strong character? You bet it is! Just spend an hour or so with Dr. German, and you will want to be on her team every day.

FRANCE TÉLÉCOM

We have seen how high-performing organizations strive for competence, character, and caring to optimize their organizational climate and promote excellence among their employees. We have also looked at examples of organizations that are lacking in one or more of the elements of competence, character, and caring and the adverse impact this has on the organization and its individual members. Implicit in our discussion is the assumption that such organizations are motivated to address these deficiencies to regain the trust of their employees and improve productivity and morale.

What happens when an organization intentionally violates the principles of competence, character, and caring so as to undermine the trust and confidence of its employees? France Télécom (formerly the national phone company, now a private company called Orange) provides such an example. In an article published in *The New York Times,* writer Adam Nossiter describes what happened when France Télécom engaged in "moral harassment" of its employees in an effort to drive them to quit the company. According to Nossiter, company executives believed they needed to reduce their workforce by 22,000 out of 130,000 to make the company more competitive. Because of French laws protecting the rights of workers, the company could not easily fire them, so the executives allegedly decided to create such poor work conditions that employees would voluntarily resign. But given the poor job market in France, most workers clung to their jobs and attempted to endure whatever tactics management inflicted upon them.[14]

Management had set about their task using a variety of means. Some workers were reportedly reassigned to jobs that they were ill prepared for or did not like. Some were given meaningless tasks or no tasks at all. In doing so, management made clear to the employees that money mattered more than the welfare of the workers. Management created a work environment that clearly communicated to the employees that the company did not care about them.

In his *New York Times* article, Nossiter describes the most horrendous impact of this strategy on workers. In a lawsuit filed on behalf of the workers, former executives of France Télécom were sued for moral harassment. Prosecutors claimed that at least eighteen suicides and thirteen attempted suicides occurred among France Télécom workers between April 2008 and June 2010. In December of 2019 Reuters reported that a Paris court found the telecom group (now known as Orange) and the former CEO guilty of moral harassment. Although Orange continued to deny that "there was any systemic plan or intention to harass employees," the telecom group said it would not appeal the verdict.[15]

The outcome of these policies by France Télécom are entirely predictable based on psychologist Martin Seligman's learned-helplessness theory. Seligman discovered that when animals and humans are presented with inescapable harm, many develop symptoms of depression. If, in this case, workers had other employment alternatives, they would likely have quit their jobs as management desired and pursued other options. But the poor job market forced most to remain at their jobs, and feelings of helplessness and depression built over time. Just like the dogs in Seligman's original studies of learned helplessness, thousands of workers suffered significant emotional stress.[16]

We hope this represents a rare example of organizational abuse of employees. Whether intentional or not, the France Télécom case unequivocally demonstrates the profoundly adverse impact that an organization's violations of character and caring have on its employees.

ASSESSING YOUR ORGANIZATION

We recommend evaluating your organization's performance on the IROC principles. Give this questionnaire (Worksheet 6.1) to all or a sample of your employees. Carefully examine their responses. High responses (4s and 5s) indicate your organization is doing well on these factors. Lower responses (1s, 2s, and 3s) may indicate areas of concern. Feedback from this evaluation may be used to develop strategies for improving your organization's climate.

WORKSHEET 6.1: IROC ORGANIZATIONAL RATING FORM

Use the following 5-point scale to rate your organization for each question below:

1 = VERY POOR
2 = POOR
3 = AVERAGE
4 = ABOVE AVERAGE
5 = EXCELLENT

Individual credibility. In my organization my senior leader is

   A.   COMPETENT:

1	2	3	4	5

   B.   DISPLAYS HIGH CHARACTER:

1	2	3	4	5

   C.   GENUINELY CARES ABOUT MY WELL-BEING:

1	2	3	4	5

Relationships. In my organization my senior leader displays _____ toward others.

   A.   RESPECT AND CONCERN:

1	2	3	4	5

   B.   OPEN COMMUNICATION:

1	2	3	4	5

   C.   COOPERATIVE INTERDEPENDENCE:

1	2	3	4	5

   D.   TRUST AND EMPOWERMENT:

1	2	3	4	5

My organization includes

A. SHARED VALUES, BELIEFS, AND NORMS:

1	2	3	4	5

B. POSITIVE POLICIES, PRACTICES, AND PROCEDURES:

1	2	3	4	5

My organization

A. READILY ADAPTS TO CHANGING CONDITIONS:

1	2	3	4	5

B. HAS FORMAL PLANS TO RESPOND TO CHANGES IN DEPENDENCIES AND NEEDS:

1	2	3	4	5

SUMMING UP

Character does not occur in a vacuum. Establishing a strong and positive organizational climate and culture that follows the IROC principles is necessary for lasting success. Organizations such as Johnson & Johnson and the San Antonio Spurs that do this win consistently. Organizations that fail to live up to the IROC principles suffer greatly. Begin with an IROC assessment, using our simple survey or by devising your own assessment. Use the results to develop a plan, if necessary, to improve your organizational climate. Winning, winning consistently, and winning the right way hinge on building a positive organizational climate.

GOOD INGREDIENTS MAKE FOR A GOOD STEW

In determining "the right people," the good-to-great
companies placed greater weight on character attributes
than on specific educational background, practical skills,
specialized knowledge, or work experience.

—JIM COLLINS[1]

Imagine that you are starting a new company and need to hire one hundred employees, ranging from entry-level workers to senior management. Knowing the importance of character as the foundation of a high-performing company, you want to make sure that your employees from the most junior to the top leaders display positive character and value it in others. To accomplish this goal you need to do four things. First, you must identify what positive character traits are most important to your organization. Second, you must select high-character individuals during the initial hiring. Third, you need a plan to continually develop your employees to optimize their role in and contribution to the organization. And finally, you must constantly monitor individuals and subcultures within your organization to ensure continued adherence to organization values.

With these goals in mind you enlist the aid of a human resources (HR) specialist. This person will have many tools available to assess intelligence and aptitude and will recommend a variety of strategies to fill the positions. These will include gathering background information on each applicant, such as work and educational history. This may be followed by background checks, a review of letters of reference, and eventually interviews.

APTITUDE MYOPIA

So far so good, but standard hiring strategies only go so far in assessing character. These strategies focus mostly on talent, narrowly defined as intelligence or aptitude-test scores. The military gives the Armed Services Vocational Aptitude Battery (ASVAB) to hundreds of thousands of potential recruits each year. Fall below the cutoff score, and you will not be allowed to join any branch of the military. The ASVAB is akin to a test you may be more familiar with—the SAT. You, or your children, have probably taken this assessment. Your score on the SAT plays a major role in determining the college or university that you will attend. A high score is necessary, but not sufficient, to elicit an offer from an elite university. Fall a bit below that and you may find yourself attending a second-tier school. Score even lower, and you will likely end up, at least initially, in a community college or a trade school. This may happen even though, with hard work and determination, you had excellent grades in high school.

If you have ever been denied a job or entry into a college because of test scores, you may have experienced aptitude myopia. This bias stems from over a hundred years of psychologists putting the bulk of their efforts into developing and refining a

variety of tests for intelligence and aptitude. Human-relations specialists like these tests because they are reliable and valid. *But at the very best they only predict about 25 percent of performance in work and academic success.* If talent assessments alone account for such a small percent of success, that means 75 percent or more of performance is related to other attributes. And here is the challenge. Psychologists and HR specialists do not have sophisticated or valid ways to identify and assess these attributes.

Aptitude myopia is problematic for organizations that want to fill their ranks with high-performing individuals. Think about the high school student who studies diligently, takes summer classes, gets tutoring when needed, and graduates with an A average. But for whatever reason, this student does not excel at standardized tests such as the SAT, scoring only average. So he or she is denied admission to top-tier universities. If you were predicting this student's success in college, which factor would you put your money on? The mediocre SAT score (accounting for fewer than 25 percent of potential success) or the grit and determination (accounting for a significant chunk of potential for success) displayed by the student over four long years of study in high school?

To be clear, the SAT and similar tests are useful in predicting college success especially when combined with high school grades, which has been the most powerful way to predict future academic performance. However, considering noncognitive attributes, in conjunction with standardized test scores, will optimize the prediction of who will succeed and who will fail. The applicant with high academic potential, as measured by the SAT, combined with high grit, self-regulation, love of learning, and so forth is the ideal combination of cognitive and noncognitive abilities. Also, test scores such as the SAT are frequently misunderstood and sometimes misused. Colleges and universities should consider SAT scores along with a host of other indicators of academic potential. The College Board itself has always advocated using test scores in this manner—as one factor among many to consider when making admissions decisions. To that end, the organization has invested in a program called Landscape, designed to help schools better understand some of these other factors, and to more appropriately employ the SAT in making admissions decisions.[2]

In hiring employees, talent assessments are important, but standard HR strategies may not allow you to tap into attributes such as grit, integrity, self-regulation, and social intelligence (among many others) that will optimize the personnel makeup of your company. Because character is so important to both individual and organizational performance, let's examine some approaches to attracting, retaining, and sustaining high-character individuals. For example, Angela Duckworth and colleagues have found that physical ability is a strong predictor of success among West Point cadets. Physical ability, along with grit, predicted graduation from West Point better than cognitive ability as measured by SAT scores. The influence of physical ability and other noncognitive attributes on success in other organizations is largely unknown. We believe that organizations of all types would do well to consider these and other noncognitive factors in selecting and assigning employees.[3]

STEP 1: IDENTIFY THE CHARACTERISTICS THAT MATTER MOST TO YOU

West Point provides a useful case study of identifying positive character traits needed for success in the organization. As part of the larger Army, West Point embraces the seven Army values—

loyalty, duty, respect, selfless service, honor, integrity, and personal courage. Its honor code ("A cadet will not lie, cheat, or steal or tolerate those who do") has long been a defining characteristic of West Point. Consider the following letter, written in 1946 by Army Chief of Staff General Dwight D. Eisenhower to West Point's superintendent, Major General Maxwell Taylor:

Dear Taylor,

Since your visit to my office a few days back I have had West Point much on my mind and have wished that I could find time to have a long conversation with you. Pending opportunity to have a personal exchange of views I am writing down in very rough fashion some of the distinct impressions I have, so that you may be thinking about them with a view of further discussion or taking such action as you may deem appropriate—if indeed any at all is indicated.

I think everyone familiar with West Point would instantly agree that the one thing that has set it definitely aside from every other school in the world is the fact that for a great number of years it not only has had an "honor" system, but that the system has actually worked. This achievement is due to a number of reasons but two of the important ones are: first, that the authorities of West Point have consistently refused to take advantage of the honor system to detect or discover minor violations of regulations; and second, that due to the continuity of the Corps and the instructional Staff, we have succeeded, early in the cadet's career, in instilling in him a respect amounting to veneration for the honor system. The honor system, as a feature of West Point, seems to grow in importance with the graduate as the years recede until it finally becomes something that he is almost reluctant to talk about—it occupies a position in his mind akin to the virtue of his mother or his sister.

I realize I feel no more deeply on this subject than you do and all other responsible officers at the Academy. My excuse for bringing it up is that we have only recently undergone an expansion at West Point and we have just now been through a war where I have no doubt the Superintendent has been hard put to keep on his Staff officers of his own selection. I sincerely trust that as time goes on this latter difficulty can be largely overcome but in the meantime it seems to me equally important that individuals now at the Academy, both officers and Cadets, clearly and definitely understand that the honor system is something that is in the hands of the Cadets themselves, that it is the most treasured possession of the Point and that under no circumstances should it ever be used at the expense of the cadets in the detection of violations of regulations.

I remember my most unfortunate experience when I myself was a Cadet, an incident where some lightbulbs had been thrown into the area. The culprits were found by the lining up of the Corps and the querying of each individual of this particular misdemeanor. Any such procedure or anything related to it would of course be instantly repudiated by any responsible officer who had the good judgment to visualize its eventual effect on the honor system; but I do think it important that a policy along this line be clearly explained to all at least once a year, certainly by an authority no lower than the Commandant himself.

The problem of maintaining a profound respect for the honor system is of course something that falls upon the shoulders of all officers on duty there as well as upon upper classmen. Active effort should fall primarily upon the first classmen and their assistants in the second and third classes, but the officer certainly has a big field in his persistent adherence to the requirements of the system and in his refusal to abuse it in any way.

A feature I would very much like to see in the curriculum

is a course in practical or applied psychology. I realize that tremendous advances have been made in the matter of leadership and personnel management since I was a Cadet. Nevertheless I am sure it is a subject that should receive the constant and anxious care of the Superintendent and his assistants on the Academic Board and these should frequently call in for consultation experts from both other schools and from among persons who have made an outstanding success in industrial and economic life. Too frequently we find young officers trying to use empirical and ritualistic methods in the handling of individuals—I think that both theoretical and practical instruction along this line could, at the very least, awaken the majority of Cadets to the necessity of handling human problems on a human basis and do much to improve leadership and personnel handling in the Army at large.

I am told that since my days as a Cadet much has been done, particularly in the first class year, in inculcating a sense of responsibility in the man who is soon to be a 2nd Lieutenant. The more we can do along this line, the better for us. The Cadet should graduate with some justifiable self-confidence in his ability to handle small groups of men, to organize any appropriate task, and to see it through in a satisfactory fashion with the men under his command.

I have not a word to say about the technique or technical work at the Academy. Not only do I feel that they are in competent hands but I am certain that they are of far less importance than the larger questions I have so briefly touched upon above. In your efforts to graduate succeeding classes in which each individual will have, as an officer, a very definite feeling of responsibility toward the country, a very lively and continuing concern for his personal honor and for the honor system at West Point, and who finally will approach all of his problems with a very clear understanding of the human factors involved in the developing, training and leading an Army, then indeed West Point will continue to occupy its present place in the national consciousness and will be worth any sum that we must necessarily expend for its maintenance.

DWIGHT D. EISENHOWER[4]

This remarkable letter underscores the importance of honor and integrity as core values to West Point. In Eisenhower's view, these are the most important character traits of cadets. He doesn't even mention talent. Perhaps he took it for granted that cadets, handpicked from a large pool of candidates, would excel on this component of excellence. We have seen the fundamental importance of trust in the military, and a big part of the character component of trust is honor and integrity.

The second remarkable piece of Eisenhower's letter is his recommendation to Taylor that West Point establish a course of instruction in applied psychology. Eisenhower observed many officers during World War II who were technically competent but did not understand the human element. By studying psychology, he believed that cadets could build leadership skills by developing a better understanding of human nature, to include character. West Point's Behavioral Sciences & Leadership Department traces its origin to this letter.

How do you identify what character strengths are most important for your organization? The first step is to determine which character strengths are most relevant to and important for the mission of your company (or school or other type of organization). Considering the twenty-four character strengths, different clusters of strengths predict success in different types of organizations and for different types of missions. Studies of Army combat leaders show that teamwork, bravery, capacity to love, persistence, and honesty are the most important strengths for functioning successfully in combat situations.[5] Kindergarten teachers use different types of strengths, including fairness, humor, kindness, and love of learning. Reflect on the twenty-four strengths and ask people who are knowledgeable about your organization to identify three or four strengths that make for an outstanding employee.

STEP 2: FOCUS ON THESE STRENGTHS TO SELECT THE BEST PEOPLE

Once you identify these strengths, you must devise a plan to select for these traits in prospective employees. If persistence is important, then you may look for a past history of successfully completing challenging tasks that require time and determination. If creativity matters, then look for indicators of it in the résumé or during interviews.

How does West Point select high-character cadets? To assess academic competence, the academy uses relatively objective measures including standardized test scores, high school grade point averages, and high school class rank. But because there are no equivalent tests for character, West Point relies on indirect indicators of character. Grit, for instance, may be inferred from a number of actions and accomplishments of high school students. Choosing a sport as a freshman and sticking with it for four years is an example. Becoming an Eagle Scout, because it requires perseverance and dedication over a long period, is also a proxy for grit. Leadership, another desired character trait, can be inferred by a student's being elected as a club president or a team captain. In this way, West Point selects cadets who not only have the talent to succeed, but also possess the character important to success at West Point and in an Army career.

We recommend caution in using existing tests of character, such as the VIA-IS, for formally screening potential employees. While they are valuable for self-reflection, these assessments are not useful in employee screening because they are transparent. Applicants can easily game the assessment to demonstrate they have the character strengths that may lead to a job offer. It is better to focus on past behavior and accomplishments.

An important axiom in psychology is that the best predictor of future behavior is past behavior. This is true with predictors of academic success. A high school student who studies diligently is likely to be a college student who does the same. This is true as well when it comes to character. As you identify and screen for character, look for objective indicators of behaviors and actions that reflect the positive character traits you seek. You should also look for evidence of traits that run counter to your organization's values. A thorough background check may reveal indicators that the person's values are not a good match for your organization.

Organizations may use creative approaches to assess character. West Point, for example, requires applicants to write an essay on an ethical situation, explaining how they would address the dilemma. From these essays, character attributes may be revealed.

STEP 3: DEVELOP CHARACTER WITHIN YOUR ORGANIZATION

Once you have selected the best candidates for your organization, the focus should shift to how to nurture and further develop desired traits. This requires regular assessment, as we saw with Johnson & Johnson. To be effective, these ongoing assessments must not occur in a vacuum. Students and workers need feedback, and this requires a good mentor to interpret the assessment, to coach employees on how to address issues, and to develop a plan for improvement.

West Point takes this seriously. Every cadet at West Point is assessed in a Periodic Development Review (PDR) three times a year—each academic semester, and during summer training. In this 360-degree assessment, the cadet is assessed by his or her superiors, subordinates, and peers.

The PDR assesses the cadet academically, physically, militarily, and in character. The character assessment is considered the most important component. Among the character traits assessed are the seven Army values, empathy, the warrior and service ethos (sharing attitudes and beliefs that embody the spirit of the profession), and discipline (self-regulation). Several questions evaluate leadership and trust. Cadets are rated on a 5-point scale, from 1 (low, needs substantial improvement) to 5 (excellent, ready to be an officer). Cadets receive feedback in a color-coded format (from black at the bottom, through red, orange, yellow, and to green at the top) that allows them to easily see how subordinate cadets, their peers, their cadet leaders, and their officers and professors perceive them. In this type of rating you can immediately see strengths (i.e., green) or weaknesses (i.e., black), and you can see trends over time.

The mentor reviews the PDR with the cadet and discusses where his or her strengths or weaknesses are, what the trends are, and what the cadet needs to do to address weaknesses. This leads to self-reflection and actionable plans to improve.

You may be thinking that this works because it's an organized, well-resourced, institution-driven assessment. Then you ask, "What about me? Since I'm not a cadet, and I'm not in a job with assessments and feedback, how can I get an assessment of my leadership capabilities that includes my character development?"

That's a great question because all students, employees, and leaders need to get an open, candid assessment of how well they are leading, and how their character impacts their work performance and leadership effectiveness. We welcome favorable feedback about ourselves, but with less favorable feedback, we often rationalize or dismiss it. If you want to know if your character is in line with the values of your institution, you need to be thick-skinned and listen to what others are saying about you. So, welcome the feedback!

You can take a number of approaches. The first thing we suggest is to make a self-assessment of your character. The tactic is similar to what we suggested in identifying traits critical to a given job. Write down the character traits you feel are critical in the work you're doing, as well as necessary traits in other activities in your life—such as parenting and volunteer work. Look to the VIA-IS for a list of the character traits. Next, make a list of behaviors associated with each of these traits. An appropriate behavior for "respect" would be "intently listen, especially to people whose worldview is not consistent with your own." An appropriate behavior for "duty" could be "always doing the right thing, even when no one is looking." Once you have this list of relevant behaviors for each character trait, evaluate each behavior on a scale of 1 to 5, similar to the cadet PDR.

Now it is time to get feedback from others. Take your character trait and behavior list and share it with your boss, with some of your subordinates, with your spouse and children, and with others in the groups with which you engage. Ask them to rate you in each of these areas on the 1-to-5 scale, and if you're really open, sit down and ask them why they rated each area as they did.[6] You will be amazed at what you discover about how others perceive you.

New tools are emerging to make character assessments that you can use to develop people once they enter your organization. Psychologist Brian Davidson is the founder of MindVue, a human-capital firm dedicated to measuring, predicting, and building human excellence. Davidson and his colleagues have developed a state-of-the-art assessment tool called the MindVue Profile.[7] This profile assesses a variety of noncognitive skills and attributes including grit, self-control, conscientiousness, hope, growth mindset, self-discipline, resilience, and integrity. This instrument, unlike other character-assessment tools discussed thus far, includes a flag for whether the test taker is being honest or consistent in answering questions. This greatly increases the reliability of the instrument.

Returning to the opening scenario of hiring and developing one hundred new employees, the MindVue Profile could be used along with our other suggestions to identify and screen job applicants. Once employees are hired, the MindVue Profile can be used in a number of ways. Employees review and reflect on detailed feedback the assessment provides them, seeing areas where they are strong or may need development. For senior management, the MindVue Profile provides a dashboard that summarizes individual scores into averages for teams and larger subdivisions of the company. This provides a useful diagnostic, providing leadership and management with reliable information on how various components of the company stand in these attributes. Teams that are low in resilience, for example, could receive additional training to help them improve.

The ability of the MindVue Profile to provide both individual and group feedback takes the guesswork out of character assessments. Combined with traditional strategies of interviews and surveys, this is a valuable tool for organizations to develop and "unlock the potential within individuals." It chips away at the 25/75 dilemma.

Giving and receiving honest feedback, especially about character, is difficult. But if you don't seek feedback and take it seriously, you'll keep demonstrating the same positive or negative behaviors, with the same positive or negative outcomes. That is not improvement and it is not growth. It is also a missed opportunity. So, we encourage you to do this—be thick-skinned, use some moral courage, and ask your colleagues and your family how they would assess your character traits and affiliated behaviors.

STEP 4: RESPONDING TO CHARACTER FAILURES

Given human nature, at times individuals or groups of individuals will behave in ways that are inconsistent with the values of your organization. Sometimes the best thing to do is to fire the employee or expel the student, depending on the transgression. But in many cases, the leader may use his or her knowledge of character and its development to correct the behavior.

The two case studies that follow illustrate, in two different types of organizations, the importance of this step. In each case, leaders had selected good individuals for the organization and assumed they would continue to behave ethically. Thinking all was well, the leaders failed to diligently monitor the actions of the organization's members. This resulted in existential crises for both organizations.

CASE STUDY 1: THE 2013 WEST POINT MEN'S RUGBY TEAM

In the summer of 2013, General Caslen, as the nominated and soon-to-be superintendent of the US Military Academy at West Point, was invited to attend the Board of Visitors' meeting with the serving superintendent. The superintendent is akin to the president of a college or university. The Board of Visitors is similar to a university's board of trustees, but does not have oversight authority. The board is composed of six or seven US senators, seven or eight members of Congress, and five or six presidential appointees. Their principal task is to write an annual report to the president of the United States on the state of affairs at West Point.

The 2013 board meeting was in June, about two weeks after graduation ceremonies, and about two weeks before Caslen was to assume responsibility as the academy's superintendent. Normally board meetings are cordial and informative. Agendas are jointly prepared ahead of time, and action items and issues are prepared before the meeting. At least this was the procedure Caslen expected. But what occurred was something for which he couldn't have prepared.

As soon as the board came to order, one of the presidential appointees, a West Point female graduate from the historic class of 1980 (the first class including women at West Point), read for the record a blistering criticism of how the academy's leaders had recently handled a sexual-harassment allegation against the men's rugby team. The situation had been going on for about five years and had surfaced a few weeks before graduation.

A series of hostile, degrading, and disrespectful emails had circulated among some rugby team members after each match. Known as the "Highs and Lows," each edition criticized team members on their performance in the match, but also criticized the opposing team, the spectators, and even went beyond the match and referred inappropriately to individual instructors, tactical officers, and other cadets.

The comments were personal and degrading and not what one would expect of a future leader in the US Army, much less a responsible citizen in any community. The emails described inappropriate actions using coarse language. What really got the attention of the board members were the comments made to a number of female West Point cadets, identified by name. The emails clearly indicated a subculture with values that were totally contrary to those of the Army and the values of duty, honor, and country.

Subcultures are not inherently bad. For example, hard-nosed athletic teams pride themselves on a subculture of tenacity, resilience, and mental and physical toughness. These values within the subculture are consistent with the institution's values. But when teams have values such as those expressed in the rugby team's "Highs and Lows" emails that has to be openly acknowledged and action must be taken to realign the offending values or to remove those who are propagating them.

Public and private values must align. Individual members in the profession of arms are expected to demonstrate leadership twenty-four hours a day, seven days a week. You do not have the privilege of turning character on when it is convenient and turning it off when it is not. You are expected to lead with the same values all the time. This should be true for any leader in any profession. Trust is the most essential element of effective leadership, and the surest way to lose trust is to demonstrate a private life with values inconsistent with those of the organization.

The criticism of the USMA Board of Visitors was not so much that unacceptable values were uncovered in the rugby team, but with how the academy's leaders handled its exposure. The problem was identified about two weeks before graduation. The superintendent and the commandant put the rugby team, including the seniors who were ready to graduate, into an accelerated mentorship program and then assessed that their change of heart made their values now consistent with what the nation expects of a West Point graduate, enabling these seniors to graduate with their class on time. The board members clearly felt this response to the crisis was not appropriate, especially the allowing of the seniors to graduate on time.

Walking into this situation as the new superintendent allowed Caslen to take an outsider's view of it. When the continuing investigation was completed, he removed the coach and the officer responsible for the team, dissolved the team for one semester, and placed all team members into a revamped mentorship program. Holding people accountable for their actions is essential for sending the right message to the organization. Caslen needed to send this message, especially as he began his tenure as superintendent. Disrespectful, disparaging behavior with values inconsistent with institution values could not be tolerated. This is not what is expected of future Army leaders.

A striking aspect of the rugby team's dysfunction was that it went on for five years before being brought to light. Why didn't someone recognize it for what it was? How can you be sure that the subcultures among athletic teams and clubs and other groups have values that are consistent with institutional values?

One must have a tool to assess the culture of the subordinate organizations. Caslen authorized the creation of a culture-assessment survey and administered it every year to every club, every club-level athletic team, and every NCAA team at West Point. The survey was anonymous and was extremely helpful in assessing subcultures. It was modified each year based on the data received. For example, one team got together and gamed the survey, influencing the outcome. Fortunately, an anonymous cadet from a different team brought this to Caslen's attention. Subsequent surveys required team members not only to assess their own team, but also to assess other teams.

This assessment was so important to Caslen that he personally reviewed all the surveys, consolidated the data for each club and team, met collectively with every cadet team captain and their officer representative, and directed the athletic director to review the survey results with every coach. If issues existed, they were identified and resolved.

West Point is not alone in facing organizational conduct that is driven by the failure to adhere to institutional values.

CASE STUDY 2: THE UNIVERSITY OF CENTRAL FLORIDA

The University of Central Florida (UCF) is one of the largest universities in the country and has been one of the fastest growing since its inception in 1968. Enrollment has been exponential—from nineteen hundred in 1968 to twenty-one thousand in 1992, to sixty-eight thousand by 2019. With an operating budget of $1.7 billion, UCF offers more than a hundred bachelor degrees and master's and doctorate degrees in numerous fields, conferring more than sixteen thousand degrees each year. These sixty-eight thousand students are taught by twenty-five hundred faculty with the support of thirteen thousand staff. UCF's research funding in 2018 was $183 million.

In the middle of its rapid growth, in August 2018, a Florida auditor general found that one of UCF's academic buildings, Trevor Colbourn Hall, had been constructed using $38 million of ineligible state funds, called education and general (E&G) funds. Further investigation revealed this was not a onetime incident. A total of $84.7 million in leftover operating dollars was spent across eleven capital projects, over the five years from 2013 to 2018. The existing Colbourn Hall was built in 1974 and needed significant repairs. University leaders said that without the repairs health and safety issues would be significant. They felt that replacing Colbourn Hall constituted an emergency and used this rationale to misuse funds. The investigation found these claims "to be rooted in legitimate concerns that . . . [university] officials faced at the time of the decisions. However, the evidence does not support a conclusion that Colbourn presented an imminent health or safety risk requiring emergency action, nor does it support the claim that there was no other alternative but to use E&G funds."[8] This rationale by the university's leadership was not accepted by any oversight authority—either the Board of Trustees or the Board of Governors.

Can someone justify unethical behavior because of health or

safety? Is unethical behavior justified at some threshold? The Board of Governors held the university's leadership accountable, illustrating that no threshold justifies immoral, unethical, or illegal behavior. And rightly so. *Whether I sell my integrity for $1 or $38 million, I am still a person of no integrity. That's a tough picture to look at in the mirror each morning.*

UCF's rapid growth in student enrollment and faculty placed increased demands on its human capital and campus physical infrastructure. Systems and procedures that had previously worked were now insufficient. Meeting the needs of administrative support was in direct competition to academic excellence and research. This dilemma meant increased difficulty in meeting the mission and compliance requirements. Or said another way, the unethical use of E&G funds for capital construction was an option to meet demands, and the temptation to make the unethical choice instead of doing the right thing was embraced. Using $84.7 million across eleven capital expenditures over five years demonstrated that the temptation was regularly embraced. The institution's leaders chose the easier wrong over the harder right.

So where lies the accountability? Florida House Speaker Richard Corcoran was skeptical that the UCF chief financial officer (CFO) was the only one who accepted responsibility and was the only one who knew of the offense. Corcoran wrote to the new UCF president, Dr. Dale Whittaker, "I am baffled by how the actions of one irresponsible officer's effort at flouting the Legislature's and State University System's budget controls could result in a four-year-long unauthorized endeavor of this magnitude. There are only two possibilities: That others within UCF were aware of and conspired in this misuse of public funds, or your administration lacks the necessary internal controls to manage its fiscal responsibilities."[9] The issue the Speaker raises is *to what degree are executives responsible for unethical and illegal actions within their organizations?*

The Florida state legislature clearly felt that the executive leadership was indeed responsible; if not for personal complicity, then for failure to have proper institutional compliance procedures or to take appropriate actions if illicit activity was discovered.

The consequence of the actions of a few was devastating to the entire university. The former president retired and lost his retirement bonuses, the chief financial officer resigned, four associate vice presidents were terminated, the chair of the Board of Trustees was forced to step down, and the previous provost who had been selected to be the new president was forced to resign. Most concerning was the breach of trust between the university and its oversight committees, its Board of Trustees and Board of Governors, and the public.

In a Board of Governors meeting, the chancellor of the State University System of Florida called this a "calamity, and this calamity is a loss of credibility because it is a loss of trust." The Florida House Public Integrity & Ethics Committee chair said the university's Board of Trustees "apparently fail to appreciate the gravity of the situation they're in."[10]

The fallout from the misappropriations at UCF affected those directly involved in making those poor decisions, and ultimately the entire university, its leadership, and its reputation. It didn't stop there. It placed upon the shoulders of the new leadership the difficult task of regaining the trust that was so unnecessarily lost. The new interim president wrote an email to the local newspaper, "What happened was wrong. The people who did this, and concealed their actions, are no longer with the university. UCF has taken multiple and aggressive steps to ensure this doesn't happen again. We are committed to regaining the trust of the Board of Governors and Florida House."

To UCF's credit, the new leadership put together an aggressive plan to address the problem. The first step was to change the organizational structure that allowed finances and construction to exist under the same leadership. Separating these responsibilities introduced a degree of accountability that was previously missing. The solution addressed policies, procedures, and regulations on how the UCF leadership and staff would work with its oversight committees (the Board of Trustees and the Board of Governors). Training and education programs were put in place to teach governance and fiduciary-responsibility procedures to the oversight boards as well as the university leadership and staff.

Training also had to address a culture that saw oversight authorities as obstacles. The new culture must embrace transparency, collaboration, and partnership. The university also instituted a whistle-blower program. Whenever faculty members or employees found themselves in a compromising situation, they were provided a means to report the unethical directive or behavior without fear of reprisal.

Under the previous leadership the organizational values, beliefs, norms, and goals at UCF had become unbalanced. The administration had failed to adhere to its own standards. The university's Employee Code of Conduct now incorporates the organizational principles that the IROC model identifies as essential to a high-character organization.[11] A clear vision statement is linked to the institution's goals. Among its five visionary goals the university aspires to "offer the best undergraduate and graduate education available in Florida," "achieve international prominence in key programs of graduate study and research," and "become more inclusive and diverse." The Code of Conduct includes four areas of focus that are consistent with a high-character organization: honesty and integrity, respect of others, responsibility and accountability, and stewardship. The latter focus—stewardship—calls on its leaders and employees to be ethical in their fiscal responsibilities. The code explicitly states four questions that must be considered when making fiscal decisions: "(1) Does this transaction influence any future business decisions I will make, (2) could this transaction appear to be a conflict of interest to anyone such as the press or media, (3) have I received prior approval to spend, accept, or manage these funds, and (4) have I been trained in proper collection practices and internal controls."

Building a modern classroom building is a laudable goal. But achieving the goal at any cost, in this case through misappropriation of funds, sent devastating aftershocks throughout the organization. The old saying is that the road to perdition is paved with good intentions. Following Step 4 prevents this from happening.

A single action by a bad actor can erode the trust that took years to build. When trust is lost, it is important to find out what caused the loss, and to fix it as aggressively and quickly as possible. Whether rebuilding trust takes a couple weeks or a couple years (or longer), it absolutely must happen to have productive relationships that will enable organizations to achieve their vision and accomplish their mission.

LESSONS LEARNED AND CLOSING THOUGHTS

A good stew requires more than good ingredients. Although you may have identified what you want in the stew, shopped around for the best meat and vegetables, and followed the recipe carefully, this may not be enough. You must attend to the stew and taste it regularly to ensure that the ingredients blend together in the right way. West Point and UCF failed in Step 4 and suffered great harm that required tremendous efforts to remedy.

In the 1992 US presidential election, candidate Bill Clinton used a simple slogan to characterize his campaign: "It's the economy, stupid!" Crafted by his campaign adviser James Carville, this statement focused voters on a powerful message. With the country coming out of a recession, Clinton correctly understood that focusing on the economy would strengthen his bid to win the White House.

When it comes to character, the message may be "It's the organization, stupid!" The task of identifying, selecting, and developing high-character people is essential to having a high-quality company, school, or other organization. And the best organizations take the further step of constantly monitoring and assessing the character and ethics of the individuals and subcultures that comprise the organization.

8

NURTURING THE SEED OF GOOD CHARACTER

Good character is not formed in a week or a month.
It is created little by little, day by day. Protracted and patient
effort is needed to develop good character.

—HERACLEITUS[1]

Farmers understand the need to purchase the best seeds to produce the best crop. Seeds contain the genetic code for their
growth. Selecting good-quality seed not only increases yield,
but it also produces plants that are resistant to various diseases
and disorders. But farmers also know that high-quality seed,
while necessary, is not sufficient to ensure a bumper crop. The
quality of the soil is also important. So, too, is the care and
nurturing the farmer provides as the crops mature. Farming
would be a lot easier if all that was necessary was to plant the
seed and wait until the beans, tomatoes, corn, or other produce
was ready to harvest. Spring and summer could be spent fishing
or traveling instead of tending to the fields!

Character is akin to seeds in this respect. Selecting people
of high character to be part of your organization is necessary
to establish a high-character organization. This is analogous to

the farmer's care and consideration in seed selection. Creating and maintaining an environment that reinforces good character is also critical. We saw how high-performing organizations such as the Spurs do this year in and year out. This is similar to the farmer planting the seed in soil that is favorable to seed growth. But just as crops need tending, so character needs to be developed. You can begin with the best seeds but still fail to produce a quality crop. And you can begin with high-character individuals in your school or workplace and still end up with a character-challenged organization.

Character must continually be developed. It is not something you have or don't have. Even people considered to be icons of character sometimes fail to behave morally or ethically. There are many examples. You may think of character failures in your own life or ones you have observed in others.

Retired general and former director of the Central Intelligence Agency David Petraeus is a case in point. A native of Cornwall-on-Hudson, New York, and the son of the commander of a World War II Liberty ship, it was almost inevitable that Petraeus would attend West Point, just a few miles down the Hudson River from his home. He excelled at West Point, graduating in the top 5 percent of his class. He had an outstanding career in the Army, commanding at every echelon. His strategy as a division commander in the Iraq War is regarded as one of the most highly effective strategies employed by US troops. He went on to several higher commands, including of the Army's Combined Arms Center, the United States Central Command, and the International Security Assistance Force in Afghanistan.

Petraeus retired from the Army in August of 2011 at the rank of four-star general. Shortly thereafter, he was sworn in as the director of the Central Intelligence Agency. Here his problems began. He was discovered to have engaged in an extramarital affair with Paula Broadwell, herself a West Point graduate, and to have shared classified information with her. Petraeus was ultimately charged with and pleaded guilty to unauthorized removal and retention of classified material. Petraeus resigned as CIA director on November 9, 2012, after serving for just fourteen months in that position.

West Point carefully selected Petraeus into its class of 1974 and provided him with an optimal environment (soil) for continued growth. For the vast majority of his Army career, he served in exemplary fashion. Petraeus's behavior when he shared classified information was clearly "out of character" for him given his decades of honorable service. While we will never know what led Petraeus to these acts, one way to inoculate ourselves and others against similar failures is to pay attention to the third piece of producing a good crop—nurturing and cultivation of character.

THE BIG THREE

Cultivating good character may at first seem like a daunting task. But high-functioning organizations use a variety of strategies to do this. When you think of high-character organizations, what comes to mind? Scouting, religious institutions, schools from K–12, and colleges and universities. What is the common denominator across these diverse institutions?

Psychologists have identified what are called the big three factors in shaping character: (1) positive and sustained mentoring, (2) skill-building curricula and training, and (3) leadership opportunities.[2] Some institutions systemically integrate all three of these factors into their development efforts, while others do so intuitively, and some fail to do it at all.

POSITIVE AND SUSTAINED MENTORING

Positive and sustained mentoring is fundamental to cultivating character. You will see this in all high-performing organizations. The San Antonio Spurs director of basketball operations and in-novation, Phil Cullen, provided us with a great example of the power of mentoring. Basketball fans are quite familiar with the legendary player Tim Duncan. For those not familiar with him, Duncan was the Spurs' leader both on and off the court in a career that spanned nineteen seasons, beginning in 1997. Along the way, he led the Spurs to five NBA championships, was on the NBA All-Star team fifteen times, and was the most valuable player (MVP) in the 2000 All-Star game. He represented the United States in the 1994 Olympic Games, while still playing college basketball at Wake Forest University, where he earned his bachelor's degree in psychology. He was twice selected as the NBA's MVP. He has many other achievements, but you get the idea.

A player of this caliber could be excused for developing an inflated ego. Fans of the NBA and other sports see this frequently. An elite player demands special treatment, is easily offended by the press, and is more concerned with individual statistics and accomplishments than the team's win/loss record. Duncan, however, consistently displayed the positive character traits of humility and teamwork throughout his great career.

Cullen told Matthews about an incident during summer practice in 2018. Summer practice gives the team's management and coaching staff a chance to observe the skills and "makeup" of players, especially newly selected draft picks or players newly acquired via trade or free agency. The word *makeup* is used in sports to describe the psychological, social, and emotional traits of a player. From our perspective, *makeup* is a shorthand way of saying the player has the positive character traits—grit, teamwork, courage—to excel in the game.

In this particular practice, a rookie draft pick was doing his best to impress the team. He gave 100 percent effort to every drill. Nearly exhausted following a particularly tough session, this player vomited on the court. This is not especially unusual in sports, but what happened next is. None other than Tim Duncan appeared, towel in hand, and cleaned up the vomit. He then encouraged the young (and perhaps embarrassed) player to keep up the hard work. In mentoring, what message did this simple act communicate not just to the rookie but to all the other players who witnessed it? If we break it down by head, heart, and guts, Duncan mentored this player and his teammates on the character traits of perspective, bravery, kindness, leadership, and humility, just to name a few.

Many other Tim Duncan stories also illustrate the power of mentoring. He was always the first to arrive at practice and the last to leave. Even now, although retired from playing in 2016, he follows the same pattern. This sets a great example for other players, who look up to him as the legend he is. Although he was not formally on the coaching staff until 2019, Duncan has always worked with players during practices to build skills, frequently spending much of his time with the second- and third-string players.

Who are the mentors in your organization? They may or may

not be managers or officially designated leaders. Positive mentoring occurs just as often, perhaps more so, among coworkers. Whom do you look up to, and why? What can you do to be more like them?

We caution that mentoring can have a dark side as well. In a dysfunctional organization, negative mentors may emerge. The boss who holds employees accountable to a strict schedule but takes two-hour lunches would be an example. The athlete (in any sport) who seeks special treatment and cares only about his or her own performance is another. Whether you are a student, an athlete, or an employee in a large corporation, people like this are always around. If they are charismatic, they can have a profoundly negative impact on you and the organization. Organizational leaders are advised to be on the lookout for such people, and to remove them from the organization if they do not respond to counseling. Phil Cullen explained that being on the lookout for positive character—and evidence of poor character—is an important consideration in deciding which players to draft, sign as free agents, trade for, or release or trade away. High character players are sought out, and those with questionable character are best either not recruited and signed, or removed from the team. Sometimes addition by subtraction works.

On being an effective mentor. Effective mentoring does not happen by chance. While peer mentors emerge within organizations and may be helpful in crafting and maintaining a positive culture, leaders and managers need to have a systematic plan to ensure that mentoring occurs, and that it is framed around the organization's goals and values. We offer the following suggestions:

1. Leaders and managers must make mentoring a priority and follow through with it in a timely manner. While day-to-day, informal interactions between leaders and subordinates are important, time should be set aside in formal meetings for in-depth discussions.

2. Formal mentoring sessions should be structured. It helps to ask employees to complete a self-development assessment plan prior to the meeting and to use that plan as the basis for discussion. The Behavioral Sciences & Leadership Department at West Point uses a simple, one-page form that provides such structure for evaluating junior officers assigned teaching duties within the department (shown in Figure 8.1). Note that the junior officer completes three columns of questions pertaining to duty performance (performing well?), professional growth (has a future?), and well-being (has a life?). This mentoring is completed quarterly, but it is not part of the officer's formal annual evaluation (the Officer Effectiveness Report, or OER). We especially emphasize the last column because of the importance of family and nonwork goals and activities to overall well-being. Corporations and other organizations may easily adapt this form to fit their mission and values. The purpose of the form is to encourage self-reflection followed by meaningful dialogue with the mentor, who in this case would be a senior officer.

3. Mentoring must be genuine. Managers who go through the motions of mentoring simply because their own supervisor requires them to mentor their subordinates will fail. People can sense insincerity instantly. Leaders and managers throughout the organization's hierarchy should be coached and trained in career-counseling skills, and their competence at this important aspect of leadership should be included in their own evaluations and feedback.

Figure 8.1

SELF-DIRECTED DEVELOPMENTAL FRAMEWORK

INTENT: EXECUTABLE STRATEGY THAT FOSTERS HIGH-PAYOFF, SELF-DIRECTED INDIVIDUAL DEVELOPMENT, TAILORED TO EACH SOLDIER, EXECUTED BY LEADERS, IN COMPLIANCE WITH ARMY REQUIREMENTS

SCOPE	DUTY PERFORMANCE	PROFESSIONAL GROWTH	WELL-BEING	NOTES
ORIENTATION	CURRENT	FUTURE	CURRENT AND FUTURE	
DOMINANT MODE	TRAINING	DEVELOPEMENT	EMPOWERMENT	
TOOLS	67-9-1	PERSONAL DEVELOPEMENT STRATEGY (SWOT)	NEEDS/ ASPIRATIONS ANALYSIS	
BS&L LEADER ROLE	PROFESSORSHIP	OFFICERSHIP	MENTORSHIP	
RESOURCES	TDY, UNIT TRAINING CONTINUNG EDUCATION TIME, FDW	GRANT/SPECIAL FUNDS ALL EDUCATION, TIME	PTDY/TIME ENTITLEMENTS KNOWLEDGE	
SPECIAL DUTY	SERVICE RELATED	EXTERNAL TASKING	DUTY EXEMPTIONS LEAVE, GRACE	
ADMINISTRATIVE RESPONSIBILITY	INDIVIDUAL	INDIVIDUAL	INDIVIDUAL	
ADMINISTRATIVE ACCOUNTABILITY	RATER	SENIOR RATER	INDIVIDUAL	
REVIEW	QUARTERLY	QUARTERLY	QUARTERLY	
LEADER QUESTION	PERFORMING WELL?	HAS A FUTURE?	HAS A LIFE?	

KEY POINTS:
• SELF-DIRECTED, BOTTOM-UP
• CAN RESOURCE WITH TIME
• LEAD WITH EXAMPLES

• NON-DIRECTIVE IN FORMAT (NO FORMS)
• ESTABLISHES MENTORING DIALOGUE
• GREEN, PURPLE, CIVILIAN ENVIRONMENTS

4. Do not confuse mentoring with performance evaluations. Mentoring is developmental in focus, not evaluative. Some aspects of performance may be discussed, but the focus is on what training and support the subordinate needs to improve, rather than on a performance rating that may impact pay or promotions.

5. Be honest. Most employees want to do well and will respond favorably when constructive feedback is included in mentoring sessions.

6. Identify the informal mentors in your organization. Encourage them and reward them for their efforts. These natural mentors often do the bulk of the mentoring in any organization, and effective leaders learn to leverage these contributions to complement formal mentoring strategies.

SKILL BUILDING

Character is not a fixed entity. Some aspects of temperament may be genetic, but character develops over time. Much of this occurs during childhood and adolescence. But character continues to evolve throughout adulthood. Moreover, this development—even among adults—is highly dependent on a person's situation. Psychologist Richard Lerner describes character development as an interaction between the individual and the environment.[3] According to this way of thinking, "good" character refers to behaviors, thoughts, and actions that are mutually beneficial to the individual and his or her social environment.

Psychologist Angela Duckworth agrees. She specifies three components to building character. These are mindset, expert practice, and a social and physical environment that provides opportunities to learn.[4] Mindset, based on Stanford psychologist Carol Dweck's research, is especially relevant.[5] People with a fixed mindset believe that attributes such as intelligence or character cannot be changed. This discourages efforts to improve cognitive or character skills. In contrast, people with a growth mindset believe that these attributes can change, with effort and feedback. Moreover, Duckworth finds that a growth mindset increases grit, and higher grit strengthens the growth mindset, resulting in what she calls "a virtuous cycle."

From an organizational perspective, this growth mindset

view of character underscores the importance of a culture deeply steeped in positive values. When individuals enter a new organization—a school, team, or business—they come to that organization with character traits that are not set in stone. To attain mutually beneficial outcomes, the individual may adapt the behaviors, thoughts, and actions that make up their character to fit the organization's stated values.

Looking at character as a malleable skill enables the organization to devise creative strategies for honing and developing character. Successful organizations think of a variety of ways to do this.

CHARACTER EDUCATION AND SELF-REFLECTION

Teaching people about character, giving them the opportunity to self-assess their own character, and leading discussions on how to use positive character to achieve personal and organizational goals are important. One example comes from the Military Child Education Coalition (MCEC), a nonprofit organization formed to advocate for the needs of military children. One of their programs is called Student 2 Student or S2S. In the S2S program, students, including children of both military and nonmilitary parents, can volunteer to form a S2S chapter in their school. Throughout the United States and in thirteen other countries, MCEC has trained more than a thousand elementary, middle, and high schools in S2S programs, helping thousands of children along the way. The S2S chapters offer social and emotional support to children who change schools frequently, often coping with one or sometimes both parents deployed in combat zones, and even dealing with the severe wounding or death of a parent from combat.

From these S2S chapters, about 120 teens ranging from high school freshmen to seniors are selected to attend MCEC's National Training Seminar (NTS), held each summer in Washington, D.C. One of the programs available to them is a character-development workshop. Prior to attending, they complete the VIA-IS and bring their results to the NTS. The workshop begins with a general discussion of character and individual strengths, but quickly transitions into a hands-on education and reflection exercise. First, they are told to list their top six character strengths and to "reflect on how you have used one of your signature strengths to accomplish something difficult, to achieve a goal, or to overcome an obstacle." Then they pair off and describe to their partner how they used the strength to address their personal challenge. The workshop facilitator then asks for volunteers to share their experiences with the group. In one session a sixteen-year-old high school student remarked, "My number one strength is humor, but it's also my weakness because my sense of humor often gets me in trouble." This is a terrific insight.

The students are then assigned to one of six groups corresponding to the character virtues of knowledge and wisdom, courage, humanity, justice, temperance, and transcendence. They are presented with a realistic scenario often faced by teens. For example:

> You have just moved to a new school (your fourth such move). Your new school is in a town where most of the other students have grown up together and have formed close cliques and friendships, and you are finding it difficult to make real friends. You feel like an outsider and are now spending much of your spare time interacting with friends from your former school

(which you liked very much and where you had many friends) on social media, and not enjoying fun times with new friends.

Think about the moral virtue your group has been assigned. Discuss among your group members how you could use individual strengths within your assigned virtue to begin making new friends and fitting in better in your new school. Be specific with recommendations and be prepared to share your ideas with the other groups.

The students discuss how they would do this. For instance, if assigned to the humanity virtue, they would talk about how to use the character strengths of kindness, capacity to love, and social intelligence to address the problem. The facilitator asks students at each table to lead a discussion on their chosen strategy. The students come up with highly innovative and inspiring ideas for leveraging character to address the problem. If time allows, they may be given a second but quite different scenario to consider, such as dealing with the death of a classmate.

The workshop concludes with a third exercise, in which the students are introduced to the ways of building character we are discussing here—positive and sustained mentoring, skill building, and opportunities to lead. They are asked to discuss how to better incorporate these principles in their own schools. Once again, their ideas are quite creative. In many cases, they take these ideas back to their schools and integrate them into existing S2S strategies.

These exercises are based on the notion that the twenty-four character strengths represent a toolbox, with individual strengths representing tools that are well matched to different sorts of jobs. The character strengths needed to excel academically differ from those needed to cope with the death of a loved one or the sadness and loneliness experienced when separated from a parent during his or her combat deployment.

CHARACTER-BUILDING TRAINING ACTIVITIES

The character traits of trust and leadership can be honed through field training exercises. The Thayer Leader Development Group, a private company located near West Point, provides leader- and character-development training for corporations. In addition to leadership education and reflection exercises on character similar to the ones used at the MCEC National Training Seminar, they have their clients complete a Leader Reaction Course (LRC). The LRC is a field exercise with a series of practical problems and obstacles that the group must overcome. Solutions require communication, mutual trust, and interdependence. A facilitator oversees the group's efforts, then provides feedback to participants on what went well and what did not. This hands-on training provides a memorable way of learning about one's character strengths and seeing how different team members may pool their strengths to complete a challenging task. Like the MCEC workshop, the goal is for participants to learn about their character and leadership styles, and to take those insights with them as they return to their parent organization. With a little research, you can probably locate a company that offers this kind of leader- and character-development training in or near your area.[6]

CHARACTER-BASED EXERCISES

Positive psychology provides a number of ways to build positive character strengths.[7] One exercise involves completing the Values-in-Action Inventory of Strengths and listing your top five character strengths, called your signature strengths. Then you are instructed to intentionally and mindfully use one or more of your signature strengths over the next week in challenging situations. This exercise builds self-awareness of strengths and inculcates the idea that your character strengths are a tool, along with your intellectual ability, for you to respond effectively to problems. This is a vital skill for leaders as well as individuals.

Another positive psychology exercise is "hunting the good stuff." In this exercise, you take a few moments at the end of each day to reflect on what went well. Then write down three or four things that went well, and include a short description of the event and why it went well. This reflective exercise builds the character strengths of perspective and gratitude, among others.

The gratitude visit is another powerful exercise. We described this earlier, in chapter 4. Reflecting on the beneficence of others and then overtly telling them about why their actions were so important is moving, with long-lasting positive effects on mood and outlook.

Besides building strengths, such exercises also pay a dividend of improved mood.[8] In this sense they build resilience. Resilience training is common in many high-stress organizations, including the military and law enforcement. Corporations that include character-strength-building exercises in their employee-development training would reap the dual benefits of enhanced character and resilience. The US Army's resilience program, Comprehensive Soldier Fitness (CSF), incorporates these and other training protocols to achieve this goal among hundreds of thousands of soldiers each year.[9]

YOUTH SPORTS

Participation in organized sports, especially among children and teens, provides an opportunity to develop and shape character traits. As General Douglas MacArthur famously said, "On the fields of friendly strife are sown the seeds that on other days, on other fields will bear the fruits of victory."[10] General MacArthur's observation reflects the widely held belief that participation in sports not only strengthens the body but also strengthens character. At West Point this notion is so firmly entrenched that its football players prior to taking the field place their hands on a plaque reflecting the importance of sports in officer development. Attributed to General George C. Marshall, the quote on the plaque reads, "I want an officer for a secret and dangerous mission. I want a West Point football player." Implicit in this demand is the notion that football prepares officers to be physically tough and to possess character strengths of grit, determination, and bravery.

While this may be true for West Point football players training to be Army officers, a fair question may be whether organized sports are linked to character development in children. Certainly, parents of the millions of children enrolled in youth sports believe this to be true. But what have psychologists learned about the nexus between youth sports and character development? More and more psychological research points to the value of participation in sports in positive youth development.

Dr. Andrea Ettekal, a professor at Texas A&M University, has addressed the issue of sports and positive youth development among military children. As we have discussed previously, military children face special challenges, including frequent moves. Ettekal's research shows that participation in organized sports makes children feel that they matter, offers social support, presents opportunities to lead others, gives a feeling of belongingness, and builds self-efficacy.[11] Her work shows that sports build both performance character (grit, self-regulation, etc.) and moral character (integrity, fairness, empathy, loyalty, etc.).

While Ettekal acknowledges that sports can result in negative outcomes such as stress or aggressive behavior, if done right, they promote positive youth development. Some elements of doing it right include positive competition versus a win-at-all-costs attitude, recruiting coaches who emphasize and explicitly teach character development through their sport, educating parents to help their children understand the character lessons that sports provide, and playing for the right reasons, including challenge and fun, and for physical and mental health.[12]

Engaging in sports for fun has been addressed by Dr. Amanda Visek of George Washington University. Visek and her colleagues brainstormed with children to learn what the components of fun were from the children's perspective. The results are fascinating. On a cluster map, the researchers classified eighty-one determinates of fun into eleven more general fun factors. These eleven facets included positive coaching, team rituals, learning and improving, team friendships, and positive team dynamics.[13] Fun as a transient positive emotion (elation or emotional high) was not a primary determinant of fun in sports. Rather, aspects of sports that addressed engagement or meaning and purpose (trying hard, learning and improving) were principal contributors to fun in sports. This is congruent with findings from positive psychology that show that engagement and a sense of meaning and purpose in life are more important determinants to life satisfaction than simple, hedonic pleasures.

Visek's research also debunks several myths about sports participation in children. For example, winning was only ranked number forty out of the eighty-one determinants of fun. And smiling and goofing around are not reliable indicators of fun. Rather, children who appear focused and are developing their athletic skills are having more fun than those who joke around. Perhaps the most important debunked belief is the cultural notion that fun for girls lies in the social aspects of the game such as forming friendships, in contrast to boys, who are thought to derive fun from competition and skill development. Visek's research shows that contrary to popular belief, what is most fun for young athletes does not vary much by their sex, age, or level at which they play. School administrators, coaches, and parents would benefit from learning more about Visek's findings, and children would benefit if these findings were integrated into the design and management of youth sports.

Ettekal's and Visek's research is consistent with Duckworth's view that mindset, expert practice, and a supporting environment are critical in building character. Sports can contribute to all three of these factors. It fosters a positive mindset by allowing children to learn firsthand that they can improve at difficult tasks. Sports allow children to build both physical and social skills through expert practice. Duckworth emphasizes that expert practice—sometimes called deliberate practice—is not "fun" in the usual sense of the word. Rather, it is fun in the ways that Visek finds in her research. Duckworth's third component of character growth requires school administrators, coaches, and parents to craft a positive environment in which children may derive the positive benefits of sports.

Framing sports as an opportunity to build a growth mindset, to engage in challenging and difficult skill development, and to be part of a team with positive organizational values may begin to shape the type of character that General MacArthur and General Marshall had in mind when thinking about sports and character development in soldiers.[14]

FORMAL CURRICULA

The College Board recognizes the importance of character education as preparation for college and being a good citizen. Leaders of the College Board, known for administering the SAT, began considering which, of all the skills and knowledge they test, are most important for success in both college and life. Their answer, which may surprise you, is computer science and the US Constitution. So, the College Board updated and revamped their advanced placement courses that cover this material.[15]

Computer science may seem obvious, but why the US Constitution? According to Stefanie Sanford, chief of global policy and external relations for the College Board, appreciation for the role of character and citizenship in student success is increasing. With this in mind, the curriculum for the AP course in US Government and Politics must now include the study of passages from nine founding documents, including the Constitution, and of fifteen critical Supreme Court cases, each of which address one or more of the five freedoms included in the First Amendment— freedom of speech, freedom of religion, freedom of the press, freedom to assemble peaceably, and freedom to petition the government for a redress of grievances.

Sanford maintains that this in-depth study of the US Constitution builds character via direct knowledge of, and appreciation for, the moral virtue of justice. Specific strengths included in this moral virtue are citizenship, fairness, and leadership. By creating this AP curriculum, Sanford and her team at the College Board have created a systematic approach to enhancing the character strengths in young people that are needed for them to become productive students, leaders, and citizens.

LEADERSHIP OPPORTUNITIES

The third component of character building is providing leadership opportunities. In leading others, a person learns how his or her character influences others. In leading and influencing others, you must learn to use a variety of character strengths. Honesty, integrity, critical thinking, social intelligence, kindness, empathy, perspective, fairness, and a host of other character strengths are fundamental to effective leadership.

Early in life, in grades K–12, students are provided a variety of opportunities to lead and influence others. This may occur in the classroom, in school clubs, or in athletics. School-aged children may learn leadership through participating in extracurricular activities such as scouting. Many icons of leadership were involved in leadership activities at an early age.

West Point recognizes this through its admissions requirements. Prospective cadets are evaluated for academic potential through high school grades, class rank, and standardized test scores. Their physical potential is evaluated by their participation in sports and through a formal assessment of physical ability, called the Cadet Fitness Assessment. The third leg of the admissions triad is leadership potential. Applicants who have held leadership positions in clubs, have been the captain of a sports team, or have shown other evidence of leadership such as being an Eagle Scout are more likely to be admitted. West Point values these applicants because years of experience have demonstrated that such young people have not only honed leadership skills through practice, but they have also developed and sharpened their positive character traits.

Our advice for other organizations is to provide progressively more responsible leadership opportunities for their members. One S2S student pointed out that school leaders need to make sure that everyone is encouraged to pursue leadership opportunities, and not just the same kids over and over. We concur. Schools may develop a more focused approach to this, to ensure all students receive these opportunities. Corporations may find innovative ways to provide leadership opportunities to as many employees as possible. A promising nonmanagement-level employee may benefit from being assigned as team leader to tackle an important task. Systematically rotating short-term leader assignments will strengthen the workforce by sharpening leadership and attendant character strengths across more workers.

DEVELOPING LEADERS OF CHARACTER: THE WEST POINT LEADER DEVELOPMENT SYSTEM

In 1802 West Point began as a military training academy focused on basic engineering and soldier skills. In the twenty-first century it has become a comprehensive undergraduate institution with academic majors ranging from engineering, math, and science to the humanities and social sciences. As part of this evolution, West Point has come to emphasize aspects of character that go beyond the honor code and to reinforce its credo of Duty, Honor, Country.

Those who educate, train, and develop cadets understand the overriding importance of character in officer development. Over the past few years, West Point refined its leader development program to focus more directly on character. The desired character traits it seeks to cultivate in cadets span the breadth of the head, heart, and gut strengths discussed in this book.

Cadets coming to West Point are nominated by their congressional representative or senator, ensuring that future Army leaders represent all of America. The cadets come to West Point with a set of values developed from the communities they grew up in, values influenced by their home, their school, teams they played on, and other community institutions of which they were a part. West Point's values are mentioned in its mission statement as duty, honor, and country, and its leader development program aims to internalize these values so that they are part of every graduate's essence. Thus when graduates are faced with a potentially compromising situation, their natural response is based on these internalized values. The cup-of-coffee analogy mentioned earlier is what West Point expects its graduates to aspire to.

Cadets come to West Point from all walks of life, and while the academy hopes they enter with the values of duty, honor, and country, this is not always the case. To transform a cadet candidate into a graduate who is a leader of character, the West

Point Leader Development System (WPLDS) was created so that cadets are immersed in it from the day they arrive until the day they graduate.

The WPLDS is designed to promote three important leader-of-character outcomes—to live honorably, lead honorably, and demonstrate excellence. To "live honorably," a West Point graduate is expected to take morally and ethically appropriate actions regardless of personal consequences, exhibit empathy and respect toward all individuals, and act with the proper decorum in all environments. To "lead honorably," a West Point graduate is expected to anticipate and solve complex problems, influence others to accomplish the mission in accordance with Army values, include and develop others, and enforce standards. To "demonstrate excellence," a West Point graduate is expected to pursue intellectual, military, and physical expertise, make sound and timely decisions, communicate and interact with others effectively, and seek and reflect on feedback.[16]

To develop each cadet into a leader, four formal programs each focus on character growth. The first program focuses on the cadet's intellectual development within the academic program. Each year, West Point enjoys top rankings among public colleges across the country. In 2017, *Forbes* ranked it the number one public college, and in 2016, *US News & World Report* ranked it number two. West Point's academic program is guided by the Thayer method of instruction, where cadets are responsible for their own learning and lecturing is rare. In a classroom that is more like a seminar where faculty members are facilitators, the unique learning experience enables the development of intellectual agility, adaptability, and thought diversity. Each year, twenty-five to thirty cadets are awarded nationally competitive scholarships (Rhodes, Draper, Marshall, Fulbright, East-West, and Lincoln Labs, among others).

In their four years at West Point, cadets complete three academic courses that specifically address leadership theory and practice. All plebes complete a course titled General Psychology for Leaders. The course covers the same topics included in psychology courses at any university, but frames the concepts in relevance to leadership. The course is taken during the plebe year because cadets can build on this knowledge outside the classroom as they are given greater and more diverse leadership opportunities at West Point. In the junior (cow) year, all cadets enroll in a course called Military Leadership. This course covers theories and good practices of leadership. During summer training following the junior year, cadets serve as leaders during field training exercises, giving them the opportunity to apply what they learned in both the plebe- and junior-level courses. Finally, during the senior year, cadets complete a course entitled Officership. This course, taught by combat-seasoned Army officers, synthesizes what cadets have learned their first three years at West Point about leadership, both from the classroom and in the field. Altogether, these academic experiences prepare cadets to be effective Army leaders.

The second WPLDS program is in the cadet's military development. Most of the military training occurs in the summer and includes everything from rifle marksmanship to land navigation, and practice leading a twenty-to-thirty-person platoon in the active Army for a month or more. The first summer is cadet basic training, a program designed to transition a civilian into a cadet.

Its purpose is to teach basic cadet military skills, and to teach one of the most fundamental lessons of leadership: how to be a good follower and team member. The second summer expands the cadet's individual and collective military training and offers the opportunity to attend a military school, such as Airborne training at Fort Benning, Georgia, or Mountain Training at Fort Greely, Alaska. The third summer places cadets in leadership positions over other cadets who are executing their freshman and sophomore military training. In these positions, cadets practice leadership, succeed and fail, receive feedback, and grow as a result. During the final summer, some cadets are placed in senior cadet leadership positions, and each cadet also travels to an active-duty Army post to assist with the leadership of an operational Army platoon. This enables cadets to experience firsthand what they'll be doing as a newly commissioned officer in the Army, after graduation. Cadets also take military-science courses during the academic year. These are designed to augment the summer military training and to enable cadets to study and reflect on previous experiences and training. In these classes, they learn from the combat experiences of their instructors.

The third WPLDS component is the physical program, which includes academic courses (survival swimming, boxing, military movement), annual physical tests (both the Army's Physical Fitness Test as well as West Point's challenging Indoor Obstacle Course Test), and participation in a team sport at the intramural, club, or intercollegiate level. Many leadership lessons are to be learned in a tough physical program. After Douglas MacArthur's World War I experience, he felt that physical acumen was essential to effective leadership. When he became the West Point superintendent in 1919, he coined the phrase "Every cadet an athlete." The physical program is designed to instill cadets with the character strengths of grit, determination, and confidence.

Leading the nation's sons and daughters in the most challenging circumstances requires officers who lead from the front and who share hardships. The physical program is designed to create those challenging circumstances so that cadets will develop the physical skills, confidence, and grit necessary to lead within this crucible experience. For example, boxing teaches a combat skill and also enables cadets to come face-to-face with fear and overcome it. The physical program nurtures the development of tenacity, resilience, grit, discipline, and perseverance.

The fourth component of WPLDS is the character-development program. Character development occurs within a culture that embraces a character ethic, which is a set of principles defined by its values and standards of behavior. Fundamental to this ethic is the Cadet Honor Code, which states, "A cadet will not lie, cheat, or steal or tolerate those who do." The ethic goes much further than not lying, cheating, or stealing. It also includes "honorable living," which is the internalization of both cadet and Army values, so that they become part of a soldier's essence. Living honorably is not something that only cadets aspire to; it also defines the behavior of the entire community, including instructors, staff, faculty, and anyone who engages with cadets. "All members of the community are expected to model both character and leadership, and by living and working within this community of models, character and leadership are built, reinforced, and refined."[17]

Going back to the Cadet Honor Code, it is important to highlight the "no tolerance clause" because that is what sets this code apart from other honor codes. Since trust is a function of character and competence, character defects among military leaders, especially senior military leaders, erode the trust between the nation and its military. To maintain the high standards that leaders of character require, the profession of arms must hold itself accountable. The profession must not forfeit this to someone else, and therefore each soldier must take full responsibility to hold him- or herself and others accountable. In this way, "nontoleration" becomes a critical component to the responsibilities leaders of character have within the profession of arms.

The "Cadet Creed" articulates these values. New cadets are required to memorize this creed during their first summer at West Point. Additional references to character and values are found in the "Cadet Alma Mater" and "The Corps," a poem that emphasizes this same set of values.[18]

CADET CREED

As a future officer,
I am committed to the values of Duty, Honor, Country
I am an aspiring member of the Army profession, dedicated
To serve and earn the trust of the American People.
It is my duty to maintain the honor of the Corps.
I will live above the common level of life, and have the
Courage to choose the harder right over the easier wrong.
I will live with honor and integrity, scorn injustice,
And always confront substandard behavior.

I will persevere through adversity and recover from failure.
I will embrace the warrior Ethos, and pursue excellence
In everything I do.
I am a future officer and member of the Long Gray Line.

Self-reflectional feedback is critical to a cadet's character development. What does my action (behavior or performance) say about me as a developing officer? What have I learned about officership and leadership? What have my experiences revealed about my strengths and weaknesses? And what do I need to do in the future to further my development? Every day at West Point provides opportunities for cadets to receive feedback. These lessons are reinforced by mentors who help the cadets understand their experiences.

Several programs are designed to encourage behavioral change so that cadet behavior becomes consistent with the values of duty, honor, and country. One program, called Leader Challenge, brings West Point graduates with combat experience back to the academy to meet with cadets in small groups, and to discuss in detail some of the ethical issues they faced on the battlefield.

The cadets also participate in small-group discussions on honor, respect, and sexual relations (designed to address sexual harassment and assault issues). The key to these dialogues is to create introspection and reflection. These sessions allow open and honest dialogue, with a peer facilitator. This becomes the engine that drives behavioral change.

Cadets sometimes make mistakes stemming from character failures. This must be addressed, both to hold cadets accountable, and to provide an opportunity for cadets to learn and grow. To facilitate growth in these situations, cadets may find themselves in a Special Leader Development Program. This intensive, reflective one-on-one program with a mentor includes projects, research, and instruction. Key to its success is the mentor-led reflection component, which drives an open, candid, and honest appreciation of the cadet's motives and behavior, and how these relate to their performance within the profession. Most cadets who complete this program are stronger in character than most of their peers, including those who never had a character issue in the first place.

Not only is the West Point Leader Development System designed to develop a cadet's intellectual, military, physical, and character skills, but it is also designed to develop the cadet's leadership abilities, first as a follower and then as a leader. In everything cadets do, they find themselves living, engaging, leading, following, and studying within a military organization that includes both cadet leaders and followers. Cadets are assigned to numerous leadership positions within the organization, and by executing their duties, they learn the trials and rewards of both followership and leadership.

THE MAGIC OF THE WEST POINT LEADER DEVELOPMENT SYSTEM

The West Point Leader Development System works because it includes all three components of character development. From the day new cadets arrive at West Point to when they graduate and are commissioned as second lieutenants in the Army, they are given constant mentoring. A notable feature of WPLDS is that the responsibility to mentor and develop cadets belongs to every single person at West Point who has contact with them.

Military trainers and professors are obvious examples. Each cadet also has a sponsor, often a staff or a faculty member, who opens his or her home to the cadet during the cadet's entire West Point experience. Sponsors provide cadets a place to relax, get away from the daily grind, enjoy a meal at a family table rather than the mess hall, or to wash their clothes. Along the way, the sponsor models the values and character strengths needed to be an Army officer. Clubs and sports teams offer mentors as well.

West Point's skill-building curricula are integrated with hands-on leadership opportunities in military training, sports, and other activities. Plebes study General Psychology for Leaders and are able to practice what they learn in their daily lives at West Point. Juniors take the leadership lessons learned in Military Leadership to the field the following summer, where they can discover what works or does not work for them. This coordination between classroom learning and hands-on learning is what makes WPLDS effective.

The third piece of character development—opportunity to lead—is emphasized throughout a cadet's time at West Point. In their plebe year, cadets learn to be good followers. During their second year, every cadet serves as a team leader, responsible for the development of his or her own plebe. During the third and fourth years at West Point, cadets serve in a variety of leadership positions at progressively more responsible levels. Positions are rotated so that all cadets have the experience of being a leader. These positions include commanding a company, regiment, or the Corps, or serving as first sergeant during the regular academic year. Summer field training provides a myriad of other leadership opportunities. Throw in clubs and inter-collegiate and intramural sports, and every cadet will have had multiple opportunities to develop leadership skills and character by the time the cadet receives an Army commission.

WHAT CAN YOU LEARN FROM THE WEST POINT LEADER DEVELOPMENT SYSTEM?

Your organization may not have the resources to fully implement a West Point Leader Development System type of approach to leader and character development. But leadership and character are critically important to all organizations, large or small, civilian or military, public service or for-profit. Corporations, schools, and other organizations may use WPLDS as a model for how to approach the three elements of character development. Although it may be done differently from West Point, a culture of mentorship can be nurtured in any organization. Similarly, organizations may adopt a variety of strategies for educating their members about character and its relationship with leadership. Finally, organizations may devise ways to increase leadership opportunities at all levels within the organization.

Taken as a whole, WPLDS and the other examples of leader and character development we have presented may serve as a blueprint for building high-character organizations. By taking the seeds you have so carefully selected (good people), planted in fertile ground (a value-driven culture), and carefully cultivated (nurtured in character), you will enjoy a bountiful harvest through increased organizational effectiveness that is sustainable.

9

THE CRUCIBLE OF LIFE EXPERIENCES

That which does not kill us only makes us stronger.

—FRIEDRICH NIETZSCHE[1]

To paraphrase Benjamin Franklin, the two certainties of life are death and taxes.[2] To this we may add a third certainty—adversity. In living we inevitably encounter adversity and challenges. Sometimes these come about unexpectedly and are beyond our control. Others may be predictable but unavoidable. Adverse events have the potential to crush our sense of well-being. Or we may respond with resilience and growth, learning from these crucibles of life, emerging stronger for the experience, as Nietzsche suggests.

Character helps us deal with adversity, but we are also shaped by it. How we respond to life's challenges, whether with despair and pathology, or with hope and growth, depends in no small part on our character. Here we explore how individuals respond to the tough situations, and the role of character in determining our response, either positive or negative. We examine what you, as an individual, may do to prepare yourself for a positive and adaptive trajectory in the face of adversity, as well as the role of leaders and organizations in facilitating a positive response.

FAILURES AND BROKEN BONES

When General Caslen was a cadet in the 1970s, cadets who violated the honor code—whether during the first few days or the last week of their four West Point years—were immediately dismissed from the academy. West Point has a history of periodic honor scandals, and during the 1976 scandal, the secretary of the army created the Borman Commission (chaired by one of West Point's renowned graduates, Frank Borman, a NASA astronaut), with the mission of recommending changes within the honor system. The Borman Commission did not recommend any changes to the honor code itself as it understood the importance of honor within character, and the importance of character in building trust within the profession of arms. But it did recommend that the superintendent be granted the authority to grant "discretion" to cadets who violated the code.

The discretion policy holds a cadet who violates the honor code accountable for the offense, but allows the cadet to enter a mentorship program rather than being automatically dismissed. In most cases, a cadet must repeat a portion of his or her time at West Point—a semester or an entire year—so the cadet has more time to internalize the honor ethic. One innovative and highly effective accountability option is to place the cadet in the Army as an enlisted soldier for a year or two, then allow the cadet to reapply to West Point, finish from where he or she left off, and graduate and receive a commission as a second lieutenant. A disciplined cadet's Army-officer mentor will lead a program lasting between six and twelve months and requiring significant reflection and introspection. The program also includes projects and classes designed to contribute to the cadet's understanding of the honor ethic, and how to move toward being a graduate of character.

In an earlier assignment as commandant of cadets at West Point, Caslen observed the summer military training program at Camp Buckner—a local West Point training area where sophomore cadets learn basic military skills, led by cadets of the senior class. During this visit Caslen was briefed by the senior cadet commander, who was responsible for the summer military development training of the entire sophomore class. Caslen had just left the Pentagon, where he served on the Joint Staff and had observed numerous professional military briefings at the most senior levels of the Department of Defense. He was extremely impressed by the professionalism of the briefing given by the senior cadet commander. Caslen knew the sophomore class was in good hands. As the summer progressed, he was not disappointed. The leadership this cadet provided was outstanding.

Later in the summer, Caslen learned that this senior cadet commander had committed an honor violation during her freshman year and the superintendent had granted discretion rather than expelling her from West Point. She was placed in a mentorship program and required to take an additional semester at West Point. During Caslen's earlier experiences at West Point, any honor violation resulted in immediate and uncompromising separation. When he returned to be West Point's commandant of cadets, while aware of the new discretion policy, he had doubts it was good for the cadets and for the institution. But after observing and getting to know this cadet commander, he saw the wisdom in providing a cadet the opportunity to recover from his or her character setback. What if this particular cadet had been separated from West Point? The academy, the Army, and the nation would be without this incredibly gifted and talented cadet.

Effective leadership requires more than competence. Effective leadership also requires great character, but sometimes character must be developed. The mentorship program comes into play here.

If you break a bone and it heals correctly, the bone becomes stronger where the break occurred than it was before the break. This is equally applicable to the recovery from a character setback. A cadet may commit an honor violation and enter a mentorship program and, through reflection and introspection with a mentor, exit with character as strong or stronger than a cadet who has never committed an honor violation. Over the seven years General Caslen served at West Point as commandant of cadets and later as superintendent, overseeing the cadet honor code violations, he became a strong supporter of the mentorship program. It is important to hold cadets accountable for their offenses, even if accountability results in extra time at West Point, leaving West Point and going into the Army for a couple years before reentering West Point, or leaving West Point altogether. Holding cadets accountable is also important for their learning development, as well as to send an important message to the Corps of Cadets. Caslen saw that the discretion and honor mentorship programs were extremely effective. Indeed, the strongest cadet advocates for the honor program were cadets who had committed an honor violation and then successfully completed a program.

Cadets do not take discretion lightly. No cadet would intentionally misbehave thinking that, if caught, discretion would be granted rather than dismissal. First, discretion is just that. A cadet can be retained and entered into the honor mentorship program only at the superintendent's discretion. Separation from the academy remains an option and is invoked when circumstances warrant it. Second, discretion when granted is not a free "do-over." Besides being enrolled in a lengthy and demanding honor mentorship program, the offending cadet is usually required to repeat a semester and often an entire year at West Point, turning the typical forty-seven-month experience into something much longer. Additionally, the embarrassment and shame of being found guilty of an honor violation are significant. The motivation for cadets to rectify their misdeeds and once again to be held in full esteem by their officers, peers, and subordinates is high.

The experience of failure followed by systematic mentoring enables personal growth in cadets. This growth stems from an organizational policy that recognizes people may learn from failure and end up stronger because of it.

TRAUMA, ADVERSITY, CHALLENGE, AND PERSONAL GROWTH

Psychologists are learning more about the ways in which difficult life experiences may produce personal growth. You don't hear much about this in the media. The saying, especially in television news, is "If it bleeds, it leads." This is certainly true about the common narrative of the impact of trauma, adversity, and challenge. Following the attacks of 9/11 and during the height of the wars in Iraq and Afghanistan, the media were quick to report on stories of soldiers suffering from post-traumatic stress disorder (PTSD). PTSD and other psychological problems including depression, anxiety, and substance abuse may follow combat, and they must be addressed with medical and psychological treatment. But 85 percent of combat veterans do not experience these pathologies, and many report growth in various aspects of their lives, including character strengths.

A few years ago, Dr. Matthews spoke to a group of army leaders who were preparing to deploy to Iraq for a combat tour. Almost all of these leaders had been deployed at least once and had experienced firsthand the challenges and horrors of combat. Knowing he was a psychologist, they expected to hear Dr. Matthews expound on PTSD and other combat-stress-related pathologies. Instead, the theme of the talk that day was on the full range of psychological responses that soldiers experience during and after combat, ranging from pathology to resilience to personal growth.

The response to this talk was overwhelming. About halfway through Dr. Matthews's comments, the commanding general interrupted to offer his support for research Matthews was planning on the effects of combat on soldier performance and adjustment and directed the brigade surgeon to assist in any way needed. After the talk, many soldiers approached Matthews to share their own stories of combat. They had experienced the trauma and adversity of war firsthand, but their personal narratives were more of resilience and growth, not pathology. Many had suffered from their experiences, but they also saw themselves as emerging from their combat tours as stronger and more adaptable. This theme of resilience and growth spoke to their own narratives of combat.

Perhaps the noted Civil War officer Joshua Lawrence Chamberlain said it best: "War is for the participants a test of character. It makes bad men worse and good men better."[3] It is up to psychology to develop a more precise understanding of just what enables us to respond successfully to the inevitable challenges we all, military or civilian, must face in our lives.

FOUR OUTCOMES OF ADVERSITY

Understanding how people may react to trauma, adversity, and challenge is important in grasping why difficult life experiences may frequently result in personal growth, including strengthening certain character traits. Figure 9.1 shows four trajectories people may experience following a challenging life experience.[4] Good functioning, depicted on the vertical axis, reflects emotional well-being, good social relationships, and positive character. Time is on the horizontal axis. The impact of adversity, broadly defined, is depicted by the change in functioning following the adverse event.

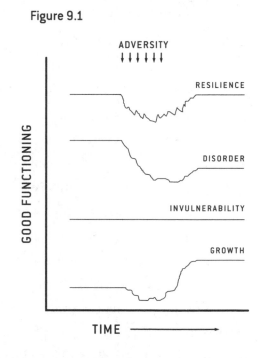

Figure 9.1

RESILIENCE

Resilience occurs when, following a period of adversity, a person's adjustment returns to baseline. Divorce, a major illness, or the death of a loved one negatively impacts one's quality of life for a time. But once the challenge is worked through, adjustment returns to normal. If this occurs, then one is said to be resilient. In a divorce, the character strength of capacity to love may temporarily be diminished, but with time it returns to normal.

Resiliency may be thought of as a form of fitness. For highly stressful or dangerous situations, establishing resilience-training programs is essential to maintaining individual and organizational effectiveness. A good example comes from the US Army. By 2008, the Army had been at war for seven years, first in Afghanistan and then also in Iraq. Compared to the Army in World War II and even Vietnam, the all-volunteer Army of the twenty-first century is relatively small. And unlike in those previous wars, where men were drafted into the service and often completed only a single tour of active duty before returning to civilian life, soldiers in today's Army are more likely to serve multiple tours, and many serve full careers. Thus the consequence of a smaller, all-volunteer Army is that soldiers are repeatedly deployed to combat.

With combat tours ranging in length from seven to twelve months or longer, by 2008 many soldiers had experienced two or more combat deployments, with no end in sight. The constant cycle of training for deployment, months in combat, and retraining for the next deployment was taking a toll on the psychological well-being of soldiers. Military suicide rates nearly doubled from 2001 to 2011 and remained high.[5] Psychological problems such as depression and PTSD were increasing, and reports from Army posts suggested that conduct issues of excessive drinking and family violence were dramatically increasing.

The army chief of staff at that time, General George Casey, sought the counsel of Army and civilian behavioral-health experts to devise a plan to improve resilience among soldiers. From these discussions, the Army's Comprehensive Soldier Fitness (CSF) program was born. Instead of hiring more clinical psychologists and psychiatrists to treat soldiers who were suffering from combat stress, CSF was designed to train soldiers in resilience coping skills prior to combat. Preventing disorders and promoting resilience is the focus of CSF.[6]

Resilience is a general term, and CSF breaks it down into four categories: emotional, social, family, and spiritual. The term *fitness* is used rather than resilience because soldiers relate better to this term. If you can make your body more fit through physical training, then by analogy you can increase your emotional, social, family, and spiritual fitness by training those skills.

Training half a million solders in resilience is no small undertaking. To accomplish it, the CSF program trains thousands of midlevel noncommissioned officers (NCOs) and certifies them as master resilience trainers. Coupled with a variety of online resilience assessments and training modules, CSF has trained hundreds of thousands of soldiers in resilience skills over the past ten years. Systematic assessments of the effectiveness of CSF have been promising, and it continues to be the primary resilience-training program in the Army.[7] The US Air Force and Navy have developed similar training programs, as have the military of other nations.[8]

The importance of resilience-training programs to law enforcement, first responders, and other high-stakes organizations should be clear. Resilience training improves individual performance as well as that of the organization. In a large organization such as the Army, this has substantial dollar savings, in addition to enhancing the well-being and adjustment of soldiers. In an Army of half a million soldiers, reducing the psychological casualties from 15 percent to 10 percent would equate to twenty-five thousand soldiers who would be psychologically healthy and capable of better performance of their duties. This would equal two or more Army divisions and would greatly increase the combat effectiveness of the force. Even in a smaller organization such as a police department of a thousand sworn officers, a similar reduction in the disorder trajectory would yield fifty more officers fully available for patrol and other duties.

DISORDER

Disorder occurs when adversity results in a negative change in adjustment, and the individual does not recover over time. Instead of showing the resilient trajectory, the individual continues to be depressed, anxious, or have PTSD. People who have divorced may find that their character strengths of humanity such as the capacity to love are permanently impaired. Trust, once compromised, is difficult to recover. One does not have to look far for examples of disorder. Environmental stress is linked to a variety of psychological disorders, ranging from anxiety to depression.

However, disorder accounts for only about 15 percent of adversity-linked trajectories. And adversity alone may not result in the disorder trajectory. Genetic predisposition and life experiences prior to encountering the adversity may also contribute to this trajectory.

Firefighters are exposed to many traumatic events, such as rescuing badly burned victims, retrieving the remains of the deceased, and a host of others. One might expect firefighters, given this exposure, to show a high incidence of PTSD and related

disorders. But this is not the case. In one study of 142 firefighters, only 4.2 percent were diagnosed with PTSD, depression,
anxiety, or alcohol-linked problems. A review of the psychological literature shows an inconsistent link between trauma and
stress-related disorders among firefighters. Instead, mitigating
factors such as social support and coping skills predicted symptoms better than adversity or stress.[9] Similar findings are typical
in other high-stress occupations.[10]

INVULNERABILITY

Invulnerability occurs when the person endures the adverse
event with no apparent change. Using our example of divorce
and the character strength of capacity to love, such a person
would maintain their capacity to love others despite the stress of
the divorce. They soldier on largely unaffected by their ordeal.

An example of invulnerability is that of retired Army brigadier general Rhonda Cornum. On February 27, 1991, Cornum
(then a major) was a flight surgeon on board an Army medical
helicopter in Iraq, supporting Operation Desert Storm. She and
her crew were dispatched to rescue a downed fighter pilot, but
were themselves shot down by enemy fire. Badly wounded with
a bullet wound to her back and suffering several broken bones,
Cornum was taken prisoner by enemy forces. Five of her Army
teammates lost their lives in this engagement. Cornum was sexually assaulted by her captors and subjected to a mock execution. In great pain and fearing for her life and those of other
prisoners, she endured significant adversity as well as trauma
until she was repatriated eight days later.

In 1992, the book *She Went to War* was published.[11] In this book Cornum relates her experiences surrounding the mission, her time as a prisoner of war, her repatriation, and her return to her family and normal Army duties. It is a fascinating account of what goes through one's mind during and after this sort of experience. In the closing chapter, Cornum talks about the after-effects on her adjustment and life. For the most part, she emphasizes that, while the experience was extremely challenging, it did not radically impact her, good or bad, subsequently. "People have asked how I am different or how the experience changed me, and I have to say that I don't think I've had any profound changes."[12]

Why was Cornum invulnerable to her experiences with adversity? First, her profession provided meaning and purpose to her life. She had much to live for, wanting to help her fellow captives and to continue serving and helping others afterward. Second, she was physically and emotionally fit going into her ordeal. Coupled with effective coping skills, this added to her resilience. And last, but of great importance, she had both strong family support and the strong support of her fellow soldiers. Had one or more of these elements been missing, she might have shown the disorder trajectory. As seen with firefighters, social support and coping skills mitigate negative outcomes.

When it comes to character, Cornum recognizes that her experience reinforced certain positive character traits. Gratitude, in particular, grew. "Being a patient for the first time taught me some personal lessons about medicine and being a doctor. I will never again underestimate the contributions of nurses, physical therapists, and other staff."[13] Interestingly, Cornum's sense of empathy for some patients may have been diminished! "I will probably be less tolerant of a patient who feels sorry for himself.

I have never liked whining. Now I am absolutely sure that whining does no good and might even slow the healing process."[14] She is one tough customer, but one that any of us would love to have as our physician.

GROWTH

Growth occurs when a person becomes stronger emotionally, builds better social relationships, or develops stronger character strengths as a result of a challenging experience. A divorced person may come to have an even greater capacity to love and be loved.

Psychological research shows that certain character strengths may grow following trauma from being assaulted, living through a natural disaster, or surviving a deadly disease. Some people who have these experiences show increases in a wide variety of character strengths, including spirituality, gratitude, and kindness, to name a few.[15] We saw earlier that adversity is linked to increases in strengths of the heart—gratitude and capacity to love—among combat leaders. In this same study, Matthews also found that the crucible of combat was associated with increases in additional strengths, specifically teamwork, bravery, and honesty.[16] Collectively, adversity may produce character growth across the six moral virtues.

We believe that post-traumatic growth is a more common outcome than disorder. You likely know people who have overcome a significant illness or experienced another major traumatic experience in life. Ask them how their lives changed as a result of their experience. They may tell you they are a better person as a consequence of their experiences, at least in part.

IMPACTING THE TRAJECTORY

The four trajectories show that we don't all respond the same way to adversity. Several factors influence the path that an individual will follow.

PREVIOUS LIFE EXPERIENCES

Our life stories are different. We learn to respond to life events in different ways. Learning to respond to frustration, blocked goals, and adversity are important life lessons. The famous psychologist B. F. Skinner in his utopian novel, *Walden Two,* described a futuristic society where children were systematically raised using principles of behaviorism to produce a well-adjusted child and ultimately a higher-functioning, pro-social society.[17] Principles of positive reinforcement, negative reinforcement, and punishment were used to shape children's behavior. Skinner recognized that adversity and challenge are unavoidable in life and included planned and systematic exposure to such events during childhood training. This, Skinner thought, would allow adults to more effectively work through and cope with such events.

While most psychologists disagree with Skinner's behavioristic model of child development, they do agree that learning to cope with and adapt to frustration is important to stable adjustment in adulthood. You probably don't need psychologists to tell you this. You have seen what happens to children who are always pampered and overly protected by their caregivers. Youth sports are often organized so that everyone wins a ribbon or a trophy—there are no losers. When, inevitably, such children encounter significant obstacles, they are often unprepared to deal with them. Frustration and anger may spiral into disorder, and their worst character traits are activated.

The character strengths you bring to the adverse situation will in no small measure affect how you respond. Parents, schools, religious institutions, sports, and other activities, such as scouting or clubs, collectively shape our character. Even as adults you can learn more about your own character strengths and practice using them to overcome obstacles.

GENETICS AND BIOLOGY

Human behavior is complex, to say the least. Genetics and biology contribute to who we are and how we respond to stress and adversity. People differ in basic temperament. Some are shy and withdrawn from childhood on, and others are extroverted. To some extent, this wiring influences which trajectory a person will take in the face of adversity. Harvard psychologist Jerome Kagan spent much of his career studying the link between the temperament of infants and their later temperament as adults. While adolescent and adult temperaments are modified by environmental factors, Kagan found that infants classified as "difficult" in temperament were more likely to get into trouble as teens than infants classified as "easy."[18]

SOCIAL SUPPORT

In adversity, going it alone is never a good thing. Rhonda Cornum benefited after her ordeal as a prisoner of war from the strong social support she had from her family and, importantly, from her fellow soldiers. Social support is a protective factor for all of us when facing adversity.

For people employed in high-risk settings, sometimes the social support offered by the work group or team may be more important even than family support. Highly cohesive teams provide a buffer for the stress, anger, and pain that soldiers, law enforcement officers, firefighters, and others experience as part of their jobs. Sadly, some of their experiences may be too horrible to share with a "civilian," even a spouse or other loved one. Only others who have shared the experience can provide the understanding and advice needed to recover properly. Members of highly skilled and cohesive military units such as the Green Berets are significantly less likely to show the disorder trajectory.[19]

While cohesive, close-knit teams may inoculate soldiers and others in high-risk occupations against the disorder trajectory, when the individual leaves the team, vulnerability may increase. Sebastian Junger's books *Tribe* and *War* capture this dynamic well. Junger describes how, when separated from their team by retirement or reassignment, soldiers are especially at risk for depression and other pathologies associated with the disorder trajectory.[20] This is a significant issue for military reservists who, after being called to active duty and deploying to combat, return to their civilian lives rather than staying with their military unit. This isolation from comrades in arms removes an essential safety net and may increase the incidence of suicide, depression, and other psychological maladies. Veterans organizations worldwide provide important social support to veterans that may be unavailable elsewhere. In the United States, the American Legion and Veterans of Foreign Wars attract large numbers of members.

We have intentionally used several different terms in this chapter to describe difficult events. Trauma, adversity, and challenge are not the same things. *Trauma* includes direct experience with situations or events that threaten a person's life or well-being or make the person cognizant of his or her mortality and vulnerability. Traumatic events are discrete, being specific and short lasting. Soldiers or law enforcement officers who take a life in the line of duty experience trauma. Being badly injured in a car accident or by a violent crime is traumatic.

Adversity equates to severe difficulty and may extend over longer periods. Often, adversity and trauma can occur together, but not necessarily. In our experience, all combat deployments involve adversity, but many soldiers do not experience trauma. For combat deployments, adversity comes from months of separation from one's family, living under constant threat of attack, and other deprivations and uncertainties from living in a high-threat zone for months at a time. While disease and injury may be traumatic, over the long haul the adversity of aches, pains, discomfort, seemingly endless medical appointments, and an uncertain outcome may end in disorder, resilience, invulnerability, or personal growth.

Challenge refers to obstacles that block or interfere with the attainment of important goals. A mother working full-time and raising young children may want to complete a college degree. This can be done, but many obstacles have to be overcome. Character strengths from the six moral virtues are helpful in overcoming challenges, even though challenges are not necessarily life-threatening.

Trauma, adversity, and challenges may affect us in different ways. Also, the duration and intensity of each may vary. Cornum's prisoner-of-war experience was eight days. Barry Bridger, whose story we told earlier, was a prisoner for more than six years. A dose-response curve is at work here—the greater the adversity, the more the impact of its effects.

MAKING THE BEST OF THE CRUCIBLE OF LIFE EXPERIENCES
AN OUNCE OF PREPARATION IS WORTH A POUND OF CURE

Nietzsche may have overstated his point, but life does deal difficult hands. How can you improve the chances of responding with a favorable trajectory? You personally can do things to optimize the outcome, and organizations may also do things to optimize the trajectories for their members.

Let's start with what you can do. Psychologists have found the characteristic of hardiness to be consistently linked to positive outcomes in the face of adversity.[21] Hardy individuals are like hardy plants or trees. They can subsist and even flourish in and through harsh conditions. Hardiness breaks down into three components: commitment, challenge, and control.

Commitment refers to seeing things through to their end no matter how difficult the task. It is similar to the idea of grit. *Persistence* or *perseverance* are other words that describe commitment. Persistence is one of the twenty-four character strengths included in the Values-in-Action Inventory of Strengths and is a skill that can be honed. Parents should think of creative ways of nurturing and developing commitment in their children. As adults, practicing persistence and commitment at work and in other contexts will allow you to build this skill for when you really need it.

Challenge is how we frame obstacles to desired goals. Viewing an obstacle as a threat is a negative reaction. This raises anxiety and may promote avoidance behavior, making it more difficult to persevere. Instead, in framing an obstacle as a challenge we see it as a way to learn new skills or to employ existing skills. This leads to a sense of competence and satisfaction.

Not all challenges are outside us. Some come from within based on personal limitations. What would you do if you had a lifelong and burning desire to be a law enforcement officer but were born with only a partial left arm? Many of us would concede that the limitations from this would prevent us from achieving this goal. We would frame the obstacle as a threat and give up. Maybe you would seek a career in something related to law enforcement, such as being a communications officer or crime-lab expert, but you would not even try to be a street officer.

Well, meet Joseph "Joe" Presley, a young man who was born with a partial left arm. The son of a convicted bank robber, Joe wanted to follow a path on the other side of the law than his father (now deceased). Looking into law enforcement career options, he received little encouragement from police chiefs and other law enforcement agencies. The more he was told he could not do it, the more he wanted to try. Joe persevered and ultimately graduated from the Law Enforcement Academy at Drury University. This rigorous 750-hour course of study certifies its graduates as eligible to be hired as law enforcement officers in Missouri. "We saw that he wanted to overcome any obstacle that he might have, and that is a good trait in any recruit. You have to work out problems. He'd done a lot of work to prepare. He'd made a commitment," commented Tony Bowers, the director of the academy.[22]

To qualify for his degree, Joe had to complete the same physical requirements as fully abled candidates, including self-defense and controlling or restraining prisoners. The sports he had engaged in previously helped him with strength and endurance, but he had to be creative to complete some tasks—such as climbing a rope, a task difficult enough for those of us with two fully functioning arms and hands. Try climbing a rope with only one hand. Joe figured out a way to use his good hand, grasp the rope under the armpit of his partial left arm, then use his legs for additional leverage to propel him to the top of the climb.

Did Presley's grit and determination pay off? You bet it did! Presley was offered a job as a full-time deputy with the Stone County, Missouri, Sheriff's Office in August of 2019. "It feels emotional, especially when he handed me my badge. It was kind of surreal time," Presley said. You can also bet that the Stone County Sheriff's Office is getting one fired-up and motivated new employee.[23]

Joe Presley shows how framing an obstacle as a challenge versus a threat is instrumental to persevering in difficult tasks. What character strengths did he utilize? Take a few minutes and review the twenty-four character strengths presented in chapter 1. Circle the ones Joe used. Then think about how you could do the same to overcome obstacles in your life.

Control. One of the most consistent findings in psychology is that a sense of control over one's fate is linked to positive adjustment. Sometimes this is called locus of control. People high in locus of control believe they have self-agency in achieving goals and dealing with adversity. They think of active ways to solve problems and to overcome obstacles. In contrast, people low in locus of control believe that chance or fate, or powers and circumstances beyond their control, determine life outcomes.

Years of research in settings ranging from soldiers in combat to sales personnel show that people with a high locus of control are more successful and less prone to negative trajectories in the face of adversity.[24] The belief that your own actions can lead to success is fundamental to good adjustment.

Hardy West Point cadets outperform less hardy cadets in academics, leadership, and physical fitness. One study found that cadets tested for hardiness shortly after arriving at West Point were rated as better leaders *seven years later* when they were in the active-duty Army, many of them in combat jobs.[25]

Cultivate character strengths that build commitment, challenge, and control. Love of learning, persistence, self-regulation, and optimism are character strengths that you may employ to achieve these ends.

DEVELOP AN ACTION PLAN FOR ADVERSITY

Sometimes you can plan for adversity, and sometimes it occurs without warning. In either case, being prepared to leverage your character strengths to cope effectively with the challenges you face will help you immensely. You should prepare for adversity just as much as you prepare for the good things in life. We recommend the following:

> 1. *Anticipate adversity and plan ahead.* Suppose you are soon facing heart surgery or another major medical intervention. It is natural to experience anxiety. But you can decrease your anxiety by forming a systematic plan for using your

character strengths to deal with the situation. You may draw on strengths from the moral virtue of wisdom and knowledge by learning more about the procedure and becoming knowledgeable on what to expect during the recovery phase. The moral virtues of courage may be invoked to help you face the challenge head-on. Drawing on strengths from the moral virtue of humanity will aid you greatly as you turn to social support and the love and kindness of others to help you. The moral virtues of transcendence may help you put your situation into perspective by drawing on gratitude, hope, and spirituality. Actively reflect on which strengths will help you the most as you prepare for surgery. Write down a specific plan on how you will use these strengths to overcome your fear and anxiety as the event draws near.

2. *Plan for after the event*. The character strengths that help you prepare for the surgery or other adversity may not be the same ones that help the most as you recover afterward. Perhaps gratitude and spirituality rise in importance as you recover. Or you use your experience to reinforce your self-concept of being a brave and wise person. Act on these strengths. Personally thank the physicians and medical professionals who performed the surgery. Write a gratitude letter to friends and family who stood by you in your time of need. Use your strengths of knowledge and wisdom to write out a plan to foster your recovery. Capitalize on your grit and self-regulation skills to adhere to a healthier diet and exercise plan. Most important, do all of this overtly. Have an *action plan* and use it!

3. *Unexpected adversity*. You cannot always plan ahead. The soldier knows when he or she will be deployed to combat and can develop a character action plan accordingly. But what if you are the victim of a violent crime or a vehicular accident? After the shock of the incident, you should take time to assess your character strengths across all six moral virtues and once again develop an action plan on how to apply those strengths to overcome the adversity. Discuss your strengths with family and close friends and call upon them to help you express your strengths during your recovery.

Being aware and mindful of your character strengths and learning to use them to succeed in life is fundamental to engendering a positive trajectory in response to adversity. This is the basis of resilience-building programs such as CSF. In dealing with adversity, an ounce of preparation is worth a pound of cure.

THE LEADERSHIP IMPERATIVE

A principal theme of this book is that leaders play a pivotal role in how character is expressed within their organization. In the crucible of life experiences, this is especially true. Leaders set the tone for how individuals respond to adversity by establishing an organizational climate that supports positive character and standards of conduct that reinforce it. The actions of individual leaders are critically important. The following case study provides an example.

STEWARDSHIP AND COMMITMENT

The West Point honor code is a cornerstone to the character development of the Corps of Cadets. The cadets generally understand the importance of not lying, cheating, or stealing, but they struggle to understand the importance of not tolerating a fellow cadet who has violated the code.

The answer is simple. We have addressed the components of trust—competence, character, and caring. These, in addition to commitment, are necessary to build and maintain trust between leaders and subordinates. In the public service professions, an additional component in the trust equation is the client. Those who tolerate lying, cheating, or stealing undermine the trust between the profession and the client and do so at great risk. When that bond of trust is broken, suspicion, doubt, and hostility follow. One need look no further than widely publicized instances of the use of lethal force by law enforcement agencies against people of color to illustrate the tremendous impact from this breakdown of trust between public service members and client. The Michael Brown shooting in Ferguson, Missouri, provides a case in point. Regardless of the legal merits of the case, the bottom line is that many people in the Ferguson community did not trust their police department. The perception was that the police were untruthful and prejudiced. The result was significant civil unrest that led to numerous violent incidents.

Picture a member of your own organization who violates the standards and values of your profession. He or she is performing just below the fine line between acceptable and unacceptable behavior. If left uncorrected, that is to say, if tolerated by fellow workers, distrust and condemnation between your organization and its clients will follow. Looking the other way and not confronting what we know to be wrong behavior allows a cancer within an organization to continue and grow. By identifying and openly addressing the behavior, the embarrassment brought upon the organization and subsequent mistrust may be avoided.

A few years ago, one of West Point's more outstanding cadets graduated, was commissioned in the US Army, and reported to his first assignment. During one of his first field training exercises, the senior noncommissioned officer (NCO) in his battery (the first sergeant) called him to his vehicle, pulled out a bottle of whiskey, and asked him to join him for a drink. Soldiers in the US military are prohibited from consuming alcohol while training and during duty hours. They certainly do not consume alcohol during a field training exercise. In combat or in a training environment, where mishaps can translate into life-and-death situations, no one wants to follow a leader who is under the influence of alcohol. Further, the American people entrust their sons and daughters to the Army to lead them twenty-four hours a day, seven days a week, and they do not expect this leadership to exist only when it is convenient. When the senior NCO in the unit is violating this sacred trust, this must be corrected. No one wants this leader to set an example that is abhorrent to the nation's values and character, and no one wants him leading America's sons and daughters.

So now, suddenly and totally unexpectedly, this brand-new, idealistic lieutenant is faced with a compromising situation caused by someone he was taught to listen to and to trust. What does he do? What would you have done? Surprisingly, and contrary to the honor ethic he was taught while a cadet at West Point, he looked the other way and failed to report the first sergeant's behavior that night. The nontoleration element of the honor code was not internalized to the point where he did the harder right and reported the NCO. The lieutenant looked the other way. Eventually, the NCO's behavior was identified and reported, and in the follow-on investigation the new lieutenant was reported to have earlier observed the errant behavior and failed to take the appropriate action. The lieutenant received a letter of reprimand from the commanding general, but to the lieutenant's good fortune, it was not placed in his official file. (If this had occurred, it would have led to his removal from service in the Army.) It was instead used as an opportunity to teach the lieutenant the importance of upholding values and standards, and this lesson hardened the lieutenant's character and commitment to institutional values. He learned a valuable lesson from adversity brought about by his failure to enforce standards.

Competence, character, caring, and commitment are four critical components in building a culture of excellence and honor. Most of us easily understand why competence, character, and caring are so important to this; however, the commitment portion is often overlooked or viewed as less important. Nothing can be further from the truth. Nothing can destroy the trust of an organization faster than when one of its members is allowed to remain a part of the organization while displaying behavior inconsistent with its values and standards. When that occurs, the individual must be corrected and his or her actions brought back within the parameters of acceptable behavior. If not, that person can drag others into similar behaviors, discredit the organization, and, most damaging, lose the trust between the organization and its client. In the profession of arms, this results in a loss of trust between the military and the citizens it serves. What a terrible indictment if that occurs.

RECOMMENDATIONS FOR LEADERS

Leaders may take a number of steps to maintain organizational values and character and to preserve and even build the cohesion of the organization.

Training. High-stakes organizations should invest significantly in resilience training. The organization should consider personal resilience skills as high a priority as job-specific technical skills. The US Army's CSF program provides a model of how this is done.[26]

Few organizations have the resources of the US Army to devote to resilience training, but smaller organizations may adopt many programs or approaches. The Hardiness Institute offers a training program in hardiness skills. Organizations send one or more members (depending on the size and needs of the organization) to the institute to be trained to execute a series of hardiness-building classes and exercises. These trainers then become the organization's source for educating and building among individual members the traits of challenge, commitment, and control.[27]

Many police and fire departments employ psychologists, and they may be asked to develop a resilience-building program with a firm grounding in character development. Other organizations, lacking a full-time psychologist, may contract for resilience and character-building services.

Team building. Positive, cohesive teams are critical to aiding individuals in coping with adverse events. Leaders should invest significant time in planning events and exercises that build a sense of common mission and shared beliefs in the organization's members.

Make standards public and enforce them. Leaders should

establish clear standards and hold employees to them. Clear expectations for appropriate behavior and consequences for failing to adhere to standards is critical in high-stakes organizations. Remember that individuals are capable of learning from their mistakes, and as in the case of West Point's discretion and honor mentorship program, leaders should have a plan to help those who err to learn from their mistakes.

Provide feedback. Leaders should provide feedback to members of the organization on character, both positive and negative. Ignoring a character problem will not make it go away, and failing to recognize exemplars of positive character fails both to reinforce that character in that individual and to express the importance of it to others. Johnson & Johnson's Credo and the company's strategic focus on character are a good example of what right looks like when it comes to leader-driven standards of positive character.

CLOSING OBSERVATION

The crucible of life experiences provides fertile soil in which to sharpen and hone character. From adversity stems the possibility of personal growth. The broken bone heals stronger than it was before. That which does not kill us makes us stronger. This does not occur by chance. Successful individuals and organizations learn to benefit from adversity, grow stronger from it, and use it as the foundation for future excellence and flourishing, providing them with a character edge in their lives.

10

AVOIDING THE POTHOLES

An ounce of prevention is worth a pound of cure.

—BENJAMIN FRANKLIN[1]

Reflect on instances in your life when you have not lived according to your values, or on such instances among family members or friends. Calculate a cost-benefit ratio. How many times did the benefits of character failure outweigh the costs? Not often, we suspect.

Throughout this book we have looked at ways that positive character, both as an individual trait and as an organizational value, is associated with good outcomes. Strengths of the head, heart, and gut give us the edge needed to live productive and fulfilling lives. Organizations that embrace positive values and develop a culture that nurtures and rewards positive character among their members create an environment that fosters both individual achievement and organizational effectiveness.

By virtue of being human, we are subject to errors of judgment and conduct. Times, settings, and conditions in life may lead us to behave "out of character." Sometimes we can pick ourselves up and get back on the right track. Other failures may be sufficiently profound as to present a major obstacle to making amends and moving forward. It may take many years to repair a reputation tarnished by failed character. In addition to the loss of reputation, such major failures may also have tangible economic consequences, including the loss of a job or a career.

To Benjamin Franklin's point, with character, an ounce of prevention is indeed worth a pound of cure. Preventing character failure is a better strategy than mending the fallout stemming from that failure. Most people know this and incorporate strategies to aid them in living a virtuous, principled life. Strong family values, religious and spiritual beliefs, and a conscious effort to give positive meaning and purpose to life help. Psychologists, too, have examined factors that are associated with character failure in both individuals and organizations. Being mindful of these factors may add to your ability to avoid character failure.

A CHARACTER RISK MODEL

Threats to exhibiting good character stem from three sources. First, *intrapersonal* factors, meaning personality traits, personal weaknesses, or habits that compromise one's ability to display positive character traits. The second source are *environmental* factors, circumstances external to the individual that create pressure or stress that may lead to character failure. Third are *social/organizational* factors, which are aspects of the social or organizational setting that create conditions that fail to properly guide and constrain behavior, making it more likely that some individuals will fail in character.

These three factors do not operate independently. Instead, they multiply together to increase risk of character failure.

Figure 10.1 represents that relationship among these three factors and character risk. The shaded area in the middle of the Figure 10.1 indicates the space where intrapersonal, environmental, and social/organizational factors come together. When this happens, character risk is greatly increased. You could call it a character-risk triple threat. Risk is also increased where two factors combine, such as a person at low risk in intrapersonal factors, but at high risk for both environmental and social/organizational factors. Looking at character risk this way helps us understand why on some occasions even people with the highest character may fail.

Figure 10.1

CHARACTER RISK

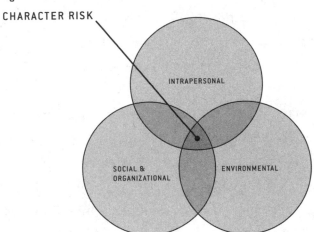

Let's use the Character Risk Model to analyze a case of character failure that General Caslen encountered while a division commander in Iraq. In an infantry battalion (consisting of eight hundred to a thousand soldiers), its senior noncommissioned officer, the command sergeant major (CSM), is, aside from the commander, its most influential leader. If this leader is under investigation for some moral or ethical issue, the entire battalion is adversely impacted. This is their leader. This is the one they are told to emulate. This is the leader who not only establishes the standards but also enforces the standards. This is the leader whom all the enlisted soldiers want to be like. He or she is their role model. All noncommissioned officers memorize the Non commissioned Officer (NCO) Creed, which says, "I am proud of the Corps of noncommissioned officers and will at all times conduct myself so as to bring credit upon the Corps, the military service and my country regardless of the situation in which I find myself. I will not use my grade or position to attain pleasure, profit, or personal safety." So, when the senior NCO is charged with character issues contrary to the standards, values, and culture of the unit and the NCO Corps, you can imagine the devastating impact it has on the morale and discipline of a unit. When that unit is in a combat environment, where stress and life-and-death situations face the troops daily, morale and discipline are exponentially affected. Such was the case with one of the battalions in Caslen's division.

Sexual violence impacts the victim for a lifetime. Knowing that one of your own teammates is a victim of sexual violence also has a crippling impact on the morale of the unit. This was the situation for this battalion when its command sergeant major was being investigated for sexual assault.

As the investigation was launched, the CSM was suspended from his position. Additional investigations soon revealed allegations by a number of female soldiers from other units. They surfaced from not only this deployment, but from previous deployments as well, indicating a lengthy pattern of predatory sexual behavior.

The exposure of his conduct had even more devastating impacts. In the middle of the investigation, the CSM took his own life. The impact on this unit's morale and discipline when they found out, in combat, their CSM had taken his own life instead of facing the charges and allegations was devastating. It was similar to the impact of the problems that faced the Third Battalion, Eighth Cavalry Regiment (described in the preface).

Caslen experienced far too many ethical issues among his senior leaders during his deployment in Iraq as a division commander. Over his twelve months of command, he dealt with more than seventy incidents of misconduct. While a few were cases of criminal conduct, most were discipline and morale issues that stemmed from character failures. Improper treatment of subordinates, hostile command climates, inappropriate relationships, sexual harassment, sexual assault, and alcohol use were common themes. These character failures among leaders are certainly disruptive in a civilian or noncombat setting, but in a war zone, misconduct of this type is a direct threat to team cohesion and therefore mission success.

INTRAPERSONAL THREATS

Using the Character Risk Model, we can examine the three classes of threats to character. First, consider intrapersonal factors. One example of such a factor that is strongly related to character failure and criminal behavior is what psychologists refer to as the *dark triad*. The dark triad consists of three personality traits—narcissism, Machiavellianism, and psychopathy. Narcissism involves a greatly exaggerated sense of self-worth and importance. Machiavellianism refers to people who use others as tools to achieve personal goals, even when it is detrimental to the others. It is a win-at-all-costs approach to life, an approach that we argue is unsustainable over the long run. Finally, psychopathy involves persistent antisocial behavior. Psychopaths are not capable of the feelings of empathy and remorse that for most people provide constraints to thoughts and behavior. Psychopaths are self-centered and egotistical.

This combination of three dysfunctional personality traits has been linked to a variety of unfavorable and criminal behaviors. One recent study examined the relationship between the dark triad and the seven deadly sins of anger, envy, gluttony, greed, lust, pride, and sloth.[2] Each component of the dark triad, including narcissism, was reliably associated with these seven outcomes.

In the case of the CSM, his behavior reflected aspects of the dark triad. His alleged history of sexually assaulting multiple women represents a consistent pattern of antisocial behavior. Spotting someone in your organization who shows one or more components of the dark triad is probably not difficult. Such people are boastful, talk a great deal about their accomplishments, are in constant need of praise, feel they deserve the best perks and special compensations the organization offers, and all the while demean and belittle others to enhance their own sense of self-worth. They may stop at little to achieve their goals and to satisfy their personal needs.

The dark triad reflects a basic personality pattern and may be difficult to change. But these traits occur on a continuum ranging from mildly annoying on the left end to pathological and sometimes criminal on the right. Nearer the left (nonpathological) side of the continuum, self-regulation may modulate the expression of narcissistic, Machiavellian, and/or psychopathic tendencies.[3] On the right, or pathological, side of the continuum, these impulsive behaviors are difficult for an individual to control. If you as a leader or a coworker see these behaviors, they should set off warning signals.

Hubris, or excessive self-pride, is another character trait that may contribute to problems in an organization. Hubris is not a personality disorder like the components of the dark triad. But if self-pride dominates a person's interactions with others, it can destroy morale. Consider the following case.

One of the staff officers in General Caslen's division was tremendously competent and demonstrated the highest standards every day. But he was such a perfectionist that any subordinate who failed to meet his high expectations was confronted in an adversarial way. This resulted in a hostile command climate. No allegations of the officer's lying, cheating, or stealing, nor of inappropriate relationships, or moral or ethical issues, were made. But if you found yourself in his staff unit, you would try your best to get out from under his authority, simply because of the antagonistic and hostile way he treated his subordinates. Although this officer did not demonstrate flaws in his fundamental character or values, his actions would be considered a violation to "living honorably" because this is not how to treat those we work with, and it destroys the trust between a leader and his or her subordinates.

This staff officer in Caslen's division suffered from an overriding sense of hubris; it was a signature of his personality, and it made him ineffective as a leader. In our character model, this reflects a low level of modesty and humility and of social intelligence. This example is from a workplace, but the negative impact of such character flaws can be found in any sort of group. A basketball player, however talented, who criticizes and dominates his or her teammates causes great harm to team morale.

Hubris undermines the trust between an organization and its clients. This is true in the profession of arms, where the erosion of trust between the military and the people it serves may have devastating consequences. The military is not alone in this way. The widely publicized outcries over the use of lethal force by law enforcement officers against minorities reflect the profound distrust between these communities and law enforcement.

Another all-too-common intrapersonal factor that compromises character is drug and alcohol abuse. The link between alcohol and sexual assault is well demonstrated. Alcohol, even in low doses, depresses the central nervous system and reduces inhibitions. Alcohol's effects are well known and include increased aggression and a variety of inappropriate and sometimes illegal behaviors. When the dark triad meets drugs and alcohol, the threat to character is significantly higher. People with the dark triad do a poor job of self-regulation, and self-regulation is further impaired by substance abuse. This creates a Venn diagram within a Venn diagram, within the intrapersonal circle shown in Figure 10.1.

Personality characteristics and substance abuse present challenges to the consistent expression of good character. But people are capable of significant change. If you have these personality traits, then you may seek psychotherapy to address narcissism, Machiavellianism, and psychopathy. Alcoholics and substance abusers may find a variety of programs to help them. At the organizational level, leaders should be fully cognizant of the problems posed by the dark triad and substance abuse and have policies in place to address them. Large organizations, such as the military, have many programs in place to accomplish this.

ENVIRONMENTAL THREATS

The second threat to character in the Character Risk Model is environmental factors. Work or other settings that result in sleep deprivation (going without any sleep for extended periods) or sleep restriction (getting inadequate sleep over extended periods) are linked to character failures. A study of West Point cadets showed that those who slept the least had higher incidents of conduct problems. This study found that cadets on average receive only 5.5 hours of sleep on weeknights, and by Friday their sleep deficit resulted in behavioral deficits similar to a blood alcohol content of .08 percent—legally drunk in most US states.[4] A recent study of Royal Norwegian Naval Academy cadets found that sleep-deprived cadets showed poorer leadership behavior.[5] Other research establishes a link between sleep and moral awareness. Sleep deprivation and restriction diminish a person's ability to self-regulate, sometimes leading to ethical/moral character failures.[6]

A particularly interesting study showed that sleep deprivation increases risk-taking due to a reduction of self-awareness. Judgment also suffers.[7] These effects may result in decisions leading to behavior inconsistent with a person's character. Soldiers deployed in Afghanistan report sleeping fewer than six hours a day. Over a one-year deployment, sleep restriction of this degree could contribute to a host of bad outcomes, including ethical/moral lapses.[8]

Other environmental factors include danger, prolonged

exposure to a hostile physical environment, frequent changes in leadership, or, in some organizations, frequent changes in work assignments or locations. In the case of the command sergeant major, both sleep restriction and social isolation may have combined with other risk factors to enable his deviant behavior.

Environmental factors may worsen intrapersonal factors that contribute to character failure. For example, a young infantry officer performed heroically in his first combat tour, where he earned several decorations for valor. Selected to attend graduate school and teach at West Point, he continued his exemplary performance as a West Point instructor, both in the classroom and as a role model for cadets and other officers. Following this assignment, he deployed again to combat and again excelled. Once again, because of his faithful and exemplary service both in combat and previously at West Point, he was sent to graduate school to obtain a doctorate degree. Upon completion he reported to West Point to serve once again on the faculty. He was the loving father of young children and enjoyed a good relationship with his wife. Thanks to his outgoing personality, he had many friends as well.

What nobody knew was that following his second combat tour he was silently dealing with the lingering symptoms of combat stress. But, like many soldiers, he hid the symptoms and did not seek treatment. When he returned to West Point, his behavior changed significantly from that of his first tour. Then he was always the first at work, arriving early in the morning to prepare for class and complete other duties. He was engaged with cadets outside of class. He was positive and energetic in his interactions with others. But in his second tour, he came to work late and left early. He seemed preoccupied and distracted and not fully engaged in his job.

About two years into his second tour, allegations came to light that he was having an affair with the wife of a fellow officer. Formal charges of misconduct were filed. Recognizing his character failure, this officer pleaded guilty to all charges. The superintendent of West Point reviewed the case and ruled that the officer would be reduced in rank and forced to immediately retire from the Army. This officer had the potential to rise to a position of high leadership at West Point, but despite his great talent, his career was ruined.

What happened? The environmental stress and responsibilities of his most recent combat deployment contributed to poor decisions associated with character failures. These environmental factors reduced his ability to self-regulate and led him to behavior that was out of character. Similarly, the environmental stress of the combat deployment may have contributed to the command sergeant major's situation as well.

SOCIAL/ORGANIZATIONAL THREATS

Social/organizational factors exert a powerful influence on positive character. This third circle within Figure 10.1 may be the most important because organizations have considerable influence over this component.

Individuals who lack supportive social networks are more vulnerable to character failures. Some people are incapable of forming close relationships with others. Some are physically removed from their normal social setting and are isolated from others. We saw earlier that soldiers in the *Black Hearts* platoon were geographically isolated from other units in the battalion. Clearly many factors contributed to the criminal actions of this platoon, including the dark triad, but social isolation was also a contributing factor.

In the case of the command sergeant major, his unit provided some social support, but probably not enough. Senior officers and NCOs have fewer close social relationships within their units because military tradition and rules discourage the establishment of friendships between leaders and subordinates. Moreover, the CSM was away from his family and thus lacked any stabilizing support they may have offered.

The values of an organization are critical to shaping and maintaining positive character among its members. When leaders overlook the importance of positive values and organizational climate, the consequences may be severe and even represent an existential threat to the organization. It is all the more distressing when the institutions are responsible for the development and education of the nation's greatest resource—its college students, who will be our future leaders.

ORGANIZATIONAL FAILURE: A CASE HISTORY

The first big scandal comes from Penn State University, where Coach Jerry Sandusky was convicted of sexually abusing children in 2012. This resulted in the termination or resignation of a number of university officials.

Then, on September 26, 2017, "the US Attorney's Office for the Southern District of New York announced the arrest of ten people for involvement in fraud and corruption schemes related to college basketball—four NCAA Division 1 college basket-

ball coaches, a senior executive and two employees at a major athletic apparel company, and three athlete advisors. The first scheme involved allegations that college coaches took cash payments from athlete advisors to steer players and their families to the advisors making the payments. The second scheme involved allegations that a senior executive at a sports apparel company worked with athlete advisors to funnel payments to high-school players and their families to obtain their commitment to attend universities sponsored by the apparel company."[9] Of the ten individuals arrested, six pleaded guilty, three went to trial, and charges were dropped for the tenth person. The trial for the three defendants who pleaded not guilty resulted in convictions, but all three are expected to appeal the decision.[10]

Another scandal occurred at Michigan State University, whose gymnastics-team physician sexually abused more than three hundred women athletes both at Michigan State and on the USA Gymnastics women's team. Penn State made the news again when a student died during a fraternity hazing incident. Then came the misappropriation of 85 million taxpayer dollars at the University of Central Florida, which resulted in the resignations of another university president and its board chair. Four senior administrators at Georgia Tech resigned after it was discovered that they had failed to disclose conflicts of interest and inappropriate business relationships with vendors. The scandals reached a new level when federal charges were filed against more than thirty parents who had allegedly paid enormous amounts of money to recruiters who then allegedly bribed officials to ensure their children were accepted in prestigious universities.

What is striking in this last case were the sheer number of

university athletic coaches and administrators who were charged with bribery, fraud, or racketeering conspiracy. These included two university soccer coaches, a sailing coach, a college aptitude test administrator, a senior associate athletic director, a water-polo coach, and a men's tennis coach. At the time of publication many defendants had pleaded guilty but a handful of defendants have pleaded not guilty and the criminal justice process will undoubtably continue to unfold for some time to come.[11]

These incidents are alarming. When the university athletic scandals broke into the public news cycle, the National Collegiate Athletic Association (NCAA) hired former secretary of state Condoleezza Rice to head a commission to recommend ways in which the NCAA could regain its ability to provide leadership and accountability. The commission's final report stated, "Everyone knows that these payments occur. That state of affairs—where the entire community knows of significant rule breaking and yet the governance body lacks the power or will to investigate and act—breeds cynicism and contempt."[12] These incidents represent a terrible indictment about the ability of university leadership to maintain ethical climates within their institutions.

What do these scandals and situations have in common? In every instance a leader, someplace, failed to lead. *You can be the best university president in the country, but if you fail in character, you fail in leadership.* Sound familiar?

Ethical fading may play a role in these examples. Ethical fading is a deterioration or corrosion of ethical standards over time.[13] When unethical behavior occurs and goes unchecked by leadership or others, it can become standard practice and, over time, is

no longer seen as wrong. This is exactly what occurred at the University of Central Florida, with its misappropriation of state funds. Failure to address unethical behavior is poor leadership.

In an examination of a university admissions scandal in 2009, Dr. Nathan Harris, assistant professor at the Warner School of Education at the University of Rochester, said, "The potential for misconduct pervades colleges and universities more than we assume—and even more than we feel comfortable acknowledging." He followed up, "A senior administrator does not wake up in the morning and say, 'Today I am going to do something that lands me on the front page of the *Chicago Tribune* for the wrong reasons.'"[14] Ethical fading strikes again.

How are universities today addressing this? And can universities develop a culture of ethics on their campuses? We believe the answer is yes.

These crises force universities to address these issues and problems directly. At Penn State, the solution was to create an independent and centralized compliance office. This office oversees compliance in a wide variety of issues, including employee conflicts of interests, use of appropriated funds, employee training in whistle-blower procedures, hiring vendors, disclosing crime statistics, and complying with NCAA and other governance statutes, such as gender-equity laws known as Title IX. University staff and faculty must comply with numerous other laws, policies, regulations, and statutes, and the university leadership is responsible for creating a culture of ethics that seeks compliance rather than trying to find ways around regulations.[15]

At many universities, offices of compliance and ethics are using a powerful "new" tool—a simple campus-wide survey.

When Georgia Tech discovered that four senior employees had inappropriate financial ties with vendors and contractors, the president, Dr. Bud Peterson, surveyed the staff, faculty, and graduate students, a population of twelve thousand. From the survey Georgia Tech's leadership learned, astonishingly, of a level of distrust that "exceeds the realm of an ethics scandal that shook the campus last summer. . . . You as administrators hope and think you're in tune with everyone on campus, but that one really came as a shock to us," said Georgia Tech's then chief of staff, Lynn M. Durham.[16]

Peterson should be applauded. Other presidents might be reluctant to survey their staff and faculty on these topics. That Peterson faced these issues head-on and was transparent with the survey findings and in the follow-on actions he took to address these issues showed the staff and faculty how serious the leadership was in addressing their concerns. This type of leadership produces an essential result—a rebuilding of trust.

Georgia Tech also appointed a new vice president for ethics and compliance, Ling-Ling Nie, who reinforced the importance of ethical compliance: "If we underscore the importance of having a workforce that is grounded in integrity and respect and articulate exactly what that means and how that manifests, day to day, as a manager or as an employee, it gets to the heart of some of those concerns."[17]

As Georgia Tech's leadership and staff and faculty continue to build this ethical culture on its campus, other newly implemented programs include regular surveys of employees to assess campus culture, instituting an ethics-awareness week, regular ethics and whistle-blower training, senior leadership meetings singularly focused on campus values, senior-level emphasis that retaliation will not be tolerated, and the requirement of all senior administrators to regularly talk face-to-face with their subordinate leaders about campus values.[18] This is leadership building a culture based on university values. This is leadership making a difference.

These examples illustrate the juxtaposition of personal character flaws, such as hubris and dysfunctional organizational values and climate of a win-at-all-costs mentality. When the university's leadership considers the success of a college football program to be more important than holding an individual responsible for years of child abuse, something is badly amiss.

ORGANIZATIONAL HAZARDS TO CHARACTER

An article by the Deloitte Center for Regulatory Strategy called "Managing Conduct Risk: Addressing Drivers, Restoring Trust" lists eight drivers of misconduct.[19] Although discussed in the context of the financial industry, these drivers of misconduct are relevant to many organizations and represent another type of pothole that must be avoided. Misconduct is associated with failures in character. Let's first take a look at these drivers of misconduct, then see how they play out in an actual organization.

> **1**. *Consumer need and suitability are not guiding product lifecycle practices.* In simple terms, this means that organizations that place sales over actual customer needs are prone to misconduct. The university that is more concerned with new buildings or winning sports championships than with the education of its students is an example.

2. *Failing to have a balanced scorecard for human resource decisions.* This means that important personnel decisions that are driven by short-term or narrow performance indicators result in misconduct. In college athletics, this is the win-at-all-costs mentality. Coaches who believe they will be fired if they do not win a championship every year are at greater risk to compromise their character in recruiting or retaining players.

3. *Individuals and leadership are not responsible or held to account for misconduct.* We have already discussed multiple examples of this driver. Failure to have and to enforce standards is a surefire recipe for misconduct.

4. *Failing to identify and manage conflicts of interest.* There must be outside checks and balances to guard against misconduct. Scientists who conduct research on human participants must present their research plans and objectives to an institutional review board to ensure ethical standards of research are adhered to. Before these institutional review boards were common practice, abuse of human subjects occurred, even when the scientists involved were well intended. In 1932, scientists with the lofty goal of developing effective treatments for syphilis began a study of six hundred black men. But while the men volunteered to be in the study, the researchers did not reveal to them the true purpose of the study or the full facts about their treatment. The researchers thus deceived the participants, ultimately resulting in a class-action lawsuit and a $10-million out-of-court settlement in 1973 to surviving participants and their families.[20] The checks and balances provided by a review board would have prevented this misuse of human participants.

5. *Complex, disconnected, or growth-at-all-costs business models.* Complexity breeds confusion, which can be followed by a focus on the wrong goals and objectives. A bigger-is-better philosophy enables focusing on short-term gains, achieved at any costs including compromises of character, over long-term success.

6. *Manual and complicated processes and procedures.* Making the job too hard leads to shortcuts. Excessive bureaucracy causes people to take shortcuts that may compromise their ethics. A recent study of Army culture concluded, "Many Army officers, after repeated exposure to the overwhelming demands and the associated need to put their honor on the line to verify compliance, have become ethically numb. As a result, an officer's signature and word have become tools to maneuver through the Army bureaucracy rather than being symbols of integrity and honesty. . . . As a result, untruthfulness is surprisingly common in the U.S. military even though members of the profession are loath to admit it."[21] Leaders must streamline their organization's policies and procedures to promote adherence to ethical standards.

7. *Weak systems for monitoring and surveillance.* Leaders must ensure that fair and objective systems are in place to track adherence to ethical guidelines. Failure to do so allows the perception that unethical actions will go undetected and unpunished.

8. *Disparate subcultures or a problematic prevailing culture.* Organizations may foster positive character, such as Johnson & Johnson, or allow unprincipled behavior to be the norm, such as the Army rugby team. Leaders must take positive and constant action to establish and maintain a positive organizational climate. This may be the most important thing a leader does. Such a strong and positive culture may mitigate against other risk factors in the Character Risk Model.

One or more of these drivers of misconduct have been found in every example of organizational failure that we have presented from the West Point rugby team to the University of Central Florida. For the rugby team, the main driver of misconduct was the formation of a subculture that had values inconsistent with the values of the parent organization, coupled with weak systems for monitoring and surveillance. Had an effective monitoring system been in place, the dysfunctional subculture would not have been able to fester and grow.

In larger and more complex organizations, such as some of the universities described previously, multiple drivers of misconduct may combine to create significant departures from acceptable and even legal procedures, bringing on a crisis that can become massive in scope and impact. Deloitte's third driver of misconduct is clearly illustrated when leadership is not held responsible for misconduct. Deloitte's fifth driver of misconduct, growth at all costs, is also seen in some of these cases. Perhaps not surprisingly, Deloitte's seventh driver of misconduct, "weak systems for monitoring and surveillance," will prevent a university from recognizing its failures and correcting them before significant damage is done. Finally, Deloitte's eighth driver of misconduct may be seen in the development of a subculture where a set of values inconsistent to the values of the institution can damage an institution's reputation and good standing.

There are several key takeaways from these situations. The

solution starts with a leader who reinforces integrity and honor. Not only does he or she demonstrate integrity and honor every day and take advantage of every opportunity to articulate the need for it, but the leader also holds subordinates accountable to these values. When subordinates are out of line, they are immediately corrected. When subordinates cross a threshold and are no longer trusted, they must be replaced. Leaders must also identify risks to their organization, their employees, and their customers. These risk assessments must originate from numerous sources including the leader him- or herself. Once risks are identified, they should be assessed for their likelihood and duration, then risk mitigation factors must be put in place.

The good news is that high-performing, high-character organizations may develop strategies to avoid these potholes. It takes attention and conscious effort, but that is what high-performing, high-character organizations do. The road to excellence has no easy shortcuts.

A COMMENT ON SOCIAL MEDIA

Social media presents a major threat to character. People say things on social media they would not ordinarily say in person. Why? Perhaps it is the perceived distance between themselves and their targets. Stanley Milgram's famous study of obedience to authority demonstrated that ordinary people are capable of doing harm to others. You may recall this experiment, where Milgram posed as an experimenter and instructed "teachers" (the subjects of the experiment) to administer painful electric shocks to "learners" (the learners were actors and did not receive actual electric shocks). One of Milgram's main findings was that teachers were far more likely to comply with the experimenter's commands to administer painful shocks when the learner was physically distant than when the learner was close by, where he or she could be seen and heard.[22] This same principle applies to social media. Because they cannot directly sense the impact of their words, some people feel unconstrained and say things that are both incongruent with their own values and hurtful to others.

The unfiltered content of social media may be especially disruptive to people who are at multiple levels of character risk as defined in our Character Risk Model. Hateful and prejudiced content has been linked to mob violence. The deadly incident in Charlottesville, Virginia, where a young woman was run over and killed by a white nationalist sympathizer, is a good example. Social media messaging incensed both the white nationalists and those protesting against their views. Evidence suggests that Russian operators employed "false-front" Twitter accounts to polarize and inflame the attitudes of both sides in Charlottesville.[23]

Riots and group violence are not a new phenomenon. Mobs are well known to bring out the worst in many people. What is new is the ease with which a virtual mob may form. Whether whipped into a frenzy either by groupthink or through intentional manipulation by outside forces, the potential threat to character is significant.

SOCIAL ISOLATION

Social isolation is a significant contributor to character failure. Sometimes your personality leads you to social isolation, as in the case of extreme introverts. Other times specific situations make direct social contact and support difficult, such as for soldiers deployed far from home for extended periods.

Senior leaders often have poor social relationships, especially in hierarchical organizations such as the military. The commanding general or CEO may have few people he or she can turn to for advice or to discuss important issues. This isolation allows problems to fester. A few years ago, an Army general committed suicide shortly after promotion to the next-highest grade. The army chief of staff tasked a three-star general to form a group to explore threats to general-officer well-being. One threatening factor the group identified was that general officers usually do not have a peer of equal rank easily available for advice. While the Pentagon and a few large military bases have several general officers, generals assigned to most Army posts have nobody of equal rank at their installation. This was true of the general who committed suicide. For others, such social isolation may result in less dramatic, but still quite damaging, lapses of character.

PREVENTIVE ACTIONS

The Character Risk Model provides strategies for avoiding character potholes. For individuals, a number of things may be done. Reflect on your character strengths, how you use them, and under what conditions you may sometimes fail to adhere to your values. Do you have personal habits that may compromise your character, such as alcohol or drug abuse? If so, get help. Evaluate your social network. Identify close friends, ones that you may reach out to in trying circumstances. Look to them and family members for balance and perspective. Changes in mood or sleeping habits may signal stress. Learn what situations trigger stress for you and work to develop adaptive ways of dealing with those situations if they cannot be avoided altogether. Be honest with yourself about your personality. Do your vanity and pride get in the way of effective relationships? Is your ego too big? Learn to self-regulate these indicators of the dark triad.

Individuals should seek a mentor with whom they can have an honest discussion about their personality and character. A powerful exercise would be for your mentor to rate you on each of your twenty-four character strengths, then for the two of you to compare his or her ratings with your own. Others may perceive you differently from the way you perceive yourself. If you learn that you are perceived as immodest or that you lack social intelligence (we are often bad at recognizing our flaws), such a discussion may stimulate personal development. Most character flaws are not pathological like the dark triad. More common are lesser flaws in one or more of the strengths in each of the six moral virtues. Once identified, these may be addressed.

At the social level, individuals should seek to establish and maintain positive relationships with friends, family, and coworkers. There is no one-size-fits-all approach. People have different needs for social support and different ways of seeking it. But we all need people with whom we can share our joys and accomplishments and seek comfort and guidance. Ask yourself, "Whom could I see or call right now, or at any time of the day, if I have something I need to talk about?" If you can't think of anyone, then you may need to put less time into your job or your schoolwork, and more time into social relationships. These social relationships help bring out good character and are central to a balanced life.

At the organizational level, leaders have the responsibility to create a positive, character-driven environment with clear goals. A public and simple vision statement combined with an equally straightforward mission statement is a beginning. But most important, leaders must genuinely believe in the organization's values and adhere to them. Workers, students, and members of all types of organizations are quick to sniff out hypocrisy.

Leaders may use Deloitte's eight drivers of misconduct to diagnose organizational character risk. Key leaders should be intimately aware of these drivers of misconduct, and units at all levels within the organization should be assessed on each. Doing so helps avoid potholes and should be a priority for all types of institutions.

THE CHARACTER EDGE REVISITED

Character lost is difficult to regain. Individuals and organizations who want to excel and win over the long term should maintain a focus on character. Our Character Risk Model provides a guide for where to look for threats to character. A proactive approach to character management prior to failure is far more effective than a reactive approach focused on repairing damage after the fact. The result is a distinct character edge, for both the individual and the organization.

11

WINNING THE RIGHT WAY

Competing at the highest level is not about winning.
It's about preparation, courage, understanding and
nurturing people, and heart. Winning is the result.

—JOE TORRE[1]

AN EXISTENTIAL CRISIS?

In the Gettysburg Address, President Abraham Lincoln spoke
to a somber crowd. It was November 19, 1863, just over four
months following the bloody battle that cost the lives of 3,150
Northern soldiers, wounded 14,529, and resulted in 5,365
missing or captured troops. Confederate losses were similar.
The American Civil War was only half over, and overall victory
was not at all certain. Democracy hung in the balance. But in
this darkest hour, with the United States facing an existential
crisis, Lincoln saw hope. He proclaimed "that we here highly
resolve that these dead shall not have died in vain; that this
nation, under God, shall have a new birth of freedom; and that
government of the people, by the people, for the people, shall
not perish from the earth."[2]

Over a century and a half later, America is facing another existential crisis. This one is not a result of civil war or a military attack by a foreign country, but is the result of a character crisis. A government "of the people, by the people, for the people" is grounded in positive values and character, of its individual citizens and even more important on the part of its leaders. A breakdown of these values leads, as we have seen, to an erosion of trust. An erosion of trust in government and other major social institutions is a precursor to the downfall of a democracy. "Of the people, by the people, for the people" hinges on trust, and without trust democracy cannot be sustained.

Elected leaders from all political parties carry the burden of responsibility for this breakdown of trust. When winning at all costs is what matters, then the elements of national trust—competence, character, and caring—are discarded. It is incumbent on today's leaders, elected by the people and for the people, to address the character crisis. The United States and many other nations appear fractured politically, resulting in discord instead of discourse. This fuels a perception among many that the government has strayed from the principles of competence, character, and caring. To be clear, this is not a partisan issue and is not unique to a particular administration. This breakdown of trust is manifested at the state and local level as well as the national level. In too many cases, getting elected and reelected seems more important than representing the best interests of the people. Elected leaders of all political parties carry at least some of the burden for the breakdown in trust between the people and their government. Trust lost can be regained. Great leaders focus on the three C's. Washington, Lincoln, and Mandela won, and they won the right way.

It is not just the government that is failing in character. The other four major social institutions—family, business, education, and religion—are also drifting away from basic human values and strengths of character. We have talked about several of these failures, from colleges and universities that place growth, profit, and winning football games above their missions to educate students, to the Catholic Church, which has failed to police its own sexually predatory priests. Many businesses will do anything to build their profits. There seems to be a breakdown in traditional family values as well. Win and win at any cost seems to be the prevailing ethic.

Foreign entities, most notably Russia, sow social and political discord through social media. Russia's well-documented efforts to impact the 2016 presidential election are a case in point. So is Russian use of social media to stir anger and discord among individual Americans by creating memes intended to antagonize and disrupt people's opinions of each other, their government, and their social institutions. But this would not work if Americans trusted their major social institutions. Russia is simply exploiting a current national vulnerability.

On June 16, 1858, Abraham Lincoln gave his acceptance speech to delegates at the Illinois Republican convention where he accepted their nomination to run for US senator. In this speech, anticipating the Civil War, Lincoln famously said, "A house divided against itself cannot stand."[3] We fear that America stands at a tipping point. Without a renewed focus on positive character, distrust in government and the other social institutions may lead to a crumbling of democracy as we know it.

But it doesn't have to be this way. There is still time to turn this around. Embracing positive individual and organizational character can turn the tide. Winning—whether it is an election, a game, or making an A on an exam—is not enough. We must learn to win the right way. And winning the right way is character driven.

WINNING THE RIGHT WAY

When the nation puts its Army in harm's way, it does not expect the Army to look good or do its best. They expect it to accomplish the mission and win. But they do not expect it to win at all costs; they expect it to win "the right way," meaning to win in accordance with national and Army values. That is, to win with integrity.

The definition of "the right way" has changed over the years, and along with the evolution of what "right" looks like, we have also observed an evolution of the nation's values on how to conduct combat operations. Near the end of World War II, on August 6, 1945, the United States dropped an atomic bomb on Hiroshima, Japan, killing up to eighty thousand citizens. Three days later it dropped an atomic bomb on Nagasaki, killing another forty thousand Japanese, mostly civilians.[4] Before this indiscriminate massacre of civilians, Allied forces in the European theater bombed the city of Dresden, Germany, in February 1945, killing around thirty-five thousand German civilians. This strategy was known as saturation bombing and was designed to destroy morale by using incendiary bombs to kill as many civilians as possible.[5]

The Allied nations persevered and won World War II, but did the calculated destruction of so many civilians represent "winning the right way"? It is not our intent to argue this question.

But can you imagine deliberately killing more than one hundred thousand unarmed civilians as part of today's military strategy? Killing any civilians whatsoever has potential devastating consequences toward the long-term success of a contemporary military strategy. This is why today's military operations include stringent rules of engagement that include progressive and measured use of force designed to minimize civilian casualties, and preferably to avoid killing civilians altogether.

Winning the right way is just as important in the civilian world. We have seen how corporations and other organizations that go about their business with values and respect for others prosper over the long run. And we have seen how organizations that fail to incorporate positive values and respect for others suffer over the long run. At the individual level, the same principle applies. Yes, a person can lie or cheat and occasionally succeed, but over the long haul a significant price will be paid for this approach to life.

Thomas Jefferson proclaimed in the Declaration of Independence, "We hold these truths to be self-evident, that all men are created equal, that they are endowed by their Creator with certain unalienable Rights, that among these are Life, Liberty, and the pursuit of Happiness."[6] We add to this the idea that character and winning the right way is not just an American principle. The twenty-four character strengths we have focused on in *The Character Edge* are thought to be universal among humans. The ideas in this book apply to everyone, regardless of culture or nationality.

Winning the right way has been discussed throughout this book. Here are some significant takeaways.

THE SCARECROW, THE TIN MAN, AND THE COWARDLY LION

Suffolk University law professor Lisle Baker welcomes three hundred new law students each fall term. Law students are admitted mostly on the basis of aptitude, assessed by a combination of undergraduate academic performance and scores on the Law School Admission Test, or LSAT. Baker became interested in positive psychology and completed a master of arts in applied positive psychology at the University of Pennsylvania in 2016. In his many years as a law professor, Baker has concluded that aptitude measures, while useful in admitting students with the intelligence to complete their course of study, are insufficient in predicting who will flourish in the profession of law.

Baker sees the other crucial ingredient to success in law as character. He invokes *The Wizard of Oz* to describe the necessary ingredients: aspiring lawyers need brains (the Scarecrow), a heart (the Tin Man), and courage (the Cowardly Lion).[7] We agree, and Baker's clever classification maps perfectly to our discussion of strengths of the head, heart, and gut. All of these tools are needed to solve difficult problems, rebound from failures, and form meaningful relationships with others. We discussed the strengths as composing a toolbox from which people may select the tool best suited to any situation. Not every problem can be solved with grit, just as not all jobs can be completed with a hammer.

STRENGTHS OF THE GUT

We learned that courage—both moral and physical courage—is an important aspect of character. Captain Barry Bridger, an Air Force pilot who was shot down and captured during the Vietnam War, demonstrated both moral and physical courage in abundance during his lengthy incarceration in the Hanoi Hilton. General Caslen visited the Hanoi Hilton more than forty-five years after Bridger was released and reunited with his family. Looking at the conditions these American prisoners lived under gives a renewed respect and admiration for their grit, courage, and character. It is said that the true test of one's character occurs not when things are going well in life, but when the worst happens and often when it is least expected. Bridger demonstrated true strength of the gut in persevering through repeated torture, disillusionment, and inhumane living conditions when hope was forlorn. Yet through all of this he remained loyal to his nation, his family, his colleagues, and himself, refusing to compromise the values he was raised with, and the values he was taught in service to his country. Bridger defines character as "the courage to do the right thing at the right time for the right reasons and is determined by what you value about life, about living, about being. Your deeply held beliefs, therefore, define who you are and how you are likely to behave."[8]

Where do men and women find the character to persevere under such horrific conditions? Bridger—and Brendan Marrocco and Rhonda Cornum, whose stories of combat we shared in earlier chapters—would tell you that they were grounded in a set of values that could never be compromised. These core values guided them through the worst conditions imaginable.

Character traits of the gut are vital to successful competition, on playing fields and battlefields. The transformation of the Army football team is an example. Playing with mediocrity, making mistakes, and not having the relentlessness and toughness to persevere resulted in an average-at-best performance that plagued this team for many years. Discipline, toughness, tenacity, relentlessness, and laying it on the line—all character strengths of the gut—allow a team to compete until the last whistle blows. Those were the character traits needed to transform Army football from a losing team to a top twenty-five national powerhouse. And it is also what America expects of its Army when it puts soldiers in harm's way with boots on the ground in the crucible of combat.

While superintendent of West Point, General Caslen was under public pressure to eliminate mandatory boxing from the West Point curriculum, mostly because of the risk of head injury to the cadets taking the course. Despite the pressure, Caslen elected not to. Instead, Caslen retained boxing because it was the only activity that pits one cadet against another in full body conflict, and it teaches cadets how to face fear and to overcome it, which is an important attribute for those who lead soldiers in combat. But West Point did not dismiss the risks of head injury. While still maintaining the program because of its intended purpose, West Point put a lot of effort into safe equipment, processes, and procedures to minimize the risk of head injury, and saw considerable reductions as a result.

Discipline, toughness, tenacity, and relentlessness are not just the purview of the military. Success in school, business, and sports requires the same attributes. Fail an exam? Study more and try again. Lost the game? Practice harder. Sales floundering? Same advice. Strengths of the gut are essential to winning. But they are not enough.

STRENGTH OF THE HEAD

In one of the most volatile and hostile environments during the surge in Operation Iraqi Freedom, a tough battalion commander demonstrated great intellectual agility in bringing stability and progress to a key province in Iraq. Rather than fighting his way to stability, this commander recognized how to get a dilapidated tomato-paste factory up and running again, knowing it would draw young men back onto the farmlands. With the backing of the local government this commander restored essential services and instilled trust between coalition forces and the local population. With the character traits of open-mindedness and creativity, Lieutenant Colonel Dave Hodne showed great perspective and wisdom dealing with some of the most complex problems in that environment.

Likewise, former secretary of veterans affairs Bob McDonald demonstrated incredible intellectual character in transforming the culture of the US Department of Veterans Affairs (VA). Embracing a set of values (articulated in "What I Believe In"),[9] he stressed these values throughout his tenure with the VA. In establishing a strong leader-development program, he changed the organization, making a huge difference in its commitment and obligation to care for veterans.

Strengths of the gut energize us to tackle the challenges of life. But strengths of the head allow us to do so in smart, effective ways. Grit, determination, and courage will take you a long way, but curiosity, creativity, and love of learning allow you to win the right way. Whether in the corporate world, higher education, the military, collegiate or professional sports, or any other complex environment, strengths of the head are critical to success. Those who are strong in the virtues of wisdom and knowledge thrive and flourish.

STRENGTH OF THE HEART

Sharing hardships in dire circumstances builds bonds of loyalty that are difficult to break. Many of today's veterans returning from Iraq and Afghanistan, having experienced some of the worst physical and mental conditions imaginable, experience difficult readjustments when they leave the bonds of their warrior brothers and sisters and try to readapt to a civilian environment. In combat, these bonds of loyalty enabled the soldier to endure hardships. But when no longer part of a team, the veteran often finds him- or herself challenged to persevere through difficult times. The unfortunate consequence for too many of these veterans is suicide. To better understand this dynamic, it is worth looking at what created this loyalty, and the character traits that define these bonds.

William Shakespeare captured the importance of these bonds in his play *Henry V*. Henry V stood in front of the undermanned British army as the soldiers prepared to face the heavily favored French army and proclaimed, "We few, we happy few, we band of brothers, for he today that sheds his blood with me shall be my brother." This speech captures a timeless message. It illustrates the character traits of the warrior heart—camaraderie, love, compassion, loyalty, and commitment—forged from shared hardships over many days and many trials and challenges.

Strengths of the heart make life worth living. You can be the grittiest person and most courageous person in your organization, but without kindness and the capacity to love, you will not meet your full potential. Strengths of the heart give you an edge in the workplace, but even more important, they allow you to have fulfilling and meaningful relationships with family members, coworkers, and friends. We have illustrated this with examples from the battlefield, but strengths of the heart matter in all human endeavors.

TRUST

The most important ingredient to effective leadership is trust. Trust is 360 degrees. It must exist between a person and his or her superiors and subordinates and among peers. We assert that trust is a function of one's competence, character, and caring. If you are in charge and don't know what you're doing (i.e., you're incompetent), it will be hard for anyone to want to follow you. Likewise, if you are my boss and your values and behavior make me question your integrity, how can I ever trust the orders you give me? And if you could not care less about my development, and my challenges and successes, and see me only as a pawn in your "empire," then why would I want to follow you?

We have seen this trust relationship numerous times in both great and not-so-great leaders. The Gettysburg battle is full of great leadership examples, with no better example of the trust between soldiers and their commander than that of the Minnesota regiment and its commander, Colonel William Colvill. When ordered to attack into the heart of the Confederate line, knowing it meant the certain death of most of his men, Colvill obeyed the order. His men carried out the assault without hesitation, despite recognizing the likely deadly outcome. Only a disciplined unit with incredible loyalty and trust could have followed that order. Despite the circumstances, the unit executed the attack perfectly and accomplished their mission. Losses were indeed heavy, but these sacrifices paved the way for the eventual Union victory.

Likewise, when Colonel Joshua Chamberlain was holding the leftmost flank of the Union Army after being repeatedly attacked, only to finally run out of ammunition, he ordered his men not to defend (as they had on the numerous previous attacks), but to "fix bayonets" and assault down the hill against the regrouping and still-supplied Confederates. Only a unit with leadership that the men unequivocally trusted could have accomplished that mission on that fateful day. Chamberlain, a highly respected and trusted commander, knew that the trust of his men would result in a successful bayonet charge against the enemy.

Doesn't this play out the same way in your organization? Your life probably doesn't depend on the bond of trust, but your performance and sense of well-being probably do. Effective teachers are competent, display positive character, and care deeply for their students. Students respond with hard work and devotion. It is no different in any workplace. Managers who are competent, are of high character, and care about their employees inspire great loyalty from their workers. Dr. Matthews once observed a custodian in West Point's Thayer Hall walking along a hallway crying. He asked her what was the matter, and she told him she was retiring at the end of the day, truly loved the people she worked with, and would miss them greatly. Would she have felt these emotions so keenly if her boss was incompetent, dishonest, or uncaring?

Effective organizations know that leaders must create a positive organizational climate that engenders trust among all of its members. One of the most effective ways leaders earn trust is by underwriting the risk of mistakes made by their subordinates. A trusted leader creates the conditions that enable subordinates to expand out of their comfort zone. This allows followers to realize their full potential. When you are in unfamiliar areas, you may make mistakes. By underwriting the risk of failure, the leader provides an opportunity to learn and improve. Leaders who are uncomfortable doing so will often harass and embarrass subordinates who make mistakes. Thus the subordinates fail to exercise initiative and only do what they are told, nothing more or less. No one wants to work in that environment. Organizations do not win under these conditions, and if there is any success, it certainly is not "winning the right way." When the boss underwrites the risk of failure, how far the organization may grow and improve is unlimited.

It is not only important to lead with character. A leader must also find ways to instill character throughout his or her organization. The leader must exemplify positive character him- or herself. Once you model character, how do you drive it throughout the organization? We have spotlighted several organizations with leaders who created a culture of positive character and the difference it made. It is worth highlighting their best practices.

INFLUENCING THE ORGANIZATION

Johnson & Johnson provides a stellar example of a character-based organization. Its CEO, Alex Gorsky, knows that trust is the essential element between his organization and its clients, and between Johnson & Johnson's leadership and its employees. This approach has been a core tenet since the company was founded.

Recognizing the importance of character to the company, Robert Wood Johnson II created a Credo that explicitly and publicly states the company's organizational values. The Credo was designed to infuse positive character and values throughout the organization. Gorsky continues this emphasis today, making a discussion of company values a part of the agenda of every meeting. He requires leadership assessments based on the principles expressed by the Credo. If you want to see how character is driven within the culture of a Fortune 500 company, look no further than what Alex Gorsky is doing at Johnson & Johnson.

If you're the CEO of a Fortune 500 company, you're going to be dealing with good and bad news every day. Johnson & Johnson dealt with this during the Tylenol crisis in 1982 that resulted in seven deaths and substantial financial loss. Alex Gorsky explained how Johnson & Johnson handled that: "Nothing is more important than not compromising your integrity to the people who trust and depend on you." The leadership in 1982 immediately took responsibility of the crisis and creatively developed measures to prevent product tampering. This led to the restoration of trust with customers and employees. A company of integrity exercises values-based leadership when a crisis like this unexpectedly arrives at its front door.

Recent events underscore the importance of Johnson & Johnson's Credo. The company now faces a new crisis. The company markets the painkiller fentanyl, a drug designed to treat severe pain that is now part of the nationwide opioid crisis. Opioid overdose deaths are at a near epidemic level in some parts of the United States, and a host of lawsuits have been brought against manufacturers and distributors of the drugs. In Oklahoma, a court found

Johnson & Johnson responsible for overdose deaths and fined it more than a half billion dollars.[10] Similar lawsuits are pending in other states. The ultimate financial cost to Johnson & Johnson may be crippling. How will Johnson & Johnson respond? Ultimately, Gorsky's response must be based on the Credo. To survive, the company must demonstrate competence, character, and caring.

Another example of caring leadership by an organization's CEO was shown by Dr. Deb German when her hospital leadership required her to cut her workforce by 10 percent. Dr. German was loved and respected by her employees. She genuinely knew their needs because she spent quality time with them on their turf listening to their challenges. Dr. German knew that by trusting her employees, she could address the hospital's financial crisis without firing a single individual. She did just this simply by going back to the people who had made a difference in her hospital all along—the employees. Harnessing the intellectual capacity of her workforce, she shared the challenge and solicited creative ideas and solutions that the employees themselves would implement. And solve this problem they did. Only a caring, compassionate leader who knew the strengths of her employees could accomplish this.

These are great examples of leaders who cultivate character throughout their organizations. This is winning at the institutional level, and it is winning the right way.

CHARACTER DEVELOPMENT

We have shown that character can be developed if the values of positive character are internalized. They must become part of one's essence, so that when facing a compromising situation, one does not have to think about what is right or not. The response must be reflexive, based on internalized values consistent with the organization's ethic. The West Point Leader Development System (WPLDS) provides us a model for how organizations may develop character among their members.

You will note that WPLDS is not called the West Point *Character* Development System, but rather the West Point *Leader* Development System, because character is the most important element of effective and successful leadership. West Point's mission statement declares that its mission is to "educate, train and inspire leaders of character." Leadership is developed across four pillars—academic, military, physical, and character. But the mission statement does *not* say the institution will educate, train, and inspire leaders of "academic excellence" or "military competence," but rather it says "leaders of character." Building leaders of character is the most important thing West Point does.

The West Point Leader Development System is quite simple. Immersed in an environment of intense academic, military, and physical programs, cadets are placed in leadership and follower roles. Cadets are required to meet the academy's high standards in each of these programs in a manner that embraces West Point's values of duty, honor, and country, as well as the Army's values of loyalty, duty, respect, selfless service, honor, integrity, and personal courage. As discussed in chapter 8, WPLDS has a set of defined outcomes around the expected behaviors of living and leading honorably and demonstrating excellence.

Notice that the *D* in *WPLDS* stands for "development," meaning that the internalization of values progresses and gets stronger over time. One of the more challenging aspects of West

Point's leadership program is the idea that new cadets may arrive at West Point in need of character development. Because the Army requires high standards and uncompromising ethical values, how does West Point treat its cadets when those standards are not met, or when a breach occurs in the ethical values that are so important to building trust?

People learn from their mistakes, and organizations that are good at promoting character growth understand this and use these mistakes as the launching pad for positive development. Each mistake is an opportunity to learn and get better. We like the metaphor of a broken bone. If you break a bone and it heals correctly, the bone is stronger than it was before the break. Likewise, if someone fails in character and is given the opportunity to reflect upon that failure with the aid of a mentor, that person can become stronger in character than before the defect.

Mentorship is essential to character development. It is hard to grow without it. Mentorship provides the opportunity for reflection and introspection guided by someone who lives and shares the proper values and has the experience to articulate their worth. This sets the occasion for genuine and lasting character development and associated behavioral change.

ADVERSITY

A wonderful proverb says, "As iron sharpens iron, so one person sharpens another."[11] A piece of iron to be sharpened is placed in intense fire and heated to a temperature that allows it to be bent and molded. Similarly, what is critical to our character development is our response when we find ourselves in a firestorm. The strength of your character is displayed not when life is going smoothly, but in the midst of adversity. No one likes to be there, but "as iron sharpens iron," adversity presents an opportunity to sharpen our character.

However, adversity does not always produce growth. Whether you grow, remain unchanged, are resilient, or experience disorder depends upon your character. Growth is supported by successfully dealing with adversity while taking advantage of a number of factors, including strengths of the gut, head, and heart. A big part of winning the right way is learning that you can experience adversity and not be overwhelmed by it. Developing the mindset that adversity breeds growth is essential to the winning spirit. Take some time and look for quotes from famous athletes about winning. Almost all of them point to losing as a gateway to learning how to win.

STEWARDSHIP

As a cornerstone to the character development of the Corps of Cadets, the West Point honor code says, "A cadet will not lie, cheat, or steal or tolerate those who do." Although the cadets are generally on board with not lying, cheating, or stealing, they struggle to understand why it is so important to not tolerate the transgression of a fellow cadet when they observe it.

The answer is simple. Leaders of character are driven by excellence, competence, caring, and their commitment to their profession. These attributes build trust between leaders and subordinates, leaders and their superiors, and leaders and their clients. To build and sustain trust, leaders must be the stewards of their profession. They must not only set standards; they must enforce them.

When a member of an organization violates its standards and values, this not only results in condemnation of the individual but also dishonors the reputation of the organization and creates mistrust by its client. This is unacceptable and creates a vicious cycle where tolerated misbehavior is implicitly condoned and enables future misconduct. We saw this in the example of the West Point rugby team.

If the errant behavior is identified and immediately corrected, the embarrassment brought upon the organization and the mistrust it created will have been avoided. High-quality organizations recognize the importance of self-policing. It is a core element of winning the right way.

ETHICAL FADING

A challenge an organization's leader may face is a dynamic called ethical fading. Ethical fading is a deterioration or corrosion of ethical standards over time. When unethical behavior occurs and goes unchecked by leadership or others, it can become a new standard practice, and over time it is no longer seen as wrong. Employees are watching what is happening, secretly hoping leaders will act and restore behavioral standards. When they don't, ethics fade, a new values standard is set in place, and unacceptable behavior slowly creeps into the organization.

We have all seen this in one form or another. In the late twentieth century, New York City was overwhelmed with street crime. Murder rates were at record levels. Times Square was not a place one felt safe to walk. The police were overworked and could barely keep up with investigating the major crimes of robbery, burglary, stealing, assault, rape, and murder. In 1994 William

Bratton was appointed commissioner of the New York Police Department, and reducing street crime was one of his highest priorities. A police prodigy, Bratton had begun his law enforcement career in Boston in 1970, rising to several leadership positions, including commissioner. To address New York City's crime problem, Bratton turned to what is popularly referred to as "broken windows" policing, an approach championed by criminologists James Q. Wilson and George L. Kelling. This approach, controversial to some, involved strict enforcement of highly visible but minor crimes, such as public intoxication, vandalism, and fare evasion—offenses that, while not especially dangerous, detracted from quality of life in a city. Surprisingly, the broken window approach was followed by a substantial reduction not just in petty crimes, but in major crimes such as murder as well. In 1994, when Bratton initiated the broken-windows policing strategy, the city recorded 1,561 murders. By 2001, New York reported just 649 murders. By June 2019, New York City was on pace to record its lowest number of murders since the 1950s.[12]

Bratton's broken-windows approach to reducing crime was based on the concept that attending to small violations would prevent larger ones from occurring. Ethical fading is similar. The organization that tolerates small ethical transgressions may soon find itself awash in a major controversy or crisis. Organizations that win the right way attack the small stuff and in doing so prevent more catastrophic failures. As Booker T. Washington said, "Success in life is founded upon attention to the small things rather than to the large things; to the everyday things nearest to us rather than to the things that are remote and uncommon."[13]

AVOIDING THE POTHOLES

It is better to prevent character failure than to deal with its personal and organizational consequences. An untarnished personal or organizational reputation is priceless. The Character Risk Model provides a basis for avoiding character failure, both for individuals and for organizations.

At the personal level, recognizing personality traits that often lead to character failure allows individuals to self-monitor their actions, and for leaders to be on the lookout for such individuals within their organizations. We have emphasized that character can and should be developed, wherever possible, and recognizing these warning flags may be of immense utility in knowing where to direct these developmental efforts. In some cases, such as the dark triad, removal from the organization may be the best tactic. Unfortunately, people who are narcissistic, Machiavellian, or psychopathic often lack self-insight. For the good of the organization, they are best removed. Those with lesser flaws, such as hubris, may benefit from self-imposed or management-driven developmental efforts.

Environmental threats contribute to character failure. Leaders may take steps to mitigate these potholes, whether it is an army platoon leader ensuring that her soldiers are well rested, or a corporate manager crafting a positive organizational climate to reduce stress. Good organizations expend a lot of time and money to foster positive conditions. Doing so may prevent some individuals from making character-based errors.

At the social level, individuals should cultivate strong and supportive relationships with their families, friends, and coworkers. These strong social bonds are a major protection against character failure and help individuals respond to stress and adversity with a resilient or growth trajectory, rather than slipping into pathology. Leaders can help here, too, by providing opportunities for employees to bond together. Coach Popovich's team dinners are a great example.

At the organizational level, being aware of the threats to organizational values and of ethical fading are critical. Every senior manager should take to heart and take great pains in avoiding the Deloitte Center's eight drivers of misconduct. These drivers of misconduct, if left unchecked, are the seedbed of ethical fading. Whether it is a university focusing on new buildings over the primary mission of educational excellence or a win-at-all-costs mentality, successful organizations must be vigilant in avoiding these potholes. When things are not right, it is critical to recognize this and take appropriate action. Doing so reinforces and maintains institutional values and sends an important message to the organization on what is acceptable and what is not.

PRIVATE LIFE—PUBLIC LIFE

It is virtually impossible today to separate your public life from your personal life. Leaders of character must show the same character in both. This has been one of our most consistent themes. You can't adhere to one set of personal standards at work and a lesser standard in your private life, especially given the ubiquity of social media. Try this little experiment. Do an internet search using the phrase *resigned because of past tweets*. You will be amazed at the number of famous and not-so-famous people who post thoughts online that are incongruent with the values of their institution. This relates to General Martin Dempsey's concept of the digital echo. Once something is posted on social media, such comments live forever and have led to the firing or resignation of countless individuals from businesses, universities, churches, and other organizations. Who would want to be led by such people?

Men and women of character will seek facts, identify what is true, and place their trust accordingly. They make sure that their private lives and thoughts align with their public lives and thoughts. They avoid the temptation to side with the majority without a critical analysis. Winning the right way must be based on facts, not the emotionally charged images and baseless assertions, rampant in social media today.

A PERSONAL ETHIC-CREED

There is a character crisis in America. *The Character Edge* is a step toward providing people with a better understanding of character, trust, and leadership. Our book is a guide toward strengthening leadership skills that lead to lasting success. It is also a passionate call to arms for individuals and organizations to pay more attention to character. Understanding character is a necessary first step to improving it. We want the importance of character to become embedded in the national consciousness—a goal that each of us should demand of ourselves and of our leadership at every level.

As we wrap up this chapter and this book, we want to leave you with the idea that winning the right way is what matters. Regardless of what you're leading, winning the right way starts with you and your character. We are impressed by organizations such as Johnson & Johnson, West Point, and many others that have publicly stated personal and organizational values. So, we leave you with a personal creed for you to consider as well. This creed is inspired by Johnson & Johnson's Credo and the creed of the West Point Corps of Cadets. Whether you like this creed or another, we encourage you to find one that defines the values and behavior to which you aspire. Read it and internalize it and post it where you can read and refresh these values often.

MY PERSONAL CREED

As a leader of my organization, I am first committed to our clients and customers, to provide them a high-quality, reasonably priced product that is safe and secure, and that is the best in the market.

My next responsibility is to our employees, who work with us throughout our entire organization. All are valued members, who will work in a safe and secure environment and will find fulfillment in their jobs. I will ensure their work environment is supportive to their imagination, creativity, innovation, and growth. I will empower and develop them to the limits of their potential, ensure that they have great opportunities for advancement and satisfaction, and ensure their compensation is competitive with the best in the nation. I am committed to their development as lifelong employees and future leaders of our organization.

My organization is emboldened by the values of loyalty, duty, respect, selfless service, honor, integrity, and personal moral courage. These are the values that I embrace and that drive everything I do, both with my organization and in my life. I am a man or woman of great integrity, who will live a private life with the same values I will live in my public life. I will live these values not only at work, but also at home and in everything I do.

I am responsible to be a strong partner within my commu-

nity, supporting my local government and my local organizations, and ensuring I am a good citizen who supports good
works and charities, and my fair share of taxes. I will be a
good steward of the environment I am privileged to use.

I will serve our clients and our customers, maintaining the
honor of our organization, living above the common level of
life, and having the courage to choose the harder right over the
easier wrong. I will live both my public life and my private life
with honor and integrity.

I am a member of an organization of excellence and will
pursue excellence in our product, in our customers, in our employees, and in all we do.

YOUR LEGACY

We opened this book by posing the question of what you want
the hyphen on your tombstone to represent. What do educational, professional, and personal achievements mean in the absence of positive character? We hope you have learned more
about the broad scope of positive character. Character is fundamental to trust, and trust is the bedrock of leadership. Great individuals know this and consciously and deliberately center their
lives around the strengths of the head, heart, and gut. These
strengths become the personal body armor needed to face life's
challenges and to not just prevail, but to flourish. Great organizations also know this and make positive character a number
one priority for themselves. In short, positive character provides
individuals and organizations with the edge they need to win
and to win the right way. Start today making positive character
the hallmark of your epitaph.

RECOMMENDED READING

Ambrose, Stephen E. *Band of Brothers.* New York: Simon & Schuster, 1992.

———. *Undaunted Courage.* New York: Simon & Schuster, 1996.

Brafman, Ori, and Rod A. Beckstrom. *The Starfish and the Spider: The Unstoppable Power of Leaderless Organizations.* New York: Portfolio, 2006.

Brooks, David. *The Road to Character.* New York: Random House, 2015.

Collins, Jim. *Good to Great: Why Some Companies Make the Leap . . . and Others Don't.* New York: HarperCollins, 2001.

Covey, Stephen M. R. *The Speed of Trust: The One Thing That Changes Everything.* New York: Free Press, 2008.

Crandall, Doug, ed. *Leadership Lessons from West Point.* San Francisco: Jossey-Bass, 2007.

Damon, William. *The Path to Purpose: How Young People Find Their Calling in Life.* New York: Free Press, 2009.

Duckworth, Angela. *Grit: The Power of Passion and Perseverance.* New York: Scribner, 2016.

Dweck, Carol S. *Mindset: The New Psychology of Success.* New York: Random House, 2006.

Emmons, Robert A. *Thanks! How the New Science of Gratitude Can Make You Happier.* New York: Houghton Mifflin Harcourt, 2007.

Engstrom, Ted W., and Robert C. Larson. *Integrity: Character from the Inside Out.* Colorado Springs, Colo.: Waterbrook Press, 1997.

Feith, Douglas J. *War and Decision: Inside the Pentagon at the Dawn of the War on Terrorism.* New York: HarperCollins, 2008.

Fisher, Roger, and Daniel Shapiro. *Beyond Reason, Using Emotions as You Negotiate.* New York: Penguin, 2005.

RECOMMENDED READING

Harley, William F., Jr. *His Needs, Her Needs: Building an Affair-Proof Marriage.* Grand Rapids, Mich.: Revell, 1986.

Hunter, James C. *The Servant: A Simple Story About the True Essence of Leadership.* New York: Crown Business, 1998.

Johnson, Steven. *Where Good Ideas Come From: The Natural History of Innovation.* London: Penguin, 2010

Kaufman, Scott Barry, and Carolyn Gregoire. *Wired to Create: Unraveling the Mysteries of the Creative Mind.* New York: Perigee, 2015.

Kidder, Rushworth M. *How Good People Make Tough Choices: Resolving the Dilemmas of Ethical Living.* New York: Quill, 2003.

Kolditz, Thomas A. *In Extremis Leadership: Leading As If Your Life Depended on It.* San Francisco: Jossey-Bass, 2007.

Marrella, Len. *In Search of Ethics: Conversations with Men and Women of Character.* Sanford, Fla.: DC Press, 2001.

Matthews, Michael D. *Head Strong: How Psychology Is Revolutionizing War.* New York: Oxford University Press, 2014. Rev. and expanded ed., 2020.

Moore, Harold G., and Joseph L. Galloway. *We Were Soldiers Once . . . and Young: Ia Drang—the Battle That Changed the War in Vietnam.* New York: Random House, 1992.

Myrer, Anton. *Once an Eagle.* New York: Holt, Rinehart & Winston, 1968.

Nagl, John A. *Learning to Eat Soup with a Knife: Counterinsurgency Lessons from Malaya and Vietnam.* Chicago: University of Chicago Press, 2005.

Peterson, Christopher. *A Primer in Positive Psychology.* New York: Oxford University Press, 2006.

Seligman, Martin E. P. *Authentic Happiness: Using the New Positive Psychology to Realize Your Potential for Lasting Fulfillment.* New York: Free Press, 2002.

———. *Flourish: A Visionary New Understanding of Happiness and Well-Being.* New York: Simon & Schuster, 2011.

Shaara, Michael. *The Killer Angels: A Novel of the Civil War.* New York: Random House, 1974.

Smiley, Scotty. *Hope Unseen: The Story of the U.S. Army's First Blind Active-Duty Officer.* New York: Simon & Schuster, 2010.

Sweeney, Patrick J., Michael D. Matthews, and Paul B. Lester. *Leadership in Dangerous Situations: A Handbook for the Armed Forces, Emergency Services, and First Responders.* Annapolis, Md.: Naval Institute Press, 2011.

Wagner, Tony. *The Global Achievement Gap: Why Even Our Best Schools Don't Teach the New Survival Skills Our Children Need—And What We Can Do About It.* New York: Basic Books, 2008.

NOTES

PREFACE

1. General Order Number 1 states that soldiers may not consume alcohol during combat deployments.

2. For an informative explanation of this seminal work, see Martin E. P. Seligman, *Helplessness: On Depression, Development, and Death* (New York: W. H. Freeman, 1975).

3. Christopher Peterson and Martin E. P. Seligman, *Character Strengths and Virtues* (New York: Oxford University Press, 2004).

4. Angela Duckworth, *Grit: The Power of Passion and Perseverance* (New York: Scribner, 2016).

1. HAVE GOOD CHARACTER, DON'T BE ONE

1. Alexander Hamilton, letter to John Laurens, from *The Papers of Alexander Hamilton*, ed. Harold C. Styrett et al. (New York: Columbia University Press, 1961–87), 2:467. Quoted in Ron Chernow, *Alexander Hamilton* (New York: Penguin, 2004), 145.

2. Martin E. P. Seligman, *The Hope Circuit: A Psychologist's Journey from Helplessness to Optimism* (New York: Hachette, 2018), 294.

3. For more information about the Positivity Project, see their website: posproject.org.

4. Michael D. Matthews and Richard M. Lerner, "Leaders of Character: Striving Toward Virtuous Leadership," in *West Point Leadership,* ed. Daniel Smith (New York: Rowan Technology Solutions, 2016), www.rowantechsolutions.com/leadership/.

5. William Damon, *The Path to Purpose: How Young People Find Their Calling in Life* (New York: Free Press, 2008), xi.

6. Peterson and Seligman, *Character Strengths and Virtues.*

7. Christopher Peterson et al., "Strengths of Character, Orientations to Happiness,

and Life Satisfaction," *Journal of Positive Psychology* 2 (2007), 149–56, https://doi.org/10.1080/17439760701228938.

8. Maria Fotiadou et al., "Optimism and Psychological Well-Being Among Parents of Children with Cancer: An Exploratory Study," *Psycho-Oncology* 17 (2008), 401–9, https://doi.org/10.1002/pon.1257.

9. Michael D. Matthews, "Character Strengths and Post-Adversity Growth in Combat Leaders." Poster presented at the Annual Meeting of the American Psychological Association, Washington, DC, August 2011.

10. Jim Frederick, *Black Hearts* (New York: Broadway Books, 2011).

11. "Yadier Molina Named Recipient of 2018 Roberto Clemente Award," MLB.com press release, October 24, 2018, www.mlb.com/news/yadier-molina-named-recipient-of-2018-roberto-clemente-award/c-299633704.

12. Jenifer Langosch, "Yadi Recognized with 2018 Clemente Award," MLB.com, October 24, 2018, www.mlb.com/cardinals/news/yadier-molina-wins-2018-clemente-award/c-299600082.

2. STRENGTHS OF THE GUT

1. Nelson Mandela quotes, BrainyQuote.com, 2019, www.brainyquote.com/quotes/nelson_mandela_178789.

2. Barry Bridger, personal communication, November 7, 2018.

3. On the Veteran Tributes website you can find the text for Bridger's Silver Star, along with "tribute pages for Medal of Honor Recipients, Prisoners of War, Generals and Admirals, as well as the Soldiers, Sailors, Airmen, and Marines that nobody has ever heard of." Veteran Tributes, www.veterantributes.org.

4. This phrase originated in the cadet prayer at the US Military Academy: "Make us to choose the harder right instead of the easier wrong, and never to be content with a half truth when the whole can be won." westpoint.edu/about/chaplain/cadet-prayer.

5. Bridger, personal communication.

6. Paul Lester and Cynthia Pury, "What Leaders Should Know About Courage," in *Leadership in Dangerous Situations,* ed. Patrick J. Sweeney, Michael D. Matthews, and Paul B. Lester (Annapolis, Md.: Naval Institute Press, 2011), 23–25. Lester and Pury base their comments on a series of studies by Christopher Rate and colleagues: Christopher R. Rate et al., "Implicit Theories of Courage," *Journal of Positive Psychology* 2, no. 2 (2007), 80–98; Christopher R. Rate, "Defining the Features of Courage: A Search for Meaning," in *The Psychology of Courage: Modern Research on an Ancient Virtue,* ed. Cynthia L. S. Pury and Shane J. Lopez (Washington, D.C.: American Psychological Association, 2010), 47–66.

7. See the book written by the sister of Hans and Sophie Scholl, Inge Aicher-Scholl, *The White Rose: Munich, 1942–1943* (Middletown, Conn.: Wesleyan University Press, 1970), for an inspiring and fascinating description of

Scholl's life and death. Several movies have also been made about Sophie and Hans, including *Sophie Scholl: The Final Days* (Zeitgeist Films, 2005).

8. David Wolpe, "The Japanese Man Who Saved 6,000 Jews With His Handwriting," October 15, 2018, New York Times, www.nytimes.com/2018/10/15/opinion/sugihara-moral-heroism-refugees.html.

9. Stephen E. Ambrose, *Band of Brothers* (New York: Simon & Schuster, 1992), 307. This quote is widely misattributed to Major Richard Winters, who quoted it in the HBO miniseries *Band of Brothers,* but who clearly attributed it to his friend Mike Ranney.

10. Capt. Chesley "Sully" Sullenberger, *Highest Duty: My Search for What Really Matters* (New York: HarperCollins, 2009).

11. Angela L. Duckworth, personal communication, June 28, 2004.

12. Angela L. Duckworth et. al, "Grit: Perseverance and Passion for Long-Term Goals," *Journal of Personality and Social Psychology* 92 (2007), 1087–1101.

13. The term *SAT* refers to the standardized test administered by the College Board. This test, along with the ACT (administered by ACT, Inc.), is widely used for college admissions in the United States.

14. Duckworth et al., "Grit."

15. Ibid.

16. Lauren Eskreis-Winkler et al., "The Grit Effect: Predicting Retention in the Military, the Workplace, School and Marriage," *Frontiers in Psychology* 5 (2014), 36, https://doi.org/10.3389/fpsyg.2014.00036.

17. As noted in John Bartlett, *Bartlett's Familiar Quotations: A Collection of Passages, Phrases, and Proverbs Traced to Their Sources in Ancient and Modern Literature,* 18th ed., ed. Geoffrey O'Brien (New York: Little, Brown, 2012).

18. Martin E. P. Seligman et al., "Positive Psychology Progress: Empirical Validation of Interventions," *American Psychologist* 60, no. 5 (2005), 410–21, https://doi.org:10.1037/0003-066X.60.5.410.

19. Lester and Pury, "What Leaders Should Know."

20. For a historical perspective on Bandura's work, see his classic article: Albert Bandura, Dorothea Ross, and Sheila A. Ross, "Transmission of Aggression Through Imitation of Aggressive Models," *Journal of Abnormal and Social Psychology* 63 (1961), 575–82.

21. Jim Collins, *Good to Great: Why Some Companies Make the Leap . . . and Others Don't* (New York: HarperCollins, 2001), 41–64.

22. Mike Krzyzewski, with Donald T. Phillips, *Leading with the Heart: Coach K's Successful Strategies for Basketball, Business, and Life* (New York: Warner Business Books, 2001), 209.

23. John Feinstein, "Feinstein's Findings: Michie Miracles Continue," *Army West Point Athletics,* November 4, 2018, https://goarmywestpoint.com/news/2018/11/4/football-feinstein-findings-michie-miracles-continue.aspx

3. STRENGTHS OF THE HEAD

1. Anne Bradstreet, *The Works of Anne Bradstreet* (Cambridge, Mass.: Harvard University Press, 1981).

2. Peterson and Seligman, *Character Strengths and Virtues,* 29.

3. The phrase *six inches between the ears* (along with variations) is commonly heard throughout the military. For example, see Jim Mattis and Bing West, *Call Sign Chaos* (New York: Random House, 2019), 166— "The most important six inches on the battlefield is between your ears."

4. David Hodne, personal communication with Dr. Matthews, September 20, 2019. The term *formation* refers to Hodne's fellow leaders throughout General Caslen's command.

5. Robert J. Sternberg and Karin Sternberg, *Cognitive Psychology,* 7th ed. (Boston, Mass.: Cengage, 2017), 502–3.

6. Ibid., 101, for documentation of Gardner's discussion of the eight types of intelligence.

7. Ibid., 432.

8. Ibid., 433–34.

9. See Peterson and Seligman, *Character Strengths and Virtues,* 134–35.

10. Gary E. Swan and Dorit Carmelli, "Curiosity and Mortality in Aging Adults: A 5-Year Follow-Up of the Western Collaborative Group Study," *Psychology and Aging* 11, no. 3 (1996), 449.

11. See Peterson and Seligman, *Character Strengths and Virtues,* 150–53.

12. Ibid., 169.

13. Ibid., 170.

14. Ibid., 189.

15. Brian K. Cooper, James C. Sarros, and Joseph C. Santora, "The Character of Leadership," *Ivey Business Journal,* May/June 2007, iveybusinessjournal .com/publication/the-character-of-leadership.

16. Brian W. Head and John Alford, "Wicked Problems: Implications for Public Policy and Management," *Administration & Society* 47, no. 6 (2015), 711–39, https://doi.org:10.1177/0095399713481601.

17. Ryan W. Buell, Robert S. Huckman, and Sam Travers, "Improving Access at VA," *Harvard Business School Case 617-012,* November 2016 (revised December 2016).

18. Procter & Gamble Company, "Bob McDonald Biography," https://www .pg.com/content/pdf/04_news/mgmt_bios/McDonald-Robert.pdf.

19. Harvard Business School interview with Robert McDonald, July 27, 2016.

20. US Department of Veterans Affairs, Office of Public Affairs, "VA Announces Single Regional Framework Under MyVA Initiative," press release, January 26, 2015, www.va.gov/opa/pressrel/pressrelease.cfm?id=2672.

21. Action Learning Associates, "Leaders Developing Leaders: 2-Day Cascade

Workshop," Department of Veterans Affairs training material (Washington, D.C., 2016), i.

22. Robert McDonald, "What I Believe In," Procter & Gamble website, www .pg.com/en_US/downloads/company/executive_team/Bob_McDonald _Leadership_Principles.pdf.

23. Ibid.

24. Ibid.

4. STRENGTHS OF THE HEART

1. Benjamin Hochman, "Shildt Is the Right Guy for Cardinals and Their Fans," *Stltoday.com,* February 16, 2019, www.stltoday.com/sports/columns /benjamin-hochman/hochman-shildt-is-the-right-guy-for-cardinals-and -their/article_a71af930-4880-5855-a984-964cd00522b3.html?mode =nowapp.

2. Sara Karnes, "Sheriff's Department Presents Restored Car to Deputy's Widow," *Springfield News Leader,* March 19, 2019, www.news-leader.com /story/news/local/ozarks/2019/03/19/sheriffs-department-restored -car-deputy-aaron-roberts-widow/3214134002.

3. Peterson and Seligman, *Character Strengths and Virtues,* 304–5.

4. Rochelle Randles, "The Handbook's Fifth Edition Brings 'Good Turns, Daily' to Scouting," *Scouting Wire,* May 5, 2016, scoutingwire.org /handbooks-fifth-edition-brings-good-turns-daily-scoutinga-good-turn -can-simple-holding-door-someone-grandiose-national-project-scouts-o.

5. Known as the Golden Rule, this is a common form of "Therefore all things whatsoever ye would that men should do to you, do ye even so to them: for this is the law and the prophets," Matthew 7:12 (Bartlett, *Bartlett's Familiar Quotations,* 33n1).

6. Eric Burger, "25 Volunteer Statistics That Will Blow Your Mind," *Volunteer-Hub,* www.volunteerhub.com/blog/25-volunteer-statistics.

7. Richard McKinney, "Op-ed: I Wanted to Kill Muslims, Too. But Then I Saw the Light," *IndyStar.com,* www.indystar.com/story/opinion/2019/03 /31/op-ed-almost-terrorist-then-found-islam/3302137002.

8. Nicholas A. Christakis, *Blueprint* (New York: Little, Brown, 2019). Christakis also made headlines in 2015 when a video of him talking with students at Yale became a viral sensation. Christakis's wife, Erika, who also taught at Yale at the time, questioned a ban on "culturally insensitive Halloween costumes," sparking protests on campus. For an overview of the controversy and the book, see Frank Bruni, "A 'Disgusting' Yale Professor Moves On," March 19, 2019, *New York Times,* www.nytimes.com /2019/03/19/opinion/nicholas-christakis-yale.html.

9. See the official US Army website for Staff Sergeant Travis Atkins: www.army .mil/medalofhonor/atkins.

10. Emma Marris, "In Our Shadow," *National Geographic,* April 2019, 126–47.

11. Nick Perry, "At Memorial, Mosque Survivor Says He Forgives Attacker," Associated Press, March 29, 2019, www.apnews.com/e787324a3036438 0b1607129da1d7ea1.

12. Peterson and Seligman, *Character Strengths and Virtues*, 447–48.

13. Janice Harper, "A Lesson from Nelson Mandela on Forgiveness," *Psychology Today*, June 10, 2013, www.psychologytoday.com/us/blog/beyond -bullying/201306/lesson-nelson-mandela-forgiveness.

14. Peterson and Seligman, *Character Strengths and Virtues*, 452.

15. Seligman et al., "Positive Psychology Progress," 410–21.

16. Matthews, "Character Strengths and Post-Adversity Growth in Combat Leaders."

17. Monica Rohr, "As U.S. Cuts Refugee Numbers, African Teens Find Brotherhood on a Texas Soccer Team," *USA Today*, December 6, 2018, www .usatoday.com/story/news/nation/2018/12/07/african-refugee-teens -brotherhood-houston-soccer-team/2136754002.

18. Ibid.

19. Caitlin Murray, "USA's Band of Sisters Have Used Their Unity to Gain a Crucial Edge," *Guardian*, July 6, 2019, www.theguardian.com/football /2019/jul/06/usa-womens-world-cup-final-soccer.

5. TRUST: THE STRAW THAT STIRS THE DRINK

1. Stanley McChrystal, "Listen, Learn . . . Then Lead," TED Talk, March 2011, www.ted.com/talks/stanley_mcchrystal?language=en.

2. Martin Dempsey and Ori Brafman, *Radical Inclusion: What the Post-9/11 World Should Have Taught Us About Leadership* (Arlington, Va.: Missionday, 2018).

3. Michael Gold and Tyler Pager, "New York Suburb Declares Measles Emergency, Barring Unvaccinated Children from Public," *New York Times*, March 26, 2019, www.nytimes.com/2019/03/26/nyregion/measles -outbreak-rockland-county.html.

4. Paul B. Lester and Gretchen R. Vogelgesang, "Swift Trust in Ad Hoc Military Organizations: Theoretical and Applied Perspectives," in *The Oxford Handbook of Military Psychology*, ed. Janice H. Laurence and Michael D. Matthews (New York: Oxford University Press, 2012), 176–86.

5. Patrick J. Sweeney et al., "Trust: The Key to Leading When Lives Are on the Line," in Sweeney, Matthews, and Lester, *Leadership in Dangerous Situations*, 163–81.

6. Janelle Griffith, "Homeless Man, N.J. Woman Accused in GoFundMe Scam Plead Guilty," NBC News, March 6, 2019, www.nbcnews.com/news/us -news/homeless-man-n-j-woman-accused-gofundme-scam-plead-guilty -n980166.

7. Stephanie Gosk and Conor Ferguson, "GoFundMe CEO Says the Company Has an Answer for Fraud," NBC News, April 8, 2019, www.nbcnews

.com/news/us-news/after-new-jersey-scam-gofundme-says-it-has-answer
-fraud-n992086.

8. Corky Siemaszko, "Pennsylvania Priest Who Molested Boys After Mass
Pleads Guilty to Abuse," NBC News, October 17, 2018, www.nbcnews
.com/news/us-news/ex-pennsylvania-priest-who-molested-boys-after
-mass-pleads-guilty-n921136.

9. Shelly Bradbury, "Catholic Priest Sentenced to Prison in Jefferson County
Sex Abuse Case," *Pittsburgh Post-Gazette,* January 11, 2019, www
.post-gazette.com/news/crime-courts/2019/01/11/david-poulson
-pennsylvania-priest-sentenced-brookville-jefferson-county-sex-abuse
-attorney-general-erie/stories/201901110119.

10. Liam Stack, "Catholic Bishops Vow to Hold Themselves Accountable for
Sexual Abuse and Cover-Ups," *New York Times,* June 13, 2019, www
.nytimes.com/2019/06/13/us/catholic-bishops-abuse.html.

11. Jeffrey M. Jones, "Many U.S. Catholics Question Their Membership amid
Scandal," Gallup.com, March 13, 2019, news.gallup.com/poll/247571
/catholics-question-membership-amid-scandal.aspx.

12. Neil Monahan and Saeed Ahmed, "There Are Now as Many Americans
Who Claim No Religion as There Are Evangelicals and Catholics, a Survey Finds," CNN, April 26, 2019, www.cnn.com/2019/04/13/us/no
-religion-largest-group-first-time-usa-trnd/index.html.

13. Christine Hauser and Maggie Astor, "The Larry Nassar Case: What Happened and How the Fallout Is Spreading," *New York Times,* January 25,
2018, www.nytimes.com/2018/01/25/sports/larry-nassar-gymnastics
-abuse.html.

14. "The Nassar Scandal and the Crisis of Michigan State's President," Special
Report, *Chronicle of Higher Education,* January 17, 2019, www.chronicle
.com/specialreport/The-Nassar-Scandalthe/179.

15. Bill Chappell, "Entire Board of USA Gymnastics to Resign," NPR News,
January 26, 2018, www.npr.org/sections/thetorch/2018/01/26
/580956170/usoc-tells-usa-gymnastics-board-to-resign-within-6
-days.

16. Lester and Pury, "What Leaders Should Know," 21–39.

17. A condensed version of General Caslen's thoughts about the Bank of Public Trust was expressed in the foreword to Michael D. Matthews, *Head
Strong,* rev. ed. (New York: Oxford University Press, 2020).

18. This text is taken from the Police Officer's Creed of the Laredo Independent
School District, http://laredo.ss11.sharpschool.com/UserFiles/Servers
/Server_328908/File/Student%20Services/Departments/Police%20
Department/Homepage/policecreed.pdf. Variations on this text are used
by police departments throughout the United States, adapted from the
Law Enforcement Code of Ethics adopted by the International Association
of Chiefs of Police (IACP) in 1957, www.theiacp.org/resources/law
-enforcement-code-of-ethics.

6. IT IS NOT JUST ABOUT YOU

1. Frances Hesselbein, "The Key to Cultural Transformation," in *Leader to Leader 2: Enduring Insights on Leadership from the Leader to Leader Institute's Award Winning Journal,* ed. Frances Hesselbein and Alan R. Shrader (San Francisco: Jossey-Bass, 2008), 267.

2. Mallen Baker, "Johnson & Johnson and Tylenol: Crisis Management Case Study," September 8, 2008, http://mallenbaker.net/article/clear-reflection/johnson-johnson-and-tylenol-crisis-management-case-study.

3. Personal communication with the authors, May 6, 2019.

4. Johnson & Johnson website, www.jnj.com/credo.

5. Baker, "Johnson & Johnson and Tylenol."

6. The term *ACT* refers to the standardized test administered by ACT, Inc. This test, along with the SAT (administered by the College Board), is widely used for college admissions in the United States.

7. Michael G. Rumsey, "Military Selection and Classification in the United States," in Laurence and Matthews, *Oxford Handbook of Military Psychology,* 129–47.

8. Eric Freeman, "New Details on What Went Wrong for USA Basketball in 2004," Yahoo Sports, August 2, 2016.

9. To learn more about Eddie Mabo, see the Eddie Koiki Mabo page on the Australian Institute of Aboriginal and Torres Strait Islander Studies (AIATSIS) website: aiatsis.gov.au/explore/articles/eddie-koiki-mabo.

10. Nansook Park and Martin E. P. Seligman, "Christopher M. Peterson (1950–2012)," *American Psychologist* 68 (2013), 403, ppc.sas.upenn.edu/sites/default/files/chrispeterson.pdf.

11. Baxter Holmes, "Michelin Restaurants and Fabulous Wines: Inside the Secret Team Dinners That Have Built the Spurs' Dynasty," ESPN, April 18, 2019, www.espn.com/nba/story/_/id/26524600/secret-team-dinners-built-spurs-dynasty.

12. Sweeney et al., "Trust," 163–81.

13. Personal communication between Dr. Deborah German and Robert Caslen.

14. Adam Nossiter, "35 Employees Committed Suicide. Will Their Bosses Go to Jail?," *New York Times,* July 9, 2019, www.nytimes.com/2019/07/09/world/europe/france-telecom-trial.html.

15. Simon Carraud, "French Telco Orange Found Guilty Over Workers' Suicides in Landmark Ruling," Reuters, December 20, 2019, www.reuters.com/article/us-france-justice-orange-sentences/french-telco-orange-and-ex-ceo-found-guilty-over-workers-suicides-idUSKBN1YO12D.

16. Seligman, *Helplessness.*

7. GOOD INGREDIENTS MAKE FOR A GOOD STEW

1. Collins, *Good to Great,* 51.

2. The authors thank the College Board for providing us with information on Landscape. To learn more, visit https://professionals.collegeboard.org /landscape.

3. For the details of this study, see Angela L. Duckworth et al., "Cognitive and Noncognitive Predictors of Success," *Proceedings of the National Academy of Sciences,* November 4, 2019, 23499–504, https://doi.org: 10.1073 /pnas.1910510116.

4. General Dwight D. Eisenhower (then US army chief of staff), letter to Major General Maxwell D. Taylor (then superintendent of the US Military Academy), January 2, 1946.

5. Matthews, "Character Strengths and Post-Adversity Growth in Combat Leaders."

6. This concept comes from Robert C. Carroll, *Building Your Leadership Legacy: It's All About Character* (Sarasota, Fla.: Suncoast Digital Press, 2017).

7. A full description of the MindVue Profile assessment tool can be found at the company's website: www.MindVue.com/profile.

8. From the "Report of Investigation; Presented to the University of Central Florida Board of Trustees," January 17, 2019, prepared by Bryan Cave Leighton Paisner, LLP.

9. Jerry Fallstrom, "The Rise and Fall of President Whittaker," *Orlando Sentinel,* February 23, 2019.

10. Personal communication with Robert Caslen.

11. University of Central Florida, "Employee Code of Conduct," March 2019, compliance.ucf.edu/files/2019/02/UCF-Code-Of-Conduct-2019-Rev .pdf.

8. NURTURING THE SEED OF GOOD CHARACTER

1. www.brainyquote.com/topics/character.

2. Richard M. Lerner, *Liberty: Thriving and Civic Engagement Among America's Youth* (Thousand Oaks, Calif.: Sage, 2004).

3. Michael D. Matthews, Richard M. Lerner, and Hubert Annen, "Noncognitive Amplifiers of Human Performance: Unpacking the 25/75 Rule," in *Human Performance Optimization: The Science and Ethics of Enhancing Human Capabilities,* ed. Michael D. Matthews and David M. Schnyer (New York: Oxford University Press, 2019), 356–82.

4. Angela Duckworth, "Growing Character" (Master Class presentation, Military Child Education Coalition 2019 National Training Seminar, Washington, D.C., July 2019), https://www.youtu.be/fcd4oZdQWxU.

5. Carol S. Dweck, *Mindset: The New Psychology of Success* (New York: Random House, 2006).

6. For example, General Caslen consults with both Higher Echelon and Academy Leadership, two companies that offer a wide array of leader-development training activities.

7. For a scientific description of these and other approaches, see Martin E. P. Seligman et al., "Positive Psychology Progress," 410–21.

8. Ibid.

9. For a description of CSF, see Rhonda Cornum, Michael D. Matthews, and Martin E. P. Seligman, "Comprehensive Soldier Fitness: Building Resilience in a Challenging Institutional Context," *American Psychologist* 66, no. 1 (2011), 4–9.

10. General Douglas MacArthur, *Reminiscences* (Annapolis, Md.: Naval Institute Press, 1964), 82.

11. Opportunities to lead represents one of three components of character development in youth. For further discussion see Michael D. Matthews, "On Teaching and Developing Character: A Systematic Approach to Cultivating Positive Traits," *Psychology Today,* May 27, 2018, www.psychologytoday.com/us/blog/head-strong/201805/teaching-and-developing-character.

12. For a more thorough description of Ettekal's ideas on positive youth development in sports, see J. P. Agans et al., "Positive Youth Development Through Sport: A Relational Developmental Systems Approach," in *Positive Youth Development Through Sport,* ed. N. L. Holt (Abingdon, UK: Routledge, 2016), 34–44.

13. For a full list and a more scientific discussion of the findings, see A. J. Visek et al., "The Fun Integration Theory: Toward Sustaining Children and Adolescents Sport Participation," *Journal of Physical Activity and Health* 12, no. 3 (2015), 424–33.

14. For youth development, the positive effects described here are found in a wide variety of organized activities that transcend traditional team sports such as soccer or baseball. Dance classes, for example, have the same beneficial effects.

15. For additional information on the changes in the College Board's advanced-placement programs, see Thomas L. Friedman, "The Two Codes Your Kids Need to Know," *New York Times,* February 12, 2019, nyti.ms/2UXlfkt.

16. "Developing Leaders of Character," the West Point Leader Development System, 2018.

17. Ibid., 9.

18. The lyrics to the alma mater and other songs can be found at the Army West Point Athletics page, goarmywestpoint.com/sports/2015/3/6/GEN_2014010166.aspx; the words to "The Corps" can be found in

the "Prayers and Songs" document on the West Point Association of Graduates website, www.westpointaog.org/file/PRAYERSANDSONGS .pdf.

9. THE CRUCIBLE OF LIFE EXPERIENCES

1. Friedrich Nietzsche, *Twilight of the Idols* (1888).

2. The full quote is "Our new Constitution is now established, and has an appearance that promises permanency; but in this world nothing can be said to be certain, except death and taxes." Letter to Jean-Baptiste Leroy, November 13, 1789, cited in Bartlett, *Bartlett's Familiar Quotations.*

3. Joshua Lawrence Chamberlain, *The Passing of Armies: An Account of the Final Campaign of the Army of the Potomac* (New York: G. P. Putnam's Sons, 1915), 295.

4. This discussion of the four trajectories and Figure 9.1 are adapted from Christopher Peterson, Michael J. Craw, Nansook Park, and Michael S. Erwin, "Resilience and Leadership in Dangerous Contexts," in *Leadership in Dangerous Situations,* ed. Patrick J. Sweeney, Michael D. Matthews, and Paul B. Lester (Annapolis, MD: Naval Institute Press, 2011), 60–77.

5. Andrew Anglemyer et al., "Suicide Rates and Methods in Active Duty Military Personnel, 2005 to 2011: A Cohort Study," *Annals of Internal Medicine* 165, no. 3 (2016), 167–74.

6. For a description of the rationale and development of CSF, see Cornum, Matthews, and Seligman, "Comprehensive Soldier Fitness," 4–9.

7. For a review of its effectiveness, see Michael D. Matthews, "Tough Hearts: Building Resilient Soldiers," in *Head Strong.*

8. Updesh Kumar, personal communication to Dr. Matthews, June 3, 2019. For further reading, see Updesh Kumar, ed., *The Routledge International Handbook of Military Psychology and Mental Health* (Abingdon, UK: Routledge, 2020).

9. Eric C. Meyer et al., "Predictors of Posttraumatic Stress Disorder and Other Psychological Symptoms in Trauma-Exposed Firefighters," *Psychological Services* 9, no, 1 (2012), 1, psycnet.apa.org/doi/10.1037 /a0026414.

10. Matthews, "Tough Hearts."

11. Rhonda Cornum and Peter Copeland, *She Went to War: The Rhonda Cornum Story* (Novato, Calif.: Presidio Press, 1992).

12. Ibid., 194.

13. Ibid.

14. Ibid.

15. Christopher Peterson et al., "Strengths of Character and Posttraumatic Growth," *Journal of Traumatic Stress* 21, no. 2 (2008), 214–17.

16. Michael D. Matthews, "Character Strengths and Post-Adversity Growth in Combat Leaders" (poster presented at the annual meeting of the American Psychological Association, Washington, D.C., August 2011).

17. B. F. Skinner, *Walden Two* (Indianapolis, Ind.: Hackett, 1966).

18. For a review of Kagan's thoughts on human development, see Jerome Kagan, *Galen's Prophecy: Temperament in Human Nature* (Boulder, Colo.: Westfield Press, 1994).

19. Michael D. Matthews, "When the Going Gets Rough, the Rough Get Going," in *Head Strong*.

20. Sebastian Junger, *Tribe: On Homecoming and Belonging* (New York: Twelve, 2016), and *War* (New York: Twelve, 2010).

21. See, for example, an excellent book by one of the pioneers in hardiness research, Salvatore R. Maddi, *Hardiness: Turning Stressful Circumstances into Resilient Growth* (New York: Springer, 2012).

22. For a full description of Joe Presley, refer to Claudette Riley, "Joe Presley, with Only One Arm, to Graduate from Drury's Law Enforcement Academy," *Springfield News-Leader,* May 16, 2019, www.news-leader.com/story/news/education/2019/05/15/one-arm-man-graduate-drury-academy-law-enforcement-officer/1151417001.

23. Claudette Riley, "'I Got Hired,' Joe Presley, Born with One Arm, Joins Sheriff's Office in Ozarks," *Springfield News-Leader,* August 8, 2019, www.news-leader.com/story/news/education/2019/08/08/joe-presley-stone-county-sheriffs-office-one-arm/1949423001.

24. Maddi, *Hardiness.*

25. Paul T. Bartone, Dennis R. Kelly, and Michael D. Matthews, "Hardiness Predicts Adaptability in Military Leaders," *International Journal of Selection and Assessment* 21 (2013), 200–210.

26. For insight into General Casey's vision for the necessity of establishing the Comprehensive Soldier Fitness program, see George W. Casey, Jr., "Comprehensive Soldier Fitness: A Vision for Psychological Resilience in the US Army," *American Psychologist* 66, no. 1 (2011), 1–3, https://doi.org:10.1037/a0021930.

27. See the website of the Hardiness Institute for more information: www.hardinessinstitute.com.

10. AVOIDING THE POTHOLES

1. Benjamin Franklin, letter to *The Pennsylvania Gazette,* February 4, 1735, cited on "The Electric Ben Franklin," http://www.ushistory.org/franklin/index.htm.

2. Livia Veselka, Erica A. Giammarco, and Philip A. Vernon, "The Dark Triad and the Seven Deadly Sins," *Personality and Individual Differences* 67 (2014), 75–80, https://doi.org/10.1016/j.paid.2014.01.055.

3. See, for example, W. Keith Campbell and Jeffrey D. Green. "Narcissism and

Interpersonal Self-Regulation," in *The Self and Social Relationships,* ed. Joanne V. Wood, Abraham Tesser, and John G. Holmes (New York: Psychology Press, 2008), 73–94.

4. Nita Lewis Miller and Lawrence G. Shattuck, "Sleep Patterns of Young Men and Women Enrolled at the United States Military Academy: Results from Year 1 of a 4-Year Longitudinal Study," *Sleep* 28, no. 7 (2005), 837–41, https://doi.org/10.1093/sleep/28.7.837.

5. See Olav Kjellevold Olsen et al., "The Effect of Sleep Deprivation on Leadership Behaviour in Military Officers: An Experimental Study," *Journal of Sleep Research* 25, no. 6 (2016), 683–89, https://doi.org/10.1111/jsr.12431.

6. See Christopher M. Barnes, Brian C. Gunia, and David T. Wagner, "Sleep and Moral Awareness," *Journal of Sleep Research* 24, no. 2 (2015), 181–88, https://doi.org/10.1111/jsr.12231.

7. See William D. S. Killgore, "Sleep Deprivation and Behavioral Risk-Taking," in *Modulation of Sleep by Obesity, Diabetes, Age, and Diet,* ed. Ronald Ross Watson (London: Academic Press, 2015), 279–87, https://doi.org/10.1016/B978-0-12-420168-2.00030-2.

8. See Matthew L. LoPresti et al., "The Impact of Insufficient Sleep on Combat Mission Performance," *Military Behavioral Health* 4, no. 4 (2016), 356–63, https://doi.org/10.1080/21635781.2016.1181585.

9. Commission on College Basketball, *Report and Recommendations to Address the Issues Facing Collegiate Basketball,* delivered to the NCAA Division I Board of Directors and Board of Governors, April 2018, www.ncaa.org/sites/default/files/2018CCBReportFinal_web_20180501.pdf.

10. Gabrielle McMillen, "Appeal Filed for Three Convicted in NCAA Bribery Scandal," *Sporting News,* August 14, 2019, www.sportingnews.com/us/ncaa-basketball/news/appeal-filed-for-three-convicted-in-ncaa-bribery-scandal/uczmeysrujnh14ce3cqabirle.

11. Bill Chappell and Merrit Kennedy, "U.S. Charges Dozens of Parents, Coaches in Massive College Admissions Scandal," National Public Radio, March 12, 2019. The US Department of Justice website lists all of the individuals charged and the current status of each case. At the time of publication, many, but not all defendants had pleaded guilty: www.justice.gov/usao-ma/investigations-college-admissions-and-testing-bribery-scheme.

12. Commission on College Basketball, *Report and Recommendations to Address the Issues Facing Collegiate Basketball,* delivered to the NCAA Division I Board of Directors and Board of Governors, April 2018, www.ncaa.org/sites/default/files/2018CCBReportFinal_web_20180501.pdf.

13. Ann E. Tenbrunsel and David M. Messick, "Ethical Fading: The Role of Self-Deception in Unethical Behavior," *Social Justice Research* 17, no. 2 (2004), 223–36.

14. Peter Schmidt, "An Admissions Scandal Shows How Administrators' Ethics 'Fade,'" *Chronicle of Higher Education,* April 1, 2015.

15. Nell Gluckman, "Can Universities Foster a Culture of Ethics? Some Are Trying," *Chronicle of Higher Education,* May 10, 2017.

16. Lindsay Ellis, "After Ethical Lapses, Georgia Tech Surveyed Campus Culture. The Results Weren't Pretty," *Chronicle of Higher Education,* May 10, 2019.

17. Ibid.

18. Ibid.

19. Kevin Nixon, "Managing Conduct Risk: Addressing Drivers, Restoring Trust" (Deloitte Center for Regulatory Strategy, Deloitte Touche Tohmatsu [also known as Deloitte Global], 2017).

20. Roger L. Bertholf, "Protecting Human Research Subjects," *Annals of Clinical & Laboratory Science* 31, no. 1 (2001), 119–27; see also the Centers for Disease Control and Prevention Tuskegee Study page at https://www.cdc.gov/tuskegee/index.html.

20. Leonard Wong and Stephen J. Gerras, *Lying to Ourselves: Dishonesty in the Army Profession* (Carlisle Barracks, Pa.: Strategic Studies Institute and US Army War College Press, 2015), ssi.armywarcollege.edu/pdffiles/pub1250.pdf.

21. Stanley Milgram, "Behavioral Study of Obedience," *Journal of Abnormal and Social Psychology* 67, no. 4 (1963), 371.

22. Michael Martelle, ed., "Exploring the Russian Social Media Campaign in Charlottesville," National Security Archive, February 14, 2019, nsarchive.gwu.edu/news/cyber-vault/2019-02-14/exploring-russian-social-media-campaign-charlottesville.

11. WINNING THE RIGHT WAY

1. Joe Torre, "Joe Torre on Winning," *Bloomberg Businessweek,* August 21, 2006, www.bloomberg.com/news/articles/2006-08-20/joe-torre-on-winning.

2. Abraham Lincoln, Address at Gettysburg, November 19, 1863.

3. Abraham Lincoln, speech at the Republican State Convention, Springfield, Ill., June 16, 1858. Lincoln paraphrased the Bible verse "If a house be divided against itself, that house cannot stand," from Mark 3:25.

4. Bombing of Hiroshima and Nagasaki, History.com, June 6, 2019, www.history.com/topics/world-war-ii/bombing-of-hiroshima-and-nagasaki.

5. Bombing of Dresden, A&E Television Networks, June 7, 2019, History.com, www.history.com/topics/world-war-ii/battle-of-dresden.

6. Thomas Jefferson, Declaration of Independence, July 4, 1776.

7. R. Lisle Baker, "Educating Lawyers for Compassion and Courage as Well as Brains: *The Wizard of Oz* Was Right," sites.suffolk.edu/educatinglawyers/resources.

8. Bridger, personal communication.

9. McDonald, "What I Believe In."

10. Sara Randazzo and Jared S. Hopkins, "Johnson & Johnson Ordered to Pay $572 Million in Oklahoma Opioid Case," *Wall Street Journal,* August 26, 2019, www.wsj.com/articles/johnson-johnson-ordered-to-pay-572-million-in-oklahoma-opioid-case-11566850079.

11. Proverbs 27:17, Bible, New International Version.

12. For more on the broken-windows theory, see George L. Kelling and James Q. Wilson, "Broken Windows: The Police and Neighborhood Safety," *Atlantic,* March 1982, www.theatlantic.com/magazine/archive/1982/03/broken-windows/304465. The 1994 and 2001 New York City murder statistics come from Chris Mitchell, "The Killing of Murder," *New York,* January 4, 2008, nymag.com/news/features/crime/2008/42603. For more information on the 2019 record-low rate, see Ben Chapman, "New York City Crime Hits Record Low in First Half of 2019," *Wall Street Journal,* July 8, 2019, www.wsj.com/articles/new-york-city-crime-hits-record-low-in-first-half-of-2019-11562625746.

13. Booker T. Washington, *Quotations of Booker T. Washington* (Tuskegee, Ala.: Tuskegee Institute Press, 1938).

INDEX